American Law and Society
(Vol. 4)
Garland Reference Library of Social Science
(Vol. 765)

American Law and Society

John W. Johnson, Series Editor

Mass Media and the Constitution
An Encyclopedia of Supreme Court Cases
Richard F. Hixson

Historic U.S. Court Cases, 1690–1990
An Encyclopedia
Edited by John W. Johnson

Sexuality and the Law
An Encyclopedia of Major Legal Cases
By Arthur S. Leonard

Sports and the Law
Major Legal Cases
Edited by Charles E. Quirk

Sports and the Law
Major Legal Cases

Edited by
Charles E. Quirk

GARLAND PUBLISHING, INC.
New York & London
1996

Library of Congress Cataloging-in-Publication Data

Sports and the law : major legal cases / edited by Charles E. Quirk.
       p.   cm.
       Originally published: New York : Garland Pub., 1996. (Garland
reference library of social science ; vol. 765. American law and
society ; vol. 4)
         Includes bibliographical references and index.
         ISBN 0-8153-3324-2 (pbk. : alk. paper)
         1. Sports—Law and legislation—United States.   I. Quirk,
Charles E., 1933–   .   II. Series: Garland reference library of social
science ; v. 765.   III. Series: Garland reference library of social science.
American law and society ; vol. 4.
     [KF3989.S675   1999]
     344.73'099—dc21   98-47218
                                             CIP

Cover design by Lawrence Wolfson Design, New York.
Cover photograph © Jim Cummins/FPG International Corp.

Printed on acid-free, 250-year-life paper
Manufactured in the United States of America

For Gale

Contents

Foreword

The formal law, its practitioners, and the culture it has engendered pervade the United States. The brilliant nineteenth-century French traveler and writer Alexis de Tocqueville maintained in *Democracy in America* that in this country virtually every political question sooner or later leads to a legal decision. Garland Publishing's American Law and Society series of one-volume encyclopedias, of which *Sports and the Law: Major Legal Cases* is one, goes de Tocqueville one better. Those of us involved in this series believe that the prism of the law gathers, refracts, reflects, and (not infrequently) blurs American life. At its best, law provides a framework that enables us to make sense out of our physical and intellectual surroundings. At its worst, it confuses, frustrates, and impedes progress. Law has affected and continues to affect virtually everything we do or think about: giving birth, rearing and educating children, marriage, work, travel, business transactions, what we read and see, and, of course, how we get along with one another.

Although studying law in its social context might be a valuable approach to use in grappling with any country's history, it is particularly appropriate for the United States. This is, after all, the country with more statutes and published case law than any in the world. D.H. Lawrence, the great British writer and critic, once referred to America as a nation of "Thou Shalt Nots." The United States has about twenty-five times as many lawyers per capita as Japan. Yet Americans are not completely comfortable with the law or with those who perform what the legal philosopher Karl Llewellyn once called the "law jobs." For example, the first lawyer who arrived in the Pilgrim colony of Plymouth in the 1620s was quickly driven out of town for being too disputatious. This may have spawned the first

American lawyer joke. Perhaps the residents of Plymouth were saying that law is too important to be left to the lawyers.

Sports and the Law: Major Legal Cases is the fourth volume to appear in Garland's American Law and Society series. Consistent with the philosophy of the series, the fifty essays in *Sports and the Law* deal with important legal issues without descending into jargon or lawyer's Latin. Although sports are ubiquitous in modern American life—the late chief justice, Earl Warren, proudly acknowledged that he turned his newspaper first to the sports page—only recently has the body of case law on sport in America reached a level sufficient to justify such an encyclopedic treatment. This volume's editor, Charles E. Quirk, has created a book that not only presents an organized catalog of material on this subject but also makes an important contribution in and of itself to the emerging field of sports law.

Charles E. Quirk holds a Ph.D. in Religion from the University of Iowa, a B.D. from McCormick Theological Seminary (Chicago), and a B.A. from Carroll College (Waukesha, Wisconsin). Professor Quirk has been a member of the history faculty at the University of Northern Iowa since 1963. He regularly teaches courses in American religious history, American urban history, and historical methods at both the undergraduate and graduate levels. Among Professor Quirk's professional contributions are articles on American religious history in the *Journal of Presbyterian History* and the *Wisconsin Magazine of History* and convention presentations on such subjects as race, religion, and urban life. For *Sports and the Law: Major Legal Cases,* Professor Quirk has drawn upon both his vocation as a historian and his avocation as a sports fan. For those interested, Professor Quirk is a passionate follower of the Chicago White Sox and the Green Bay Packers.

John W. Johnson
University of Northern Iowa
Editor, American Law and Society Series

Preface

When informed that I intended to edit a volume about sports law, most colleagues and friends expressed amazement that such a field existed. Even a cursory review of several indicators, however, discloses not only the reality of the field or discipline but also its continuing growth and significance. Among the tokens of the flourishing of sports law during the past two decades are the publication of specialized treatises, articles on facets of sports law in traditional law reviews, appearance of legal journals or reviews devoted solely to sports law, and courses on the subject in law schools.

These aforementioned items, of course, derive from an arena ordinary people are most unlikely to enter. The common run of humanity in the United States does, however, watch sports coverage on television and read about sports in newspapers and magazines. It is difficult in this more general arena not to encounter stories related to sports and law. The news often appears to deal with controversies surrounding the rights of players and owners, or litigation due to injuries to participants or fans.

Both professional and amateur observers of the dynamics of life in the United States testify to the central roles played by both sports and law. Americans are a sports-loving people. They also are increasingly willing to go to court. The abundance, if not oversupply, of lawyers in the nation provides legal resources for owners, players, and fans. It is not surprising, therefore, that a linkage of sports and law has occurred.

With the expansion of television beginning in the 1950s, the increase in the number of major league baseball franchises, and the growing popularity of sports such as professional football and basketball, the field for litigation increased enormously. Labor unions, frequently associated with blue-collar factory workers, moved into the ranks of players who performed on baseball diamonds, football fields, and basketball courts. Collective bargaining, therefore, provided a focus for legal disputes. Franchise owners in various sports saw opportunities to expand leagues and to move their clubs from one location to another. Cities abandoned by teams took their claims to court.

College sports also offered numerous opportunities for litigation. Court battles occurred over a wide variety of issues, including the constitutional rights of college student-athletes, the power of regulatory organizations, and the relationship between agents and student-athletes.

Discrimination in sports provided another fertile area for litigation. The past two decades, in particular, produced numerous cases related to gender or racial discrimination.

The topics mentioned above represent a sampling of the essays published in this volume devoted to sports law and are examples of the existence of a field or discipline that promises continued vitality in the forthcoming decades.

Sports and the Law: Major Legal Cases should attract the interest of a variety of audiences. Authorities in the field of sports law will want to examine how their colleagues as well as nonspecialists treat specific cases and broader issues. Also, lawyers who lack familiarity with sports law may desire an introductory exposure to the rapidly expanding field. Scholars in fields other than law may seek relatively brief descriptions of cases and broader movements. Finally, sports fans who know names such as Oscar Robertson, John Mackey, and Curt Flood may discover their significance in the legal arena.

In the preparation of the volume, the general categories were chosen before deciding upon particular cases. The four major divisions of the book, therefore, remained fairly constant from beginning to end. One of the categories, "Liability and Legislation," is enshrined in the standard treatises. In the second major division, "The Regulation of Organized Sports," readers will find cases and issues related to some of the most familiar persons and events in the history of sports in the United States. Another popular area, antitrust, is treated under the rubric of "The Rights of Players and Owners." The fourth and final classification, "Racial and Gender

Discrimination," embraces essays touching upon an area of increasing importance in society.

Several characteristics of the essays as a whole deserve recognition. All of the essays were written specifically for this volume; phrased differently, none of the essays are reprints or glosses of articles published elsewhere. Most of the essays treat cases that appear in standard books in the field of sports law. The cases under examination were decided at either the state or federal levels of the judicial system. Many of the essays deal with conventional areas such as antitrust, but some discuss recently emerging areas, such as liability suits alleging misrepresentation or unfair treatment by coaches. Chronologically, the cases range from the latter part of the nineteenth century to the last decade of the twentieth. Finally, several of the essays do not deal with court cases but with actions of authorities, such as commissioners of sports leagues, or the policies of governing bodies, especially the National Collegiate Athletic Association (NCAA).

Readers of the volume deserve to know and to pass their own judgment on the reasons for the selection of the cases and issues. Some of the cases represent landmark decisions, establishing crucial precedents. Other cases, although not leaving behind important legal markers, possess features that may spark the interest of lawyers and general readers. A portion of the essays touch upon issues which have been significant in the past and promise to remain influential in the future. Another group of essays deals with persons in the field of sports who enjoy widespread public familiarity.

A somewhat related topic concerns the criteria for selection of essayists. The editor possessed either personal or reliable secondhand information on three measures: first, the prospective author's deep interest in sports in general and solid familiarity with the sport specifically related to the essay of assignment; second, the person's ability to conduct research in the area of sports law; and third, the scholar's competency in writing both for a general audience and for readers with legal training.

The editor also sought diversity among the contributors of essays. Included in the mix were considerations of occupation, age, gender, and geography. Forty-five authors produced the fifty essays published in the volume. In regard to occupations, seventeen are professors, five are practicing lawyers, and ten were students in law school when preparing their essays. Other occupations represented include physicians, ministers, high school teachers, computer consultants, and librarians. The ages of contributors range from the mid-twenties to the early sixties, with the average age around the late thirties. In terms of gender, females constitute eight contributors. Data on the place of residence at the time of writing indicates that twenty-two contributors lived in the Midwest, fifteen in the West, and four each in the Northeast and the South.

In regard to their personal involvement in sports, the authors filled out a personal and professional information form. The most frequently mentioned participatory sports, in descending order, were basketball, baseball, football, tennis, softball, track and field, golf, swimming, and racquetball. As for spectator status, the most frequently listed sports, again in top to bottom order, were football, baseball, and basketball.

How might readers explore the volume? Some might wish to read straight through. Others might opt to sample essays in each of the four major parts. Still others might begin with the introductions to each part for information on the focus of the essays. Another group of readers might start out by selecting the part that most interests them and then proceed in the order imposed by the editor or randomly.

Each essay ends with a selected bibliography. The publications listed are intended not to demonstrate the author's scholarly erudition, but to provide directions to readers who wish to know which works proved most helpful to the writer and, perhaps, merit perusal by readers. The authors and, in some instances, the editor, sought to list books whenever possible. Law reviews represent another top priority in the bibliographies. In some essays, important material was found in periodicals such as *Sports Illustrated* or newspapers such as the *Chicago Tribune* and the *New York Times*. In a few essays, the writer or editor discovered significant information in local newspapers.

As a professional historian rather than a lawyer, I relied heavily upon experts whose writings have shaped the field of sports law and definitively influenced the form and substance of this volume. The following academicians made significant, albeit unknowing, contributions to *Sports and the Law: Major Legal Cases:* Robert Berry, Boston College Law School; Lionel Sobel, Loyola Law School of Loyola Marymount University; John Weistart, Duke University School of Law; and Raymond Yasser, University of Tulsa College of Law.

For those readers who wish to probe more thoroughly into the field of sports law, the volumes listed below receive frequent citation in the selected bibliography component of the essays. The editor also used these books in the selection of cases and in the interpretation of legal decisions.

Berry, R. and G. Wong. *Law and Business of the Sports Industries.* Two volumes. 1986 and second edition in 1993. This two-volume publication is a "casebook" in the field. The first volume deals with professional sports leagues, and the second volume treats issues in both amateur and professional sports.

Champion, W., Jr. *Fundamentals of Sports Law.* 1990. A volume that is intended primarily for practicing lawyers but is also of use to a wider audience.

Sobel, L. *Professional Sports and the Law.* 1977 and 1981 Supplement. A major text in the field of sports law. Includes discussions of virtually all of the major cases. Nonspecialists will find the volume quite readable.

Weistart, J. and C. Lowell. *The Law of Sports.* 1979 and 1985 Supplement. Undoubtedly the single most important publication in the field. Widely acclaimed and rightly so. Comprehensive in its coverage of both amateur and professional sports.

Yasser, R. *Sports Law: Cases and Materials.* 1985. This helpful volume provides an informative selection of cases related to amateur athletics, professional sports, and criminal and civil liability for sports activities.

Charles E. Quirk
Cedar Falls, Iowa

Acknowledgments

Living with a scholarly project for several years generates a lengthy list of persons who deserve recognition for their contributions. Certainly the forty-five authors who wrote fifty essays deserve plaudits. I enjoy a personal acquaintanceship with twenty-nine of the authors. The remaining essayists I know through a personal and professional information form which each completed, correspondence, and in some cases, telephone conversations.

Several of the authors provided valuable counsel and assistance throughout the development of the book. John W. Johnson, Series Editor for Garland Publishing's American Law and Society volumes, offered direct advice when requested, prodding when needed, and friendship always. Eldest son Wayne S. Quirk took time away from his scientific research activities to help structure the volume and to keep his father on task. Legal Consultant Thomas P. Frerichs found ways to maintain his law practice and family responsibilities while scrutinizing essays for legal accuracy. Timothy Wiles generously helped me navigate through the ever-changing waters of on-line searching at the same time that he worked toward the M.A. degree in history and fulfilled his professional librarian duties.

During the years in which the project evolved, I received considerable support from various individuals at the University of Northern Iowa. Many colleagues in the Department of History expressed special interest in the volume, particularly Joanne Abel Goldman, Kenneth Lyftogt, Robert Martin, Robert Neymeyer, and David Walker. The Department of History generously underwrote the costs for photocopying, supplies, telephone, and postage. Acting upon the recommendation of the Professional Development Leave (PDL) Committee, the University Administration and the Iowa State Board of Regents awarded a PDL during spring 1993, which provided five months of released time from usual classroom and committee responsibilities. Graduate College Dean John Somervill and Associate Graduate Dean David Walker approved my requests for two grants that helped cover travel expenses to law school libraries.

I am indebted to the librarians at several institutions of higher education for their interest and assistance. Many productive research hours were spent in the intellectually stimulating atmospheres of the University of Iowa Law Library, Iowa City; the University of Michigan Law Library, Ann Arbor; and the Wayne State University Arthur Neef Law Library, Detroit. The librarians at the University of Northern Iowa surpassed their reputations for efficient, competent service. Herbert Safford, Director of the Donald O. Rod Library, granted the use of a faculty study for several successive semesters. Larry Kieffer, Head of Reader's Service, and the superb group of professionals which he leads, made locating needed materials a pleasure. Reference Librarians Stanley Lyle and Timothy Wiles in particular deserve formal recognition for their valuable assistance.

In the early stages of the project, I assumed that locating qualified authors and matching them with suitable cases or issues represented a major challenge. This task proved relatively simple and enjoyable. Most of the scholars I approached accepted the invitation to contribute an essay on the topic I suggested.

In a few cases, talented researchers and writers turned down the opportunity due to other academic commitments. David Walker and John Wunder, however, provided leads to highly competent writers. Others who suggested either cases or authors include Marchell Austin, Tom Frerichs, Sharon Huddleston, John Johnson, Wayne Quirk, and Tim Wiles. Jan Stiglitz, Professor of Law at California Western School of Law, not only wrote a major article, but also recruited several authors from his fall 1992 class in sports law.

Several essayists participated in the Advanced Placement Reading session in United States History at Trinity University, San Antonio, Texas, in the summer of 1992. At this event, conducted under the auspices of the Educational Testing Service, I enjoyed informal conversations with many readers. Some of these exchanges were partially intended to identify potential contributors. I appreciate the acceptance of the invitation to write an essay for the volume by these colleagues who experienced what is sometimes termed a "boot camp for historians": Patrick Allitt, David Allyn, Lester Brooks, Michael Flamm, Susan Pingel, Terry Radtke, and Richard Terry.

During the summer of 1991, historian Bob Martin led a seminar at the University of Northern Iowa on the theme "Sports: A Mirror of American Culture, 1865–1980." Bob and the participants in the seminar patiently listened as I explained what I knew about the world of sports law. More importantly, they developed a long list of sports-related situations that lent themselves to court suits. I am indebted to Bob and the seminar scholars: Joseph Bohr, Andrew Doyle, Marlis Horgen, Frederick Johnson, Steve Moon, Al Rabenold, and Kenneth Stark.

In editing the essays, I benefitted from the suggestions of those who read all of the articles, namely, Tom Frerichs and John Johnson, and three friends and relatives who thoroughly examined most of the manuscripts, Mary K. Eakin, Wayne Quirk, and Tim Wiles. Mary K., a former university colleague and very close friend of the Quirk family, continues to read widely in her retirement years. She took time off from relishing literary classics and occasionally watching golf and baseball games featuring the North Side Chicago team to meticulously inspect the essays and to offer helpful suggestions for improving literary style. Mary K., Kathy Linda, Steve Quirk, and Wayne Quirk provided valuable assistance during the late innings of the editorial process. The published version of the essays will show that I followed the recommendations of the other readers nearly all of the time. In relatively few cases I persevered in what they will, perhaps correctly, regard as my folly. As editor of the volume, I bear responsibility for whatever stylistic deficiencies remain, as well as for the general organization of the volume and the choice of cases or issues.

From the inception of the idea of a sports law encyclopedia, through the years of recruiting authors and assigning cases, to the editing and publication process, Garland Editor Kennie Lyman proved a reliable source of counsel, a careful critic of several sample essays, and a constant dispenser of encouragement. She knew exactly when I needed definite directions and when I required some space to wander. Sylvia Ploss and Jill Sarkady at Garland Publishing are due much appreciation for their skilled work in turning the manuscript into a book.

Judy Dohlman, the highly competent secretary for the Department of History at the University of Northern Iowa, cheerfully applied her talents to many aspects of the preparation of the volume. In the final stages of editing, Judy proved especially valuable both as a professional and as a friend.

Family involvement in the project made the work especially rewarding. Reading some of the essays induced pleasant memories of my late father, Ralph, and my mother, Irma, showing an interest in my mediocre performances in high school football, basketball, and baseball. They also took me to watch American Association baseball at Borchert Field in Milwaukee, to observe the big league variety at Wrigley Field in Chicago's North Side, and to my favorite stadium, Comiskey Park, on the South Side. Their parental generosity allowed me to witness such memorable events as Casey Stengel coaching at third base while holding an umbrella during a Sunday rainstorm at Borchert Field, Bill Veeck distributing boxes of cereal at a Saturday morning Milwaukee Brewers game, and Larry Doby making his big league debut at Comiskey Park.

My in-laws, the late J. George and Lorena Senty, spent many evenings with their daughter and her future husband at Milwaukee's County Stadium. Pleasant recollections abound of Henry Aaron, Warren Spahn, Lou Burdette, Eddie Matthews, and the other members of the talented Braves' teams of the mid-1950s as well as of the pre- or postgame visit to Gilles Custard Stand on Blue Mound Road.

Russell, my deceased younger brother, loved his family, his profession, and playing both golf, in which he excelled, and Milwaukee's favorite card game, Sheepshead, at which he proved erratic. Russ's brilliant medical career and admirable life ended at the age of forty due to brain cancer. The power of his engaging personality and the insight of his witty observations about the worlds of medicine, politics, and sports remain with his wife, Sue, and daughters, Sarah, Rebecca, and Rachel, and with members of my immediate family.

Our four sons all participated in athletics in school and, unlike their father, distinguished themselves. We enjoyed spectator status as they competed in swimming meets, and in football, basketball, and baseball games. They all contributed in various ways to the project. Wayne transferred his research skills from otolaryngology to helping organize a sports law volume. Youngest son Steve took time out from his studies in the Masters of Public Policy program to review some of the essays and to serve as computer consultant for the project. He also prepared the statistical analysis of the authors that is summarized in the Preface. Because of their professional obligations, Brian and Bob could not work directly on the volume but they constantly displayed interest and encouragement. Our sons' spouses, Kelley, Cheri, Jan, and Toni, provided inspiration as they attended numerous sporting events in outdoor parks when midwestern weather offered discomfort to veteran and rookie fans alike.

Gale Senty Quirk, to whom the volume is dedicated, shared the opportunity to watch our children experience the successes and disappointments related to participation in formal athletics. Over the years she has cheerfully attended games played in rain and snow, stifling heat, and bitter cold. During the period that this project received a major share of my time and interest, Gale provided both mental working space and loving support.

Contributors

Patrick Allitt
Department of History
Emory University

David M. Allyn
Fairport, New York

Marchell M. Austin
School of Health
 Physical Education
    and Leisure Services
University of Northern Iowa

Lester S. Brooks
Department of History
Anne Arundel Community College

Sara L. Cohen
Colorado District Court
Jefferson County, Colorado

Joseph J. Craciun
San Diego, California

David F. Dolan
Kresge Hearing Research Institute
University of Michigan Medical
    School

Heather M. Feuerhelm
Cedar Rapids, Iowa

Michael W. Flamm
New York, New York

Thomas P. Frerichs
Fulton, Frerichs, Martin,
    & Anders P.C.
Waterloo, Iowa

L. John Gable
Crossroads Presbyterian Church
Mequon, Wisconsin

James W. Hewitt
Lincoln, Nebraska

Brenda Holliday
Chicago, Illinois

H. Daniel Holm Jr.
Ball, Kirk, Holm, & Nardini P.C.
Waterloo, Iowa

Ted Hovet Jr.
Department of English
Western Kentucky University

Sharon Huddleston
School of Health
   Physical Education
   and Leisure Services
University of Northern Iowa

John W. Johnson
Department of History
University of Northern Iowa

Chris Kanzius
Superior Court
San Diego, California

Scott Katz
San Diego, California

Jack Kolbe
Presbytery of Wyoming

W.H. Lee-Sammons
Department of Psychology
California State University–
   Sacramento

M. Philip Lucas
Department of History
Cornell College

Robert F. Martin
Department of History
University of Northern Iowa

Scott McEthron
Department of English
Southern Illinois University

Donald M. McKale
Department of History
Clemson University

Daniel J. Murphy
Cedar Falls, Iowa

Michele Murphy
Baltimore, Maryland

Robert Neymeyer
Department of History
University of Northern Iowa

Frederic Pepe
Superior Court, Newark
New Jersey

Susan F. Pingel
Skaneateles, New York

Charles E. Quirk
Department of History
University of Northern Iowa

Wayne S. Quirk
Department of Otolaryngology
School of Medicine
Wayne State University

Terry Radtke
Milwaukee, Wisconsin

Stephen J. Rapp
Waterloo, Iowa

Steven D. Reschly

Division of Social Science
Northeast Missouri State University

David Rodgers

Kresge Hearing Research Institute
University of Michigan Medical
    School

Steven Schulte

Department of Social and Behavioral
    Sciences
Mesa State College

Eric A. Seiken

Law Offices of Dan Zeidma
El Cajon, California

William L. Siler

Department of Physical Therapy
St. Louis University

David Sitz

San Diego, California

Jan Stiglitz

California Western School of Law

Richard M. Terry

Legal Assistant Program
Baltimore City Community
    College–Harbor Campus

Jennifer Turner

San Diego, California

William L. Wegman

State Public Defender of Iowa
Des Moines, Iowa

Timothy J. Wiles

Research Department
National Baseball Library
    and Archive
Cooperstown, New York

Part One

Sports Law: Liability and Legislation

At their most elemental level, sports are games. But games can be hotly contested and may occasionally result in physical injuries to participants or spectators. Personal injuries offer a subspecies of what lawyers and judges call "torts," that is, miscellaneous civil wrongs. Since sports injuries often spark high-profile treatments by the print or electronic media, it makes sense to begin a volume on sports law with a series of eight essays, in roughly chronological order, examining some of the most interesting recent court cases involving injuries on or close to the field of play.

"Tortious Impact" leads off the volume and the essays on liability. Readers here will find a description of the vicious blow delivered by Los Angeles Laker forward Kermit Washington to the face of Rudy Tomjanovich in a National Basketball Association game in December 1977. The attack by the Laker player against the Houston Rocket forward led to a fascinating lawsuit which culminated in a lucrative financial settlement for Tomjanovich and a clear statement on the responsibility of an employer to provide adequate supervision. The next essay, "In Jeopardy: Football Helmet Manufacturers and Wearers," concentrates upon the conditions under which manufacturers encounter products' liability charges. "Negligence and Liability: A Coach's Nightmare" explores the responsibilities of coaches to properly instruct athletes, with a focus on an important case in baseball. The succeeding essay, "The Coach's Legal Duty to Properly Instruct and to Warn Athletes of the Inherent Dangers in Sport," pursues the same theme, concentrating upon a significant case in high school football.

"Injustice Uncovered? Worker's Compensation and the Professional Athlete," provides a thorough discussion of the complex relationship between liability and legislation. The next essay, "Fans Strike Out with Foul Ball Litigation," treats the legal ramifications of a fairly common occurrence, namely, an errant baseball hitting a spectator. "The Application of the Attractive Nuisance Doctrine to Sport" probes the responsibilities of various types of property owners to those who enter their premises. The final essay on liability, "Not the Same Game," deals with several recent examples of athletes bringing lawsuits against coaches on various grounds not encountered in the previous essays.

The final three essays in Part I offer perspectives on sports legislation, specifically, why the games that athletes play prompt regulation by legislative bodies. Note that, unlike the specifically focused essays on authority and discipline in organized sports in Part II, the final three essays in Part I offer broadly ranging historical treatments of sport and the law. "Sports versus the Sabbath: Professional Baseball and Blue Laws," provides a sociocultural analysis of the late nineteenth- and early twentieth-century conflict between those favoring professional baseball on Sunday and those opposing the break with tradition. The following essay, "Amateurs, Professionals, and Eligibility for Americans in the Olympics," examines the historical developments leading to an expansion of player participation in the Olympic Games. Lastly, "Fading in the Stretch: Live Horse Racing in the 1990s" discusses the Interstate Horse Racing Act of 1978 and subsequent features of the sport.

Tortious Impact

Steven D. Reschly

Rudy Tomjanovich v. California Sports, Inc. No. H-78-243 (S.D. Tex. 1979)
The sound reminded Kareem Abdul Jabbar of a watermelon dropped on cement. Referee Bob Rakel compared it to a baseball bat hitting a concrete wall. The "crack!" seemed to Dwight Jones like a tree branch breaking. The sickening sound effects resulted from Los Angeles Laker power forward Kermit Washington punching Houston Rockets forward Rudy Tomjanovich during a National Basketball Association game on December 9, 1977. Jack McCloskey, Laker assistant coach, called it "the hardest punch in the history of mankind." The blow caused serious, life-threatening injuries to Tomjanovich's face, and resulted in the first successful civil damages action ever brought by a professional athlete against an opponent or an opposing team.

The episode in the Los Angeles Forum occurred when Houston center Kevin Kunnert and Washington skirmished after a Rocket rebound. Laker center Jabbar grabbed Kunnert in an attempt to break up the fight, but Washington hit Kunnert several times, and Tomjanovich trotted toward his injured teammate to assist him. NBA referee Rakel had already whistled and ejected Washington from the game for a fighting foul, when Washington turned and hit the approaching Tomjanovich, who did not expect the blow. Both players were 6'8", though Washington was ten pounds heavier. Tomjanovich toppled like a felled tree. He spent two weeks in the hospital, suffering from facial and skull fractures, a broken nose and separated upper jaw, a cerebral concussion, smashed sinus passages, and a detached retina. In effect, the bone structure of his face was knocked loose from his skull. Physicians compared the surgical repairs to putting a broken eggshell back together with Scotch tape.

Tomjanovich sued California Sports, Inc. (doing business as the Los Angeles Lakers), seeking actual and punitive damages on the basis of tort law. He did not file suit directly against Washington, although the primary purpose of tort law is to compensate for injuries sustained by one person as the result of the conduct of another. Criminal harm to another, or assault and battery, requires evidence beyond a reasonable doubt of intent to harm. Civil lawsuits based on reckless or negligent acts require a less rigorous standard of proof than "beyond a reasonable doubt." The standard of proof in a civil action requires that a claim be supported by a mere preponderance of the evidence.

Civil lawsuits alleging a reckless or negligent use of excessive force in sporting activity have been defended using the common-law principle of "to one who is willing no wrong is done" and the doctrine of "assumption of risk." In brief, participation in a sport implies willingness to assume the risks inherent in the activity. Given the controlled violence in professional sports such as football and hockey, and in light of the fact that intimidation just beyond the rules is often considered part of the game, sorting out provocation and self-defense is nearly impossible. A key precedent in this area is *Hackbart* v. *Cincinnati Bengals, Inc.* (601 F. 2d 5166 10th Cir. 1979), in which a player and his employer were held accountable for reckless misconduct resulting in a professional football injury. Before *Hackbart* and *Tomjanovich,* however, sports injuries rarely resulted in tort liability, excepting those cases in which violence far outside the rules, such as hitting another player with a baseball bat, indicated actual intent to commit an assault.

Internal league controls had also failed to stop excessive violence in professional sports. During the 1976–77 NBA season, there were forty-one fights among players, according to a *Sports Illustrated* story published on October 31, 1977. Given high player salaries, fines tended to be relatively minor, and league officials imposed few suspensions. Although Lawrence O'Brien, NBA Commissioner, ordered Washington suspended from play for a minimum of six days without pay and fined him $10,000 (at that time the largest financial penalty in sports history), professional franchises usually continued to pay player fines and to encourage violent play to achieve victories. Attempts to pass federal legislation against sports violence also failed. The only avenue of control and redress seemed to be civil liability intervention. Players, however, were usually reluctant to sue, preferring to handle problems "in the family" through informal retribution.

Lawyers for Tomjanovich followed two innovative approaches to hold the Laker organization liable, rather than Kermit Washington personally: vicarious liability and negligent supervision. In the former, an employer is held liable for the wrongs committed by an employee if they were committed within the scope of employment. The lawsuit charged that the Lakers created an atmosphere in which the players believed that violence was an acceptable, if not a desirable, mechanism to ensure winning. As for negligent supervision, the lawsuit accused the Lakers of knowing about Washington's violent tendencies and not acting to curb them. Lawyers for California Sports Inc. responded by charging that Tomjanovich was negligent and assumed the risk of violence. They argued that the Houston forward showed reckless indifference to his own welfare by charging into a fight. Finally, they contended that Washington was exercising the right of self-defense.

The federal jury trial in the Southern District of Texas, Houston, took place under California law, the site of the incident, and lasted ten days. The plaintiff and defendant introduced testimony from eyewitnesses and experts, and the jury reviewed films and photographs of the events. Tomjanovich showed evidence that he was acting as a peacemaker and was unprepared for the punch. In effect, he ran right into the blow, an excessive punch that violated professional basketball rules and was not part of the risks of the game that a player assumed. In regard to negligent supervision, Tomjanovich introduced evidence that the Lakers encouraged overly aggressive play; did not discipline violent players and, in fact, paid the fines for players penalized for violent action; encouraged Washington to be featured in an October 31, 1977, issue of *Sports Illustrated* that dealt with basketball's "enforcers"; and ratified Washington's actions against Tomjanovich by paying his fine and by not disciplining him, even though Washington had participated in seven fights in three years.

The defendant's evidence tended to show that basketball was an inherently physical game in which scuffles and fights were foreseeable. Washington's lawyers contended that Tomjanovich did not act reasonably to protect himself and should have known the risks of approaching a fight at rapid speed. In their scenario, Washington believed he was in danger when he glimpsed the Houston player approaching him. The Lakers also claimed that they were trying to deal with the problem of on-court violence by threatening loss of playing time and even employment. Finally, the Lakers asserted that, to a certain extent, violence was to be expected in professional basketball because it was an intrinsic part of the game, and Tomjanovich consented to the risks involved by participating.

The federal district judge, John V. Singleton, gave a broad interpretation to the scope of employment and negligent supervision in his instructions to the jury. In his view, an employee need not act only in the employer's interests for the employer to be held responsible; the act must be committed during duties which the employee "was employed, ordered, or empowered to perform." A sports employer, according to Judge Singleton, could be held liable for negligent supervision if it knew, "or by the exercise of an ordinary care should have known," that an athlete had violent propensities that might endanger other players.

On August 17, 1979, the jury found Washington and the Lakers liable. It rejected the self-defense argument and faulted the Lakers for negligent supervision. Washington had, in fact, committed a battery and had acted with "reckless disregard for the safety of others." The jury awarded Tomjanovich $3.2 million, of which $1.5 million was for punitive damages. The jury had been instructed to award punitive damages if they found that the Lakers had ratified Washington's malicious act, as claimed by Tomjanovich. In civil suits, punitive damages can be awarded for punishment and as a warning to others. The case was settled out of court for approximately $2.13 million on April 14, 1981, one week before arguments were scheduled to begin in the United States Court of Civil Appeals for the Fifth Circuit in New Orleans.

The Houston Rockets also claimed that the Lakers intentionally interfered with the contractual relations of the team and Tomjanovich. Following the trial verdict, the Rockets and the Lakers settled this claim for approximately $750,000, to compensate the Rockets for loss of services, gate receipts, and money spent replacing their roster player.

To that point, Tomjanovich had had an eight-year career in the NBA. Four times he had been named to the All-Star team. After his injury, Tomjanovich played two more seasons, averaging nineteen points a game and making the All-Star team in 1979–80. He retired after the 1980–81 season. Tomjanovich scouted for the Rockets and assisted several head coaches, and in 1992 took over as head coach. At the end of the 1993–94 season, Tomjanovich coached the Rockets to their first NBA championship. Surprising many professional basketball commentators and fans, the Rockets repeated as champs the following season. Washington played on four NBA teams after the Lakers traded him, and he retired in 1988. Spectators might have expected that the lawsuit that resulted from the Tomjanovich-Washington encounter served to deter violence during professional sporting events. But the bench-clearing brawls in baseball and the continued fighting in basketball reveal that in a society that condones violence and worships winning, eradicating violence in sports has proven an elusive goal.

Selected Bibliography

Carroll, J. "Torts in Sports—'I'll See You in Court!'" *Akron Law Review* 16 (Winter 1983): 537–553.

Gulotta, S., Jr. "Torts in Sports: Deterring Violence in Professional Athletics." *Fordham Law Review* 48 (April 1980): 764–793.

Kirkpatrick, C. "Shattered and Shaken." *Sports Illustrated.* January 2, 1978: 46–47.

Tucker, N. "Assumption of Risk and Vicarious Liability in Personal Injury Actions Brought by Professional Athletes." *Duke Law Journal* 1980 (September 1980): 742–765.

Yasser, R. *Sports Law: Cases and Materials.* Lanham: University Press of America, 1985.

In Jeopardy
Football Helmet Manufacturers and Wearers

William L. Siler

Rawlings Sporting Goods Co. Inc. v. Daniels,
Tex.Civ.App., 619 S.W.2d, 435 (1981)

On November 19, 1992, Dennis Byrd of the New York Jets ran head-first into the chest of a teammate. The collision led to Byrd's paralysis from the waist down. Millions of people viewed the incident on national television. Byrd subsequently regained use of his legs, but the incident served to renew discussions about violence in football and the amount of protection provided by football helmets. One year before the injury to Byrd, Detroit Lions' offensive guard Mike Utley suffered severe spinal damage and lost the use of his legs when a Los Angeles Rams defensive player fell on his neck and head.

In 1975, about 6 percent of every 100,000 high school football players suffered neck injuries. For the same number of college players the rate rose to almost 30 percent. Of those receiving neck injuries, approximately one-third were rendered quadriplegic. The rate of neck injuries contributed to drafting of rules prohibiting "spearing," the deliberate use of the helmet to punish a ball carrier. By 1989, the rate of neck injuries had decreased to less than 1 percent per 100,000 players at the junior and senior high school levels and under 2 percent for 100,000 players in college. Catastrophic injuries, such as those experienced by Byrd and Utley, however, continue to occur. Wearers and manufacturers of helmets, therefore, find themselves engaged in lengthy and expensive lawsuits.

An important case in the field of product liability and negligence concerned Mark Daniels, a Texas high school player, and the Rawlings Sporting Goods firm. Daniels played quarterback for the Franklin High School football team. While taking part in a team practice on August 20, 1974, he collided with a teammate. The force of the impact produced an indentation in Daniels' helmet. The young player gave the helmet to his coach and resumed practice. While participating in workouts the next day, Daniels passed out. He was subsequently taken to two hospitals. Physicians diagnosed his injury as a subdural hematoma. Following surgery, Daniels returned to school in mid-September. The injury, however, left Daniels with severe and permanent brain damage.

Early in the 1980s the courts dealt with a suit brought by Daniels against the helmet manufacturer. The 20th Judicial District Court, Robertson County, awarded a $1.5 million judgment against the Rawlings company. The manufacturer appealed, but unsuccessfully. Judge C. McDonald of the Court of Civil Appeals affirmed the ruling of the lower court. He held that the company had indeed manufactured the helmet, and that the defectively made helmet was a "producing cause of player's injuries." Judge McDonald went on to declare that the manufacturer had a duty to warn users that its helmet would not provide protection against head and brain injuries. He ruled that the "manufacturer's failure to warn that its helmet would not protect against subdural hematomas exposed [the] player to unreasonable risk of harm, that the failure to warn was [a] producing cause of his injury and that the failure to warn was negligence and a proximate cause of the injury." Judge McDonald concluded that Daniels was entitled to the award of $750,000 in exemplary damages.

Every football helmet now includes the following statement: WARNING: DO NOT STRIKE AN OPPONENT WITH ANY PART OF THIS HELMET OR FACE MASK. THIS IS A VIOLATION OF FOOTBALL RULES AND MAY CAUSE YOU TO SUFFER SEVERE BRAIN OR NECK INJURY, INCLUDING PARALYSIS OR DEATH. SEVERE BRAIN OR NECK INJURY MAY ALSO OCCUR ACCIDENTALLY WHILE PLAYING FOOTBALL. NO HELMET CAN PREVENT ALL SUCH INJURIES. YOU USE THIS HELMET AT YOUR OWN RISK.

Since that warning appeared, there has been a decline in successful law suits against helmet manufacturers. They are still likely to face liability damages, however, if the helmet is found defective and if that defect is not "open and obvious." Manufacturers have been found liable for damage attributable to factors such as faulty design, dangerous construction, inadequate testing, and failure to warn the user of potential risks associated with the intended use of the product. The success of the failure-to-warn strategy has been dependent upon the age and experience of the plaintiff. The court may decide that a manufacturer has little obligation to warn an older, experienced athlete of the risks inherent in a sport, whereas the manufacturer bears responsibility for failure to provide detailed directions for use and warning for younger, inexperienced athletes.

Because helmet manufacturers have developed effective strategies for combatting product liability suits, coaches and school districts have increasingly found themselves named as defendants in negligence suits when catastrophic neck injuries occur. Ultimately, escalating liability insurance costs may force school districts to discontinue football. In *Torts and Sports*, Raymond L. Yasser noted that helmet litigation might result in the death of football. Yasser, a major contributor to the field of sports law, contended that "football as we know it is really socially undesirable."

Selected Bibliography

Ausness, R. "Retribution and Deterrence: The Role of Punitive Damages in Products Liability Legislation." *Kentucky Law Journal* 74 (1985–86): 1–125.

Cantu, R. and F. Mueller. "Catastrophic Spine Injuries in Football (1977–1989)." *Journal of Spinal Disorders* (1990): 227–231.

Champion, W. *Fundamentals of Sports Law*. Deerfield: Clark, Boardman, Callaghan, 1990.

Yasser, R. *Torts and Sports: Legal Liability in Professional and Amateur Athletics*. Westport: Quorum Books, 1985.

Negligence and Liability

A Coach's Nightmare

W.H. Lee-Sammons

Passantino v. Board of Education of City of New York,
395 N.Y.S. 2d 628 (N.Y. App. Div. 1976)

"The mere happening of an accident does not constitute negligence."
This statement depicts a main area of controversy in case law involving liability. Consider the following high school baseball incident. The squeeze play was called but the bunt attempt was missed, the runner dove into home plate and only the catcher got up. Where is the fault? The court awarded the experienced, now paralyzed, high school base runner a hefty settlement. Upon appeal some years later the judgment was reversed. This case is one example of the plethora of sports-related injury litigation in recent decades. *Who* is responsible for the athlete's misfortune, the player or someone else?

In the highly publicized case summarized above, a sixteen-year-old baseball player, who was a junior in high school at the time, suffered a tragic, paralyzing accident. The young man, Ray Passantino, was on third base when the coach signalled for a squeeze bunt. This plan required Passantino to break for home plate shortly after the pitch was released toward the batter, who stood in the bunt position. The idea behind this strategy is for the runner to score before the bunt can be handled by either the catcher, pitcher or another fielder.

In this instance, however, the hitter missed the ball and the catcher caught it. Passantino continued full speed in an attempt to score by sliding headfirst, using his head as a "battering ram," in order to run over the catcher and, hopefully, knock the ball loose. As a result of the collision, Passantino was permanently paralyzed and is quadriplegic. Passantino filed suit claiming negligence against the New York City Board of Education and his baseball coach.

The plaintiff contended that the coach had praised him for sliding similarly in another game and that this praise had motivated
him to behave in the same manner again. In Passantino's eyes, the
coach was solely responsible for his crippling injury. The Court
awarded $1.8 million in damages. The Appellate Division of the
New York Court deemed this award excessive and reduced the
amount to $1 million. In a powerful opinion, however, Justice
Cohalan reversed the decision on the grounds that Passantino participated voluntarily and, as such, his resultant misfortune came under
the doctrines of contributory negligence and assumption of risk.

Justice Cohalan took the view that voluntary participation in a
sports-related activity, outside of that in a normal physical education class, involves inherent risks of possible injury, and since
Passantino had volunteered to participate, he alone was responsible
for his misfortune. The key case controlling the general notion of
inherent or primary assumption of risk involved a skier who, upon
colliding with a tree stump, suffered a serious injury and then sued
the resort for failing to maintain safe ski slopes. The skier was denied recovery on the grounds of the inherent risk of participation
(*Wright* v. *Mt. Mansfield Lift, Inc.,* 96 F. Supp. 786 [Dvt. 1951]
cited in Nygaard and Boone [1989]).

In addition, Justice Cohalan claimed that Passantino should have
assumed the risks associated with sliding headfirst. He also asserted
that the boy "for one unfortunate moment permitted his aggressive-
ness to overcome his common sense," and this action "solely and
wholly," *contributed* to his own negligence. According to Justice
Cohalan, therefore, both doctrines of the assumption of risk and
contributory negligence were carried by Passantino.

This case spurred considerable interest in the legal community
regarding the determination of responsibility in sports injury litiga-
tions involving negligence. In particular, the ensuing judicial review
of coaching methods inspired concern on the part of school district
administrators over possible liability of their physical education staff.
The possibility of potential liability suits for neglecting to adequately
teach students the fundamental inherent dangers of participating in
any sport obviously affected administrators, teachers, coaches, and
school boards.

Questions still arise as to whether it should have been the *duty* of the coach to teach Passantino how to slide headfirst or at least to warn him of the dangers of doing so. Does failing to do so constitute a breach of duty on the part of a coach? If so, can such a breach of duty be considered a proximate cause of injury to a plaintiff? Perhaps, but in the eyes of the law at the time, denial of recovery in this case was substantiated because the player *volunteered* to participate.

Selected Bibliography

Appenzeller, H. and T. Appenzeller. *Sports and the Courts*. Charlottesville: The Mitchie Company, 1980.

Nygaard, G. and T. Boone. *Coaches Guide to Sports Law*. Champaign: Human Kinetics Publishers, Inc., 1985.

Nygaard, G. and T. Boone. *Law for Physical Educators and Coaches*. 2nd ed. Columbus: Publishing Horizons, 1989.

Sobel, L. *Professional Sports and the Law*. New York: Law-Arts Publishers, Inc., 1977 and 1981 Supplement.

The Coach's Legal Duty to Properly Instruct and to Warn Athletes of the Inherent Dangers in Sport

Sharon Huddleston

Thompson v. Seattle Public School District (unpublished decision, 1982)

Sport litigation trends over the past few decades have resulted in the development of a legal duty for coaches to instruct athletes in the proper execution of sport skills in such a way as to insure safe participation. Also there exists the duty to warn both athletes and their parents of specific dangers inherent in a sport. These two points of law, combined with others, make it a coach's responsibility to conduct a program accordingly.

The first known case identified as a "failure to properly instruct" was *Bellman* v. *San Francisco High School District* (1938). In that case the plaintiff claimed that the head injury she sustained while performing a gymnastics move was due, in part, to the improper instruction received from the teacher. The judgment was for the plaintiff, but the teacher was not allowed to present evidence, curriculum guides and other information relevant to the activity, regarding his quality of instruction. Since 1938 a number of other cases, such as *Pirklev* v. *Oakdale Union Grammar School District* (1953); *Vendrell* v. *School District No. 26c, Malheur County* (1962); *Smith* v. *Consolidated School District No. 2* (1966); *Lueck* v. *City of Janesville* (1973); and *Garza* v. *Edinburg Consolidated Independent School District* (1979) concerning the propriety and adequacy of instruction prior to injuries have been heard. It was not until 1982, however, that the precedent was set for requiring proper instruction and the warning of risks inherent within an activity or sport.

In the landmark case of *Thompson* v. *Seattle Public School District*, an unpublished decision on Feb. 14, 1982, a high school football player was awarded $6.4 million for an injury that occurred in

1975 and left him quadriplegic. The injury occurred in practice, when Christopher Thompson lowered his head while being tackled. The coach and the school district were sued for failure to warn the athlete of the dangers inherent in the sport and for improper coaching instruction. The Thompson case was important because it shifted a great deal of the responsibility for the inherent risks involved in sport from the participant to the administrators and coaches. The Thompson decision weakened the "assumption of risk" doctrine that had been used as a common defense in sports-related injury cases since the 1962 decision in *Vendrell.* The two cases are almost identical except for the decisions. In the *Vendrell* case the judge ruled that "no prospective player need be told that a participant in the game of football may sustain injury. . . . the plaintiff assumed all of the obvious risks of which tackling was one." As a result of the *Thompson* case, the "assumption of risk" doctrine can only be used as a defense if the coaching staff can prove that the plaintiff knew of the inherent risks involved, understood the full implications of the risks, and then voluntarily chose to participate.

Another point critical to the *Thompson* decision was that the defendants could not document adequate instruction in relation to football skills, specifically running without lowering the head. In 1973, a judgment for the defendant in *Lueck* v. *City of Janesville* was rendered largely due to the fact that the teacher was allowed to submit lesson plans containing detailed notes on safety procedures and progressions used in a gymnastics unit. The provision of documentation regarding progression of skills, teaching methods, and conditioning and safety drills might have helped the defendants in the *Thompson* case support their claims of adequate instruction.

The ramifications of the *Thompson* case impact the day-to-day operations of activity and sport programs nationwide. The two legal duties of warning of risks and proper instruction require administrators, teachers, and coaches to take action designed to protect the athlete against possible catastrophic injury and the professional against litigation. Legal experts advise educational officials that this can be accomplished, in part, by instituting a comprehensive warning system within activity and sport programs at every level.

Perhaps the most important aspect of a comprehensive warning system is a meeting organized by athletic administrators and coaches for athletes and their parents. This meeting should be scheduled at the beginning of each competitive season/year for the purpose of informing athletes and parents of the dangers inherent in each activity or sport. The law requires that parents and athletes also receive written information regarding specific injuries such as sprains, lacerations, contusions, and concussions, and their consequences. Visual aids such as photographs, drawings, and videotapes should be used to illustrate the injuries discussed verbally and in written information. Discussion and written materials should also include information on risky behaviors, for example, spearing in football, that can lead to injury and therefore should be avoided. At the end of the meeting a consent form should be distributed for signing by athletes and parents, which includes a paragraph stating that the individuals who sign have been informed and warned about the inherent danger of participating in athletics. In addition, this paragraph should include a warning about the possibility of catastrophic injury and death. All materials used in such a meeting should be retained to be reused in future meetings with parents or athletes, or to be submitted in court as evidence that all concerned had been informed and warned of inherent dangers.

Another important aspect to a warning system is to advise students and athletes what to do if a dangerous situation should occur during an activity. Participants should be made aware of the location of exits and fire extinguishers in activity areas. Participants should also understand that if they are experiencing any discomfort, or are feeling weak, tired, or thirsty, that they should inform the coach or teacher and take steps to alleviate their discomfort.

Finally, warning and safety posters should be prominently displayed in locker rooms and activity areas. Equipment warning labels should be prominently displayed and legible.

Steps must also be taken by athletic administrators, coaches, and teachers to ensure proper instruction in all activities. Policy should be implemented that requires teachers and coaches to use appropriate conditioning and training exercises to enable participants to meet the physical demands of the activity or sport without undue risk of injury. Ability level and size should also be considered before allowing any individual to participate in an activity or sport. The use of appropriate drills and the proper progression of skills introduced with language appropriate to the age and experience of the athlete or student are crucial. Risky activities posing a danger to the participants should be eliminated from lesson and workout plans and no students or athletes should be required to perform a skill or activity against their will. All progressions, drills, cautions, safety measures, conditioning exercises should be carefully recorded in daily lesson and workout plans for future reference or to be used as evidence against litigation.

Finally, equipment should be kept in good repair and old or defective equipment should be replaced before it can contribute to injury. Facilities should be clean, well illuminated, and free from hazards that could jeopardize the safety of the participants.

In general, athletic personnel at every level should adopt a "safety at any cost" approach to coaching and teaching and become good record keepers. While there is no guarantee that attention to these recommendations will prevent injury or litigation, athletic programs will be improved and risks will be minimized.

Selected Bibliography

Adams, S. *The First Aider* (September 1983): 1, 6.

Champion, W., Jr. *Fundamentals of Sports Law.* Deerfield: Clark, Boardman, Callaghan, 1990.

Lubell, A. "Insurance, Liability, and the American Way of Sport." *The Physician and Sports Medicine* 15 (September 1987): 192–198, 200.

Injustice Uncovered? Worker's Compensation and the Professional Athlete

Frederic Pepe and Thomas P. Frerichs

***Palmer* v. *Kansas City Chiefs Football Club*, 621 S.W.2d 350 (Mo. Ct. App. 1981)**

***Bayless* v. *Philadelphia National League Club*, 472 F. Supp. 625 (E.D. Pa. 1979)**

***Miles* v. *Montreal Baseball Club*, 379 So. 2d 1325 (Fla. App. 1980)**

***Hendy* v. *Losse*, 54 (Cal.3d 723 1991)**

Years ago state legislatures recognized that employees injured on the job needed some protection or "compensation" from their employers. The system that was created for injured employees is called "worker's compensation." In accordance with worker's compensation statutes, employees surrender the right to sue their employer in a court of law for a full, but uncertain, recovery for work-related injuries. In exchange for this concession, workers are granted a strict, or absolute right for a fixed and limited recovery for their work-related injuries based on the nature and permanence of their injuries.

This relatively clear approach begins to cloud over when it is applied to an area of employment where employees are routinely injured on the job. Professional athletes are employed in a profession where injuries not only regularly occur, but are an expected part of the job. With several notable exceptions, most states treat injured professional athletes the same as any other injured workers. Florida and Massachusetts are the only states that specifically exclude professional athletes from coverage under their worker's compensation statutes. As a result, there is very little in the way of legal precedent to address how the domain of professional sports interacts with the system of worker's compensation laws.

The seminal case in the area of applying worker's compensation comes from the Missouri Court of Appeals. In *Palmer* v. *Kansas City Chiefs Football Club* (1981), a professional football player sued his employer for benefits under the worker's compensation law of Missouri. The Missouri Court of Appeals denied benefits to the injured player because it determined that professional football was "inherently dangerous with an expectation of injury" and that a person injured in an area of employment where there are deliberate collisions between human bodies in the usual course of an occupation cannot be considered the victim of a work-related accident.

The rationale of the Missouri Court of Appeals has been a consistent source of criticism in subsequent court decisions and resulted in the amendment of many state worker's compensation statutes. Many state statutes now specifically include those employees injured while participating in professional sports. The criticisms that have arisen relate to the underlying rationale of the *Palmer* decision and the legislative reasoning behind the current statutory exclusions of professional athletes in Florida and Massachusetts.

There is a common perception that professional athletes are overpaid and therefore do not need the legal protection afforded ordinary working people. But the fact is that many professional athletes are not grossly overpaid, and are not stars, but rather play in relative obscurity in the minor leagues. They finish out their careers without the benefit of million-dollar contracts. Also, a professional athlete's career is generally very short-lived; a National Football League running back should expect to play no more than three and a half years before completing his career. In rare instances, a fortunate male athlete may extend his career to ten years. But for the most part, a professional athlete has only a few years to maximize income and prepare for a future without sports.

Another notion about "grossly overpaid athletes" is that they sign long-term contracts and therefore don't need to be protected by a worker's compensation system. But in most cases, a typical three-year contract for a professional athlete is actually a series of three one-year contracts. If an athlete is injured during the contract period the team will usually continue to pay salary and medical expenses for the remainder of the year; however, if the athlete cannot pass the following year's physical examination, the contract may be considered void and the athlete could end up paying medical expenses for a lifetime of chronic work-related physical problems.

The primary criticism of the *Palmer* decision and the statutory exclusions of professional athletes targets the emphasis given to the fact that participation in professional sports often includes an expectation of injury, or at least constant exposure to situations placing the athlete at risk of injury. The *Palmer* Court focused on the general rationale behind the creation of worker's compensation, which was to ensure that employees injured in work-related "accidents" should not suffer for things beyond their control. It is only natural to conclude that when certain occupations expect violent physical confrontations between employees and insist on a constant demand to push the human body beyond its normal limits, the resulting injuries should not be considered work-related "accidents."

The criticism to this type of reasoning examines other occupations that could be considered inherently dangerous. For example, should those employed as police officers or fire fighters not be extended the protection of worker's compensation statutes simply because the nature of their work involves increased exposure to possible injury? If such protection were denied, it might be exceedingly difficult to find people willing to perform potentially dangerous, but greatly needed, services to the community.

Despite the difficulty created for injured athletes by the *Palmer* decision and the statutory exclusions in Florida and Massachusetts, an interesting inconsistency exists in Florida. A Florida appellate court has determined that a professional athlete, injured while attending a press party for which his contract mandated his appearance, could be awarded worker's compensation benefits despite Florida's statutory exclusion of professional athletes. In *Miles* v. *Montreal Baseball Club* (1980), the court found that the Florida statutory exclusion did not apply to athletes injured while *not* participating in their athletic field. If an athlete is injured while participating in a peripheral activity to his sporting expertise, there is coverage. If the athlete is injured while participating in the sport she or he is trained and paid to participate in, there is no coverage. This paradox has not been resolved in the years following the *Miles* decision.

A reading of the cases applying worker's compensation statutes to professional athletes gives the impression that athletes generally favor the application. This is not always the case. Many of the professional athletes who rise to the top levels of their profession do not favor the application of worker's compensation coverage because it precludes their opportunity to sue for a "full" recovery.

Though it is difficult to generalize, a typical worker's compensation statute will set a specific rate of compensation, or "schedule" for an injury to a particular body part. For example, a knee injury to a professional football player may be severe enough to end his entire career; however, that same injury may result in a doctor determining that he has only a 25 percent impairment to his leg.

Generally the scheduled rates for worker's compensation statutes are based on a maximum number of weekly pay periods determined to be appropriate for the type of injury suffered. For example, the Model Workmen's Compensation Act suggests a maximum of 240 weeks for the permanent loss of use of a leg. Additionally, worker's compensation statutes provide a set limitation on the maximum amount of weekly pay that can be claimed by an employee. A high average of state worker's compensation statutes for the maximum claimable weekly pay is $800 per week. As a rule, the subsequent earnings and earning capacity of the injured employee are immaterial to the determination of benefits. The same maximum amount of weekly pay periods is paid under the schedule to a tax accountant for the loss of use of a leg as would be paid a professional football player, yet losing the function of a leg could hardly be considered a career-threatening injury for an accountant.

A body of case law now exists as a result of these potential inequities. In *Bayless* v. *Philadelphia National League* (1979) and *Hendy* v. *Losse* (1990), athletes challenged the application of worker's compensation to their injuries. In *Bayless* a pitcher for the Philadelphia Phillies suffered through a period of low back and leg pain. The doctor for the Phillies administered large doses of a pain-killing drug. Bayless maintained that his pitching performance continuously deteriorated as result of being compelled to pitch in a drug-induced state. Bayless was eventually given his unconditional release by the Phillies.

Within thirty days after his release Bayless collapsed and underwent an emergency surgical procedure on his spine. After the operation Bayless's condition continued to deteriorate and he became severely depressed and exhibited erratic behavior. Bayless was eventually diagnosed as a paranoid schizophrenic and confined to a mental institution. The former pitcher was able to establish that the drugs administered to him by team trainers were, in part, responsible for his mental condition and sought to recover damages from the Phillies for both his back injuries and mental illness.

The Phillies responded to Bayless's claim by asserting that any compensation owed to Bayless was under the Pennsylvania Worker's Compensation Act. Inasmuch as Bayless could successfully establish that his mental condition was a direct result of the treatment provided to him by team doctors, his potential recovery under a tort action was much higher than the fixed compensation under the worker's compensation schedule. But the Pennsylvania Supreme Court held that Bayless's injuries fell under the umbrella of the Worker's Compensation Act and limited his recovery accordingly.

A similar case was decided by the California Court of Appeals. In *Hendy* v. *Losse,* however, the California Court expanded the coverage afforded to the injured athlete and provided him a dual recovery under both worker's compensation and tort law.

John Hendy was a professional football player with the San Diego Chargers. In August 1986 he injured his right knee on the playing field. Pursuant to his contract with the Chargers, Hendy was provided with the medical services of team physician, Gary Losse. In May 1987, Losse advised Hendy to continue playing on his injured knee. Soon after receiving the advice Hendy reinjured his knee in training camp. Hendy again consulted with Losse and was advised to keep playing. In September 1987 the San Diego Chargers released the player. Hendy then sought a second opinion from another physician. The second physician indicated that it was Losse's failure to properly diagnose and treat Hendy's condition that caused his injuries. In 1988 Hendy sued the San Diego Chargers and Losse, alleging among other claims, medical malpractice against the team physician. Ultimately the case was dismissed because of the exclusive right of recovery under California's Worker's Compensation law. Hendy appealed the dismissal and the appellate court, while agreeing in principle that the worker's compensation statute provided Hendy's sole and exclusive remedy against the Chargers, permitted the additional medical malpractice claim against Losse, a Charger's employee.

The *Bayless* and *Hendy* cases show a clear judicial preference for including professional athletes within the umbrella of worker's compensation statutes. A contradiction exists in requiring professional athletes to fall within the strict limitations of worker's compensation laws in some cases, and flatly denying them any of the protection of worker's compensation laws at all in others. It appears that without further legislation, professional athletes will continue to risk their livelihood and future each time they step onto the playing field.

Selected Bibliography

Blum, A. "Fair Game? More and More Pro Athletes Seek Compensation for Their Injuries." *National Law Journal.* March 7, 1988: 1.

Larson, A. *Workmen's Compensation for Occupational Injuries and Death.* New York: M. Bender, 1972–1994.

"Worker's Compensation and Injured Athletes." *The Sports Lawyer.* July/August 1992: 1.

Fans Strike Out with Foul Ball Litigation

Robert Neymeyer

Wells v. *Minneapolis Baseball and Athletic Association,* 122 Minn. 327; 142 N.W. 707 (1913) [Supreme Court of Minnesota]

Spectators injured by foul balls while attending professional base-ball games have compiled a poor batting average in winning judg-ments against stadium operators. Before 1992 nearly all cases were decided in favor of the defendants. The basis for the decisions was that fans assumed the risk for their own personal safety when seated in an unprotected area and that the stadium operator, having pro-vided reasonable protection, was not the insurer of the patron's safety.

The courts have consistently ruled that individuals attending a baseball game should recognize potential dangers. The most com-mon danger is that foul balls can inflict serious injury. In 1913, the Minnesota Supreme Court, in *Wells* v. *Minneapolis Baseball and Ath-letic Association,* held that the baseball club was not responsible for damages incurred by a teenage girl hit by a foul ball. The ruling as-serted that baseball was the national game and there was common knowledge of how it was played, and of the dangers of balls being hit into the stands. The stadium operator had met his responsibility by providing screened protection for the most vulnerable area of seating behind home plate. Spectators requesting or accepting seats outside this protected area recognized, and assumed, the risk of injury.

The courts have also ruled on several occasions that ignorance of the game does not constitute grounds for claiming damages; simple observation should quickly indicate to a reasonable person that a batter cannot always control the direction of the ball and that its speed and hardness constituted a threat to anyone who might be struck by it. For example, in *Schentzel* v. *Philadelphia National League*

Club (1953), a woman who claimed to know nothing about baseball was denied damages because she had watched the game for ten
minutes and therefore should have become aware of the potential
danger. In other cases it was found that injured spectators could be
expected to know about the game because spouses or children were
avid fans or because they had viewed games on television.

The dangers are not limited to foul balls. Stadium operators
have also been found blameless for injuries sustained by fans from
errant throws and thrown bats. Several cases have involved fans hit
by pitches during the pre-game warmup. Since this is an integral
part of the game, fans are expected to display alertness to the possible peril. Other decisions found the same applied to overthrows by
infielders. Bats slipping out of the hands of the batter were also viewed
as an anticipated hazard.

There have been some exceptions to these rulings. In *Maytnier*
v. *Rush* (1967), the case concerned a spectator who was hit by a
warmup pitch from the bullpen while watching the action. Here the
court ruled against the defendant, the Chicago Cubs, because the
club did not provide additional protection when a new risk factor
was introduced. Faulty screens have also resulted in judgments against
some baseball clubs.

Stadium owners and operators have argued their responsibility
to protect spectators is met by providing a screen behind home plate.
Until 1992, decisions have allowed baseball clubs to define the extent and nature of the screen protection. Operators have also argued
that complete protection requires screening along the entire foul
line, which would detract from the quality of the game. They point
out that many people sit in this area in hopes of catching a souvenir
foul ball, and others find the view from home plate behind the screen
unpleasant. Some clubs have taken the additional step of warning
fans of the risks of sitting in unprotected areas. Warnings are printed
on ticket stubs and posted at the entrance to the ballpark, and public address announcements are made before the game. There has
been resistance, however, to posting signs inside the park for fear
that a spectator might be struck in an area where the warning was
not visible. A judgment for $180,000 against the Houston Astros in
Friedman v. *Astrodomain Corporation* (1985) prompted several clubs
to intensify their warning procedures before the decision was over-

turned. Despite the general lack of success by the plaintiffs, there continues to be a steady flow of foul ball injury claims, including one for the death of a man in Seattle and another by a California woman who charged her breast cancer spread after she was hit on the breast by a foul ball.

A new direction in injury claims may have been established by *Yates* v. *Chicago National League Baseball Club* (1992). The plaintiff, a ten-year-old boy, was struck by a foul ball while seated beyond the safety of the home plate screen. The plaintiff argued that, while the stadium owner did not have to ensure absolute safety, there was a duty to provide reasonable care to the fans. A jury granted Yates $67,500 to cover medical costs. No punitive damages were asked. In April 1992, the 1st District Illinois Appellate Court affirmed the verdict and the Illinois Supreme Court rejected the case for review. Here is the first verdict in favor of a fan injured while seated in an unprotected area without extenuating circumstances. Baseball owners and stadium operators must now determine exactly what "reasonable care" means.

The response of the Chicago Cubs and Chicago White Sox baseball clubs was to seek immediate legislative protection. In September 1992, the governor of Illinois signed a "foul ball law" passed by the General Assembly which greatly restricted the ability of an injured spectator to sue for damages. Anyone unintentionally hit by a foul ball or errant bat cannot file a lawsuit for damages unless defective equipment or reckless behavior is evident.

There are many who claim organized baseball has received excessive legal and legislative protection. Exemption from antitrust laws and the reserve clause have allowed baseball owners to operate with few external restrictions. Until the Yates case, owners were able to avoid injury judgments because they effectively defined what was adequate protection for fans. Now that this definition has been successfully challenged, organized baseball has used its powerful influence to obtain further protection through legislation.

Selected Bibliography

Rigelhaupt, J. "Liability to Spectator at Baseball Game Who Is Hit by Ball or Injured As a Result of Other Hazards of the Game." *American Law Reports* 91 (1979): 24–132.
"Scorecard: Legal Defense Question." *Sports Illustrated.* March 3, 1986, 7.

Van Der Smissen, B. *Legal Liability and Risk Management for Public and Private Entities.* Vol. 2. Cincinnati: Anderson Publishing Company, 1990.

The Application of the Attractive Nuisance Doctrine to Sport

Sharon Huddleston

The attractive nuisance doctrine is a very limited principle, but one which has broad implications for application to playgrounds, sports facilities, and sports equipment. The doctrine is one component of the common law governing the duty of owners of all public or private property in relation to the safety of those who might enter the property or premises.

The traditional approach to premises liability cases turns on the legal status of the person entering onto the property. The three primary classifications of injured parties are an invitee, a licensee, and a trespasser. The legal duty owed to someone on the property depends upon their legal status. An invitee is generally regarded as one who enters a premises by either express or implied invitation or for a specific purpose which is of mutual interest to both the owner and the invitee. For example, an invitee is a patron of a shop who enters the establishment with the purpose of shopping, a benefit to both the invitee and the shop owner. It is the duty of the property owner to reasonably inspect the premises for unsafe or dangerous conditions and, in turn, to exercise reasonable care to protect the invitee from danger.

A licensee is generally regarded as one who enters upon the land or property of another without objection or by the acquiescence of the owner solely in pursuit of the licensee's business pleasure or convenience. Social guests are generally classified as licensees even though they may be in a sense "invited." The duty owed to a licensee is to exercise ordinary care and, if the owner knows, or reasonably should know, that a dangerous condition exists, and the licensee is unlikely to discover it, then the owner has a duty either to correct the dangerous condition or warn the licensee of it.

A trespasser is identified as one who is not rightfully upon the land or property of another, who nevertheless enters the property without the consent, express or implied of the owner. The duty owed to a trespasser, once the presence of the trespasser becomes known, is to not intentionally injure the trespasser and to exercise reasonable care to avoid injury.

The attractive nuisance doctrine is considered an exception to the general rule that governs the liability of landowners in relation to trespassers. In the United States the doctrine originated when first recognized by the Supreme Court in what has been known as the "turntable case." In *Sioux City & Pacific Railroad Co.* v. *Stout* (1873) the court found in favor of a six-year-old plaintiff who was injured while playing on a railroad turntable. Pacific Railroad was found guilty of negligence for not taking proper precautions to protect children who might wander onto the property and encounter unsuspected danger. Since the 1873 decision the attractive nuisance doctrine has been recognized, to some extent, by most states. It requires a higher level of care from the owner when the trespasser is a child too young to appreciate danger or even to understand that she or he has trespassed. Owners are liable if they fail to take proper safety precautions to prevent injury to young children, even though they may be trespassers, by a potentially dangerous object or condition that exists on the premises. The attractive nuisance doctrine has been used in cases regarding swimming pools that are inadequately secured, and has broad application to other sport and activity facilities.

Due to early inconsistencies in the application of the attractive nuisance doctrine, a section of the Restatement of Torts was written in 1934 which set uniform guidelines for application in section 339. Minor changes were made in a Restatement (Second) of Torts section 339 in 1965. This Restatement (Second) rule has become the precept adopted by the majority of states.

Section 339 of the Restatement titled "Artificial Conditions Highly Dangerous to Trespassing Children" specifies five conditions of the rule. The first condition states that a property owner is liable for injury, caused by a dangerous or artificial condition upon the land, to trespassing children where the owner knows or should have known that children might trespass. The second stipulates liability if the owner knows or should have known that a certain condition on the property posed a risk of serious injury or death to trespassing minors. The third aspect stipulates liability for the owner in relation to children who are too young to recognize a potentially dangerous condition. The fourth part indicates liability for the owner of property if the risk to the child is greater than the burden of eliminating the risk for the owner. Finally, liability is indicated if the owner fails to execute reasonable care by taking necessary precautions to eliminate the risk in order to protect trespassing children. Although section 339 of the Restatement (Second) of Torts does not specify the age range of individuals referred to as "young children" or "minors," the rule customarily applies to children of up to fourteen years of age.

In *McWilliams* v. *Guzinski* (1976), the parents of a four-year-old boy were awarded damages when their son drowned in a neighbor's swimming pool. The court found that the type of fence surrounding the pool was inadequate, that the gates were unlocked, and that the defendants should have known that children were likely to trespass. In *Gibbons* v. *Orleans Parish School Bd.* (1980) a six-year-old girl was injured while sliding down a tetherball pole located adjacent to a set of monkey bars upon which she had been playing. A screw protruding from the pole caused injury to the child's leg. The court awarded damages based on the location of the tetherball pole, the dangerous condition of the pole, and the fact that it should have been anticipated that a child might attempt to swing over to the pole from the monkey bars. In both cases, the owners and/or administrators of the property failed to exercise reasonable care to protect minors who could be anticipated to frequent or trespass on the premises.

The attractive nuisance doctrine does not require, however, that an owner of property anticipate every possibility of injury when dangerous or artificial conditions do not exist. In *Alop* v. *Edgewood Valley Community Association* (1987), for example, a six-year-old girl was injured when she attempted to turn around in the middle of a playground slide and fell to an asphalt surface. The plaintiffs charged that a slide on an asphalt surface created a dangerous condition. The court, however, ruled for the defendant, noting that the child's parent had allowed the child to play on the slide, that the child was aware that she could hurt herself if she fell, and that she was also aware that it was dangerous to turn around on the slide. The slide was not in need of repair and its location was not considered to be a dangerous condition.

Owners or administrators of playgrounds, sports facilities, and sports equipment must understand that the attractive nuisance doctrine makes them responsible for the reasonable care of young children even when the youngsters have trespassed upon the premises. Administrators should recognize that sports facilities and equipment are attractive to children and that children are likely to trespass upon such areas. Reasonable care requires that periodic inspection occur in order to identify and correct dangerous conditions. Areas, equipment, or conditions likely to pose dangers to young children require security or should be kept inaccessible at all times.

Selected Bibliography

"A New Beginning for the Attractive Nuisance Doctrine in Georgia." *Mercer Law Review* 34 (1982): 433–448.

Clement, A. *Law in Sport and Physical Activity*. Indianapolis: Benchmark Press, Inc., 1988.

Nygaard, G. and T. Boone. *Law for Physical Educators and Coaches*. Columbus: Publishing Horizons, Inc., 1989.

"TORTS-North Carolina Adopts the Restatement to Attractive Nuisance and Expands Its Application to *Non-Possessors-Broadway* v. *Blythe Industries Inc.*" *Wake Forest Law Review* 22 (1987): 405–424.

Not the Same Game

Thomas P. Frerichs

A new tide is rising in the world of big-time college athletics. While it has been the dream of most scholarship athletes to one day sign a lucrative professional contract, very few ever realize the dream. For some, injury kills the dream. For others, high expectations are never met. A number of recently filed lawsuits suggest that disappointed athletes are beginning to look to the nation's courtrooms as a forum for their disappointment and the loss of their hopes.

These lawsuits, if successful, threaten to change the nature of college athletics and the role of student-athletes. Several notable dissatisfied student-athletes have filed suits claiming that their future in the world of professional sports has been thwarted by the actions of coaches, athletic departments, and university administrations.

In October 1992, Antonio Pena filed suit against the Arizona Board of Regents, Arizona State University, and several members of the baseball coaching staff alleging, among other things, that by forcing him to throw a pitch known as the "hard slider," the coaching staff ruined his opportunity for a lucrative career in professional baseball.

Pena came to Arizona State University in the fall of 1989 on a full baseball scholarship. He was a highly regarded pitcher, known for the velocity of his fastball. Pena claimed to have given up a contract with the Chicago Cubs in order to sign his letter of intent to play for Arizona State.

Pena pitched well enough to play for the varsity team in his freshman year. During the 1990–91 year Pena alleged that the coaching staff of Arizona State compelled him to learn and throw the "hard slider." He claimed that the motion of the new pitch caused him to injure his valuable pitching shoulder. He also contended that despite his injuries, the coaching staff pushed him to pitch and play through the pain, thereby further injuring his pitching shoulder.

Eventually Pena was no longer able to pitch with the same skill and proficiency that he had shown when he came to the university. Pena then claimed that the coaching staff initiated a pattern of harassment in an effort to have him give up his scholarship. Pena refused to abandon his scholarship voluntarily. In 1991 Arizona State terminated Pena's scholarship on the grounds of unsatisfactory scholastic progress. Pena then sued the University and the coaching staff alleging, in essence, that his career was over because of the actions of the coaching staff. Arizona State denied Pena's allegations.

Ryan Harmon was a highly sought after high school football prospect from Indiana. He chose to cast his football fortunes with coach Jim Colletto and Purdue University. Harmon claimed that while he was at Purdue, Colletto physically and emotionally battered him to the point of forcing him to leave the university and give up his dream of a career in football. After leaving school Harmon filed suit, bringing a number of provocative allegations against Purdue and the coach.

In addition to Colletto's alleged abusive coaching methods, Harmon contended that the coach and the athletic staff at Purdue University made damaging academic decisions for him, provided tutors who would perform class work for him, advised him to enroll in classes that would ensure his academic eligibility rather than enhance his academic standing, encouraged him to falsify paperwork for the NCAA, and enticed him into conduct that involved consuming alcohol and fighting. Harmon argued that the actions of the Purdue Athletic Department had made it impossible for him both to complete his education at that institution and to pursue his dream in a Purdue football uniform. Purdue denied Harmon's allegations and threatened a countersuit against Harmon and his attorney. Early in 1994 Harmon dropped his lawsuit.

Bryan Fortay is another student-athlete who alleged that a coaching staff and a university administration spoiled his dreams for a lucrative future in professional sports. In 1988 Fortay was one of the most vigorously recruited high school quarterbacks in the nation. Fortay was swayed by the recruiting of the coaching staff of the University of Miami Hurricanes. Bearing the nickname "Quarterback U," the University of Miami had a record of sending its quarterbacks into profitable careers in the National Football League. Fortay was impressed by coach Jimmy Johnson and the great success the football program at Miami had enjoyed.

Shortly after he signed a letter of intent to play with the University of Miami, Johnson left for the Dallas Cowboys of the NFL. Fortay, like some other Johnson recruits, sought release from his letter of intent. Miami refused to let him out of his contractual agreement to play for the Hurricanes. Fortay alleged that he was persuaded to honor his letter of intent, in part because of the representations made by the new coach, Dennis Erickson, that Fortay would indeed be the heir apparent for the starting quarterback job at "Quarterback U."

Fortay was never made the starting quarterback at Miami and eventually transferred to Rutgers University to begin his football fortunes anew. But Fortay's problems at Miami were far from over. Just after starting his career at Rutgers, Fortay was advised that he was implicated in a scandal at Miami involving the fraudulent acquisition of student loans. Fortay contended that the loan scheme was carried out by Tony Russell, the athletic department employee who was assigned to provide him counseling. Fortay maintained that he was an unknowing dupe for Miami University officials who were intent on a scheme to defraud the college loan program of the United States government.

The prosecuting attorneys for the United States Attorney's Office in Miami allowed Fortay to enter into a deferred prosecution program where he would not face formal indictment on the charges but instead would be placed on a period of probation. Fortay contended that the University of Miami was fully aware of the scheme carried out by Russell and was seeking to make Fortay and others scapegoats for the athletic department. Fortay asserted further that the stress and confusion of the scholarship representations and the student loan scandal had ruined his reputation and hampered him from focusing on his athletic career at Rutgers, thus thwarting his opportunity to play professional football and prohibiting him from being offered a multimillion-dollar contract with the National Football League. The University of Miami has steadfastly denied Fortay's allegations.

These three instances show that a new trend in sports litigation may be emerging. Student-athletes in big-time college athletics place a lot on the line when they agree to enroll in a particular university. As the world of college athletics more closely resembles the world of professional sports, student-athletes can be expected to seek every avenue available in order to protect the investment they have made in their athletic prowess.

University athletic departments will follow the developments in these cases very carefully. The stakes are very high. If these student-athletes are able to support their claims, the universities could be held liable for the loss of high earnings in professional sports as well as damages to the reputation of their respective athletic departments. If even one of these suits proves successful, drastic changes are bound to occur within the college athletic system. Universities will fear being held even more accountable for the actions of their employees and coaching staffs, and the problems student-athletes claim to suffer at their hands. The power of student-athletes also will be considerably enhanced.

Selected Bibliography

"Football Player Sues Purdue." *Chicago Tribune*. August 4, 1993: Sports, 3.
"Glimmer of Miami QB Glory Fades into a Bitter Lawsuit." *Chicago Tribune*. November 14, 1993: Sports, 6.
"Playing Ball with Colleges." *USA Weekend*. January 23, 1994: 8.

Sports versus the Sabbath
Professional Baseball and Blue Laws

Robert F. Martin

Ex Parte Joseph Neet, 157 Mo. 527 (1900)

Statutes restricting commercial and recreational activities on Sundays have been common in the American experience, especially in the East, Midwest, and South, from the colonial era into the twentieth century. Such prohibitions, often known as "blue laws," were indicative of Protestant cultural hegemony and were intended to buttress the "American Sabbath," a day that stressed passive relaxation and a devotion to religious duties. From the mid-nineteenth century into the early twentieth century, industrialization, urbanization, and immigration began to erode the value system of Protestant, rural America. One sign of that erosion was the progress of professional baseball's assault on the "American Sabbath."

Seeking respectability and acceptance, the National League, organized in 1876, initially prohibited regularly scheduled games on Sunday and expelled teams that violated the restriction. There was, however, considerable popular demand for professional Sunday baseball in urban America and soon a battle took place between supporters and opponents of statutes that prohibited it. The struggle over "blue laws" involved class, cultural, geographical, economic, and political variables. The conflict tended to pit rural folk against urbanites, older American stock against the more recent immigrant groups, the middle and upper classes against the lower, and sometimes, Republicans against Democrats.

Barriers to professional Sunday baseball began crumbling first in the late nineteenth century in midwestern cities. In places such as Chicago, Cincinnati, and St. Louis, tradition was less firmly established. Also, large numbers of nonpietistic immigrants or their descendants, accustomed to the more relaxed "Continental Sabbath," disliked strictures against Sunday recreation. Consequently, to the chagrin of Sabbatarians, there was, frequently, little effort to enforce state statutes or local ordinances prohibiting Sunday recreation in metropolitan centers. Following the merger of the National League with the rival American Association in 1891, teams were allowed to decide for themselves whether they wanted Sunday baseball games.

Although some players had reservations about the loss of an off day or declining prestige resulting from Sunday contests, the most vehement opposition came from Sabbatarian groups such as the International Sunday Observance League. This organization, unsuccessfully, tried to pressure local authorities in Chicago to enforce laws that would prohibit professional Sunday baseball. When this failed, the League secured an injunction against A.G. Spalding's White Stockings barring Sunday games on the grounds that these constituted a public nuisance and would undermine property values and the quality of life in the vicinity of the ball park. The Sabbatarian victory was only temporary. The injunction was overturned on a technicality and soon Sunday games were routine in the Windy City. The Chicago experience was typical. Sabbatarians frequently took professional baseball teams to court in an effort to protect the "American Sabbath." While they sometimes won ephemeral victories in the form of injunctions or fines for Sabbath desecration, jurists, relying less upon precedent and more upon sociocultural considerations, increasingly found grounds on which to legitimize Sunday baseball. In 1887, for example, a St. Louis judge ruled that baseball, rather than being a public nuisance, was in fact a source of wholesome popular recreation.

In *Ex Parte Joseph Neet* (1900), a Missouri appellate court held that baseball was not subject to restrictions against Sunday amusements since such laws had been passed years prior to the development of the game. The justices contended that the legislation in question was intended to prohibit "pernicious amusements" such as horse racing and cockfighting, not wholesome ones such as baseball. By the first decade of the twentieth century, residents of most midwestern and western cities could enjoy professional baseball on the Sabbath without fear of intrusion by local authorities.

The "American Sabbath" was more firmly entrenched in the East than in the Midwest. In the East, urban middle and upper classes often supported restrictive Sabbath legislation, but the greatest enthusiasm for such laws was among the rural and small-town people, who apparently believed them conducive to piety and useful in controlling and acculturating the expanding urban masses.

In New York the conflict over professional Sunday baseball began in the 1880s and continued until just after World War I. Many of the early skirmishes between Sabbatarians and teams such as the Brooklyn Dodgers took place in the courts, which found first in favor of one side, then the other. Ultimately, however, the state judiciary upheld New York state's "blue laws," thus making it clear that only legislative changes would open the way for professional Sunday sports. From 1897 to 1919, proponents of Sunday baseball, including such unlikely allies as apostles of the Social Gospel and members of the Tammany Hall political machine, repeatedly sought to modify the Empire State's "blue laws," but the legislature, dominated by rural and largely Republican interests, consistently thwarted these efforts. In a sermon delivered on the evening of May 1, 1917, in New York City, the baseball player turned revivalist, Billy Sunday, declared, "I will say to the people that try to erase the Sabbath from our statute books, we will swim our horses in blood to their bridles before you will ever get us away from it." By the end of World War I, however, support for Sunday baseball had gained sufficient momentum, even in some rural areas, to achieve the passage in 1919 of the Walker Act which, among other things, permitted professional baseball on Sundays between 2:00 and 6:00 P.M.

The protracted struggle in New York was not atypical. Washington, D.C., did not permit Sunday baseball until 1917, while the "blue law" barrier stood in Boston until 1919 and in Baltimore until 1932. Pennsylvania, where both tradition and rural interests remained firmly entrenched, was the last eastern state to remove strictures against commercial sporting events on Sunday. Philadelphia Athletics owner and manager Connie Mack began challenging the state's "blue laws" in 1926, but it was not until 1933 that changing mores and the potential enhancement of state and local revenues combined to facilitate the passage of an act enabling Pennsylvania's cities to authorize baseball on a local option basis. In 1934 Philadelphia and Pittsburgh became the last major-league cities to allow professional baseball on Sunday.

With the exception of some parts of the South and scattered localities elsewhere, the "blue law" barrier to professional baseball on the Sabbath had fallen by the end of the Great Depression. The demise of prohibitions against Sunday games augmented the gate receipts of the teams, enhanced the tax revenues of their home cities, and made the "national pastime" more accessible to the working classes. Ironically, as Steven A. Riess has surmised, by exposing the urban masses to the tradition, discipline, and ambiance of the game, Sunday baseball may have served something of the acculturating function attributed to "blue laws."

Selected Bibliography

Lucas, J. "The Unholy Experiment—Professional Baseball's Struggle against Pennsylvania Sunday Blue Laws, 1926–1934." *Pennsylvania History* 38 (April 1987): 163–175.

Lucas, J. and R. Smith. *Saga of American Sport*. Philadelphia: Lea & Febiger, 1978.

Riess, S. *Touching Base: Professional Baseball and American Culture in the Progressive Era*. Westport: Greenwood Press, 1980.

Amateurs, Professionals, and Eligibility for Americans in the Olympics

Sara L. Cohen

The Amateur Sports Act of 1978

Avery Brundage, International Olympic Committee President from 1952 to 1972, passionately believed in amateurism. "An amateur," he said, "does not rely on sports for his livelihood. The devotion of the true amateur athlete is the same devotion that makes an artist starve in his garret rather than commercialize his work." Brundage idolized amateurism and refused to tolerate the concept of professionalism: taking money for performance.

In 1896, when the modern Olympic Games began, few professional sports and athletes existed. By the latter part of the twentieth century, however, sports in general, and the Games in particular, had become a multibillion-dollar-a-year industry. The United States athletic federations, along with the International Olympic Committee (IOC), began to adapt to these changes in the sports world, and correspondingly, the criteria of eligibility for athletes to compete in the Olympic Games also changed.

The 1992 Barcelona Summer Games might evoke memories of the introduction of baseball as an Olympic sport or the year of the first Israeli medalist. But they will certainly be remembered as the year of the "Dream Team"—the year Michael Jordan, Magic Johnson, Larry Bird, Charles Barkley, and David Robinson, among others, went to Barcelona to compete not for their professional teams in the National Basketball Association, but for the United States of America. To have multimillion-dollar NBA players competing would once have violated the spirit of the Games. Because of the changes in the sports world since 1896, however, the spirit of the Olympic Games has also changed.

The original Olympics ran from 776 B.C. until the Emperor

Theodosius canceled them in A.D. 393. The Games began as tributes to the gods, whom the ancient Greeks believed gifted the competitors with speed or endurance. For the Greeks, winning the competition was the most important thing about the Games. Athletes were not classified as "amateur" or "professional," because these words and concepts did not exist in ancient Greece. Athletes simply had to be freemen who had committed no crime or sacrilege. Women, foreigners, and slaves could not participate. The athletes took a vow not to cheat while competing, and were supported so they could train during the year preceding the Games. A winner would receive free meals and lodgings, and large sums of money.

When Pierre de Coubertin founded the modern Olympic Games in 1896, he felt differently about the spirit of the Games. He thought the most important aspect was competing to the best of the athlete's ability, not necessarily winning. To that end, he believed that full-time professionals, persons paid to compete, should not participate in the Games because, in the spirit of fairness, such professionals would have an advantage over part-time amateur athletes.

The concept of amateurism began in the late nineteenth century as a result of the British upper-class bias against the lower classes. In effect, amateurism prevented the working class from competing with the aristocracy. Athletes who made their living competing in sport could not afford to give up their income in order to compete as amateurs; therefore, the only persons who could compete were those who had an independent source of income, namely, the aristocracy. Amateurs were thus defined as persons who did not earn compensation for playing a sport. The United States Olympic Committee (USOC) and the International Olympic Committee (IOC) enthusiastically adopted this view.

Caspar Whitney, USOC president from 1906 to 1910, said it was "evil to bring together in sport the most divergent elements of society, that never by any chance meet elsewhere on even terms. The laboring classes are all right in their way. Let them go their way in peace, and have their athletics in whatever manner suits their inclination. Let us have our sport among the more refined elements." Whitney's prejudiced comment reflected the European aristocracy's negative feelings about poor and persons of color.

The most notable American athlete who felt the sting of the

definition of amateur was Jim Thorpe. In 1912, at the Stockholm
Summer Games, Thorpe won the pentathlon and the decathlon,
finished fourth in the high jump and seventh in the long jump.
King Gustav V of Sweden called him the greatest athlete in the world.
In 1913, however, the IOC discovered that Thorpe had been paid
$25 a week, in 1909 and 1910, to play baseball in a North Carolina
minor league. Because he had received money to play a sport, the
IOC stripped him of his Olympic medals and struck his name from
the record books. In reflection of the changing world, the IOC entered Thorpe's accomplishments in the record books on October
13, 1982, and in 1983 returned his medals to his children.

Thorpe was not the only American athlete who suffered because of his "professional" status. In 1984, former Olympic medalist
Brian Oldfield was not allowed to compete in the shot put because
he had signed a contract with the International Track Association.
Track stars Dwight Stones and John Smith were also forbidden to
compete due to their professional status, although they were reinstated as amateurs in 1980, and Olympic figure skater Brian Boitano
was not allowed to compete in 1992 because he had skated professionally.

Several factors, which Coubertin and Whitney could not have
anticipated, resulted in the recent changes in rules of amateurism
and eligibility. First, the Soviet bloc nations developed state-spon-
sored athletic programs whose athletes did not fit neatly into the
distinction between professional or amateur. Second, the growth of
professional sports resulted in a higher level of competition and correspondingly higher expectations by the viewing public. Third, the
growth of television coverage, advertising, and corporate sponsorship, made sports a multibillion-dollar-a-year business. The rationale behind the notion of amateurism simply grew outdated.

The advent of the Cold War resulted in competition between
East and West on many levels, including the playing field. From
1956 through 1988, East Germans and Soviets won 121 medals in
the Winter Games, and the United States 25. The Soviet bloc countries designated these athletes as amateurs, an appellation which the
IOC accepted. This definition was strained, however, given the highly
developed sports programs under which the athletes trained. Children were removed from their homes at young ages and raised to do

little more than train and compete in their sports. Athletes were given free housing and provided with the most modern training facilities available. They did not have to find sponsors or work in order to eat or pay rent while they trained, and were paid for playing their sports, even if they did not have sports contracts. In light of this, Juan Antonio Samarach, current IOC president, indicated that a professional athlete was the same as a state athlete. Additionally, Richard W. Pound, current IOC board member, noted that "professionalism has been anathema to the spirit of the Olympics for many decades, but we realized that we had reached a point where it was less of a problem of professionals than it was a question of fair play."

Because the modern Olympic Games were founded before the advent of television, the founders could not have anticipated the impact television would have upon them. In 1936, the Berlin Summer Games were the first to be televised, albeit on closed-circuit television. The first mass television coverage was of the 1972 Summer Games in Munich; over one billion people watched the opening ceremonies via satellite. New technologies such as satellites, videotape, slow motion, and instant replay, allowed faster and more dynamic coverage on television.

Currently, the Games are televised internationally for huge sums of money. In 1992, CBS paid $243 million for televising 116 hours of the Winter Games and paid $300 million for the 1994 Winter Games. NBC paid $401 million to televise 161 hours of the 1992 Summer Games. For the first time, in 1992, NBC offered a pay-per-view package, so that for varying prices Americans could receive round-the-clock Olympic coverage.

In order to make money from the Olympic Games, the networks had to recoup through advertising revenue. In 1988, a total of approximately $8.5 billion dollars was spent for television advertising in the United States. Over $1.25 billion went to advertising on sports. However, in order for advertisers to want to pay for coverage of the Games, the networks needed to broadcast Olympic competitions that the public would want to see. Facing the competition of professional basketball, football, hockey, baseball, tennis, and golf, the Olympic Games also had to acknowledge that viewers were more likely to tune in to events which were exciting, played by experts. Furthermore, with cable television and ESPN, Prime Ticket, WGN and TNT, the American public had become accustomed to a heavy diet of sports on television, and also expected the highest caliber of competition. Thus the Games, to draw viewers, had to provide an equally high level of competition.

The current definition of an eligible athlete reflects the changes that have occurred since 1896. American athletes become eligible for the Games under several criteria. They must meet the definition in the Amateur Sports Act of 1978, the IOC definition, the definition of their National Olympic Committee (NOC), and the definition of the individual federation governing their sport. The United States Amateur Sports Act (36 USCA §373) defined an amateur athlete as "any athlete who meets the eligibility standards established by the national governing body for the sport in which the athlete competes," and set up the United States Olympic Committee (USOC) as the corporation which would guide and control American participation in the Games.

The USOC agreed with the standard set by the International Olympic Committee (IOC) in recognizing that the standard set in 1896 no longer functioned properly. In 1981, the Eligibility Commission of the IOC deleted the word "amateur" from the Olympic Charter, preferring the term "eligible athlete." Rule 26 of the IOC charter, also modified in 1981, said that competitors must observe IOC rules and those of their individual federation. Any athlete was eligible to compete except one who had been registered as a professional athlete, or who had signed a contract as a professional before the closing of the Games, or who had accepted, without knowledge of their NOC, money for preparation or participation in sports.

These regulations were loosened in 1986, when track and field, equestrian events, ice hockey, and tennis allowed professional participation. Since that point, individual sports federations have continued to loosen regulations and Samarach pushed for an "open" Olympics where all athletes could compete regardless of status. As a practical matter, the definition of an eligible athlete was left to the individual bodies of international sports federations. For various reasons, differing federations have allowed athletes who received compensation for playing sports to compete in the Olympic Games.

In the United States, the impact has been diverse. In 1984,

hockey was the first sport to allow professionals to participate. Eligible players came from the minor American Hockey League, the now defunct World Hockey Association, and various European leagues. National Hockey League (NHL) players, however, could not compete until 1986. In the United States, hockey eligibility was determined through a ranking system. In 1988, all NHL players were ranked and those classified in the bottom ten in ability for each team could compete for the United States. The reason behind this system is that the Winter Olympics take place during hockey season, and NHL owners decided that their best players are too valuable to their franchises to leave in mid-season to train and compete in the Olympics.

For its part, the United States Amateur Hockey Association (USAHA) wanted stability for the team it sent to the Games. It wanted a team chosen six months in advance of the Games so that it could have time to practice together. The USAHA also did not want to have a team made up of famous athletes, fearing dissension and lack of cooperation among the premier players of the hockey world. Additionally, the USAHA feels that amateurs better represent the Olympic spirit, and fears that the American public is not going to give desperately needed funds to support the team if its athletes already earn millions of dollars.

Tennis, which draws no distinction between amateurs and professionals, became a full Olympic sport in 1988 in Seoul. The International Tennis Federation allows any tennis player, regardless of previous winnings or competition, to compete as long as they are not paid for playing in the Games and suspend all commercial endorsement contracts for a period of two weeks before the Games. Tennis is unusual among international sports. For tennis players, the Games are merely another in a long string of competitions. Continually in the international spotlight, the players do not need another competition to enhance their reputation or ranking, especially one which occurs only every four years. In that regard, the Games need tennis more than tennis needs the Games, and can always use another attraction to get viewers to stay tuned to their sets.

In 1992, Brian Boitano, the 1988 men's figure skating gold medalist, was not allowed to compete, because he had skated professionally for Dick Button's professional showcase. In 1994, however, figure skating allowed professionals to compete. Skaters who want to have their eligibility reinstated must apply to the United States Figure Skating Association. The USFSA will establish a trust fund for each skater, and the skaters will have to give 5 percent of their future earnings to the USFSA to manage the trust. Furthermore, the skaters can only compete in approved competitions.

In equestrian events, the Equestrian Federation made a very simple rule. In 1986, the IOC said that professional riders may compete in the Games, probably because the only equestrians skilled enough to compete in the Olympic Games also compete in Grand Prix (prize money competition) events. Only horses and riders displaying the name of a commercial company or product are ineligible.

In 1988, in a meeting of the International Amateur Basketball Federation, the United States voted against admission of professionals. The United States, however, lost in the voting, and the Federation allowed professionals to play. Then, in 1992, the United States sent twelve of its most highly talented and well-known athletes to play basketball. The only one of them who might have been considered an amateur was Christian Laettner, who, in 1992, had not yet played in the National Basketball Association.

Two likely reasons exist why NBA players competed in Barcelona. First, in recent international competition, the United States men's basketball team has been less than successful. The United States failed to win a gold medal in the 1972 Olympics, the 1987 Pan-Am Games, the 1988 Summer Games, 1990 Goodwill Games and the 1992 Pan-Am Games. The second factor was the recognition of the economic impact. Having the "Dream Team" play guaranteed the United States a gold medal which, in turn, guaranteed major revenue to advertisers and sponsors. Corporate sponsors had a premium marketing tool and NBC had a sport which drew international attention. With the entertainment dollar becoming a rarer premium, fans will not watch mediocre level sports and especially will not pay for a premium cable package to see the United States lose. The 1992 Summer Games coverage centered around these stars. The "Dream Team" greatly outmatched its opponents, but it also created enormous interest in the Games, and thus television and corporate sponsors' profits.

Selected Bibliography

Johnson, W. "Goodby Olive Wreaths; Hello, Riches and Reality." *Sports Illustrated.*
    February 9, 1987: 168.
Nafziger, J. "The Amateur Sports Act of 1978." *Brigham Young University Law Re-
    view.* 1983 (Winter 1983): 47–99.
Schapp, D. *An Illustrated History of the Olympics.* New York: Alfred A. Knopf, 1975.
Wallechinksy, D. *Book of the Olympics.* New York: Penguin Books, 1984.

Fading in the Stretch
Live Horse Racing in the 1990s

Stephen J. Rapp

Interstate Horse Racing Act of 1978, P.L. 95-515

In the 1990s it appears that the heyday of thoroughbred horse racing has passed. Stories of racing rarely reach the first page of the sports section. Young people come of age without knowing how to read the *Daily Racing Form*. The Nathan Detroits of our time speak of "point spreads" instead of "that horse right here." Even the equine heroes that occasionally catch some public attention seem pale by comparison to the legendary Man o' War, Citation, or Secretariat.

There is also objective evidence of racing's decline. In Central Kentucky, where the bids at the Keeneland yearling sales are followed as closely as the prices of corn and beans in the Midwest, the 1992 "Select Summer Sale" topper brought only $1.7 million, compared to the $13.1 million paid for a colt in 1985. In the same period the median prices were down 38 percent and the national thoroughbred "foal crop" dropped from 52,000 to 36,000.

Yet, in 1992 racetracks in North America distributed a near record $775 million in purses. Total "attendance" exceeded fifty-eight million and more than $10 billion was legally wagered. On the other hand, patrons in 1992 were less likely than ever to have attended and wagered on the races at the racetrack or even to have been in the same state where the horses were running.

On a typical weekend afternoon in February 1993, one could find fans at sites in more than twenty states watching and wagering on the simulcast of the "whole card" of races from Santa Anita in Southern California. Some were at tracks that were closed for the season. Others were at tracks that were closed because they could not afford to put on live racing. Some were at tracks where the live action still went on, but where the local horseflesh paraded to the post almost unnoticed while fans cheered at the flickering images on television monitors.

The impact of all of this on a simulcasted track such as Santa Anita has been dramatic. During its seventy-eight-day, winter 1992–93 meeting, some $140 million was wagered from out-of-state simulcast locations. As a result the track was able to offer bigger purses and attract the better horses, trainers, and jockeys. Other "super tracks" in California, Florida, Kentucky, Illinois, and New York, were trying to do the same.

What did this mean for the more than 75 percent of the tracks that were not so "super," where most of the 36,000 horses born in 1992 would have to race, if they race at all? What of the roughly two hundred thousand people who would raise these horses, train them, keep them healthy, strong, and clean, and who, given luck, ability, and courage, would race them to minor glory?

The impact has not been as devastating as might be expected. The reason is the Interstate Horse Racing Act of 1978, P.L. 95–515, 15 USC sec. 3001–3007. This law was passed by Congress explicitly to save the "minor leagues of the racing industry." As the Senate Judiciary Committee stated in its report,

Unregulated interstate off-track parimutuel wagering could result in a decline in attendance and wagering throughout the country which, in turn, would result in loss of revenue to the States and the racing industry. This could force the closing of a number of small race tracks and that could, in turn, seriously harm the racing industry and the States which derive revenue from those tracks.

At the same time it is recognized that properly regulated and properly conducted interstate off-track betting may contribute substantial benefits to the States and the horseracing industry. These benefits would result from expanded market areas that would enable increased numbers of fans to participate in racing.

P.L. 95–515 requires that, before interstate simulcasting can take place, the racetrack sending the signal must have a written agreement with its local equestrian group, consenting to the simulcasting and establishing terms and conditions relating to it. Additionally, the racing commissions in both the sending state and the receiving state must grant their consent.

The law has turned out to have been a useful tool in the hands of the national Horsemen's Benevolent and Protective Association (HBPA), which through its twenty-eight member organizations, represents equestrians at a majority of the North American tracks. Since its founding in 1941, the HBPA has developed into something similar to a labor union for horse trainers and owners. Its members include a disparate lot ranging from one-horse trainers to oil sheikhs. They all have a common interest in seeing that the greatest percentage of money wagered at the window (the "handle") comes back to those who "put on the show." Through long struggle and by occasionally carrying out boycotts of the entry box, local organizations of the HBPA have reached the point at many tracks where they periodically sit down with management to negotiate the percentage of handle that will go to purses and the size of the purses that will be offered at all levels of competition.

By requiring the consent of the equestrian's group at the sending track, the Interstate Horse Racing Act of 1978 gives the track's HBPA substantial power. While the law does not require the consent of the horsemen's group at the receiving track, if there were solidarity within the national HBPA the group at the sending track could withhold its consent, if the group at the receiving track had objections, thus giving the group at the receiving track the ability to negotiate an arrangement to protect local racing. This appears to have been the intent of a resolution adopted at the national HBPA convention, in January 1991, urging equestrian groups at the sending tracks to withhold consent to simulcasting, if the signal were going to a place where there was no live racing or where the equestrian's group at the receiving track had not been able to implement a satisfactory agreement regarding simulcasting with their local track.

However, when Florida and California equestrian's groups supported Alabama equestrians by withholding their consent to simulcasts into Alabama when the Birmingham Turf Club ceased live racing, the Alabama simulcast operator sued the Florida and California equestrians and the national HBPA in federal court on the grounds that the equestrians were engaged in a conspiracy to violate the antitrust laws. The litigation that followed was inconclusive. The federal district court held that if there were an explicit or implicit agreement between the equestrian's groups at the sending and receiving tracks this would violate antitrust legislation. At the same time, the court denied the simulcast operator the preliminary relief that it sought because it had not shown that the equestrians at the sending tracks were withholding their consent for the benefit of the receiving track equestrians, because they might in fact have been only looking out for their own long-term economic interests.

In the meantime, equestrian's groups in states with super tracks have generally been able to keep out all but the simulcasts of those nationally significant races which have the potential of bringing in new fans who will stay to bet on the local competition. Equestrian's groups in states without supertracks have reconciled themselves to letting in even "whole card" simulcasts at the same time local horses are running, but have tried to negotiate agreements that provide that a large share of simulcast handle must go to local purses.

It is far from certain, however, whether "whole card" simulcasting can long coexist with live racing. When fans have a choice between betting on the horses running at the local track or at the super track, the larger bettors tend to bet on the super track because superior horses may be easier to handicap and because a large wager will not depress the odds in the enormous national betting pools which simulcasting makes possible. Given these common pools, the successful simulcast wager generally carries the same payoff at every outlet. The receiving track, however, must pay 4 to 6 percent for the signal from the super track. The receiving track is thus reluctant to pay its local equestrians, who are not "putting on the show," the same percentage for purses that it is paying for live races. But if the local equestrians agree to a lesser percentage, their purses will dwindle as more of the local betting money goes into simulcast wagering. Few equestrian's groups have been strong enough to obtain an equal percentage. Those that did not obtain it at the beginning have found themselves powerless to acquire it later. The threat to stop "whole card" simulcasting once it has started is not really credible. Where equestrians have tried after a so-called trial period, they have run into strong resistance and discovered that the fans will not return, in the earlier numbers, to bet on the live competition.

So far the Interstate Horse Racing Act has helped keep the minor leagues alive. But track management has chafed at even the limited power that it gives to the HBPA. Several super tracks have argued that they did not need the consent of their equestrian's group to send out their signal because the consent is already granted by each local horse owner and trainer when they enter a horse in a race and sign the standard entry form which contains "fine print" authorizing simulcasting. In late 1992, Turfway Park in Kentucky refused the request of its HBPA for a share of simulcast revenue and began sending simulcasts out of state without the group's approval, in apparent defiance of the Interstate Horse Racing Act. The Kentucky HBPA filed suit in federal court to stop the track, and while the judge would not grant a preliminary injunction, he stated that he believed the equestrians would prevail in the end on the merits. Thereafter, the Kentucky Racing Commission decided to halt the simulcasts until the dispute was resolved.

Equestrians hoped that Turfway would back down or that there would be a judicial determination that the Interstate Horse Racing Act of 1978, at least, gives power over simulcasting to the equestrian's groups at the sending tracks. If the law does not mean this much, there will no barrier to unlimited simulcasting, and before long at most tracks in America live horses will no longer turn into the homestretch.

In September 1993, the HPBA was dealt a setback when the U.S. District Court held the Interstate Horse Racing Act unconstitutional on the unexpected grounds that it violated the sending track's right to commercial free speech. The equestrians appealed the ruling. In April 1994, the U.S. Court of Appeals for the 6th Circuit reversed the District Court and upheld the constitutionality and enforceability of the Act.

Selected Bibliography

Alabama Sportservice vs. *National HBPA*, 767 F. Supp. 1573 (M.D. Fla. 1991).

Bernet, G. "1991: The Year in Review." *Daily Racing Form.* March 22, 1992: 1, 18–25.

Legislative History: Interstate Horse Racing Act of 1978, P.L. 95–515, *U.S. Code Congressional and Administrative News 4* (95th Congress, 2nd Session, 1978), 4132–4154.

Paulik, R. and others. "Simulcasting, a Special Report." *The Blood Horse.* January 30, 1993: 454–514.

Seebauer, H. "The Interstate Horseracing Act of 1978: An Evaluation." *Connecticut Law Review* 12 (Summer 1980): 883–919.

Part Two

Sports Law: The Regulation of Organized Sports

Sports may be games, but at times they are also businesses. High-profile amateur and professional sports teams are elaborately organized into associations (often called "leagues" or "conferences"). These associations are bound by federal and state constitutions, statutory law, the judge-made common law and, of course, the rules of their own associations. The guarantee of "due process of law," found in the Fifth and Fourteenth Amendments to the U.S. Constitution and in most state constitutions, figures prominently in the treatment of cases in Part II.

Most of the sixteen essays in Part II deal with problems that well-known sports figures have encountered when their actions produced friction with the associations that govern(ed) their sports. A few of the essays treat little-known athletes or sports figures whose activities, nevertheless, ignited legal turmoil in their respective sports. The seven essays grouped together at the end of Part II highlight cases involving gambling, a seemingly perennial threat to the integrity of organized sports.

The opening essay, "The NCAA and the Courts: College Football on Television" explores the relationship between the National Collegiate Athletic Association (NCAA), member institutions, and the powerful medium of television. "Books and Bulldogs: Athletes and Academic Standards Abuses" examines a case of the mid-1980s related to academic standards and the treatment accorded athletes at the University of Georgia. The third essay in the section, "Switzer, a Sooner Scofflaw?" explores the highly publicized incidents that occurred during the last phase of Barry Switzer's coaching career at the University of Oklahoma. "The Win at Any Price Syndrome: Steroids in Athletics" essay trails the use of steroids by athletes. The succeeding essay, "To Play or Not to Play: Substance Abuse Policies of Three Major Sports Leagues," analyzes the strengths and weaknesses of policies related to substance abuse in professional basketball, football, and baseball.

The next three essays, on authority and discipline in amateur and professional sports, deal with the exercise of authority in notable incidents in professional sports. "Two All-Pros Collide with the Football Commissioner" reveals the display of power by National Football League Commissioner Pete Rozelle when confronted with evidence of gambling by two of professional football's star players, Paul Hornung and Alex Karras. This essay was not placed with the essays on gambling because its focus was more on the exercise of authority rather than gambling. The following essay, "Commissioner Kuhn Victorious over Owner Finley," treats the 1970s conflict between Major League Baseball Commissioner Bowie Kuhn and Charlie Finley, the controversial owner of the Oakland Athletics. "George Steinbrenner's Bronx Zoo" examines another battle between a baseball commissioner, Fay Vincent, and a contentious owner, George Steinbrenner of the New York Yankees. The final essay in the "Sports Law: The Regulation of Organized Sports" subsection deals with the conflict between two powerful personalities in the world of golf. "In the Groove? The Legal War over Golf Clubs" investigates the importance of the design of golf clubs as it played out in a long-running clash between Karsten Solheim and Deane Beman.

Essays on gambling are presented in chronological order. Readers here will discover detailed treatments of some of the most highly publicized personalities and events in twentieth-century sports history. "Baseball's Big Inning: The Sacrifice of the 1919 Black Sox" delves into the complicated story of the infamous gambling scandal involving several superstar players of the 1919 Chicago White Sox. The next essay, "Beating the Spread: College Basketball Point Shaving," calls attention to the outbreak of scandals from the 1950s to the 1980s. "Jack Molinas: A Basketball Player With Great but Unclean Hands" trails the career of a highly talented but thoroughly corrupt hoopster whose bizarre life generated fictional depictions.

The next three essays probe into gambling's disastrous effects upon selected highly talented professional athletes. "Fastballs and Fast Bucks Don't Mix" examines the achievements, failures, and apparent rehabilitation of Denny McLain of the Detroit Tigers professional baseball team. The next essay, "A Gridiron Hero Self-Destructs," investigates the career of Art Schlichter, former quarterback great at Ohio State University. "Charlie the Hustler and the Hall of Saints" recounts both the on-field exploits of Pete Rose and his banishment from baseball for gambling. The essay concludes with a discussion of Rose's admissability into baseball's Hall of Fame.

"Fantasy Sports and the Law," the final piece on gambling , explores a rapidly growing sector of the wild world of sports, rotisserie baseball leagues.

The NCAA and the Courts
College Football on Television

Eric A. Seiken

NCAA v. *Board of Regents of the University of Oklahoma*, 468 U.S. 85 (1984) [U.S. Supreme Court]

The National Collegiate Athletic Association is a private, nonprofit organization of over one thousand member institutions, organized to regulate and govern amateur athletics at the college level. The NCAA has inherent rule-making powers which are essential to its governance of sporting events. These rules have either direct or indirect implications for the financial status of member institutions.

Since the 1950s, the NCAA has controlled the televising of intercollegiate football games. Until 1982, the contracts were always made with a single network, although all three networks could make bids. The basic rationale for the NCAA's control of the televising of football games was the fear that unregulated televising of football games would cause a decrease in live gate attendance at other games being played simultaneously in the viewing area. But whatever the rationale, each television policy adopted by the NCAA placed restrictions on the ability of member institutions to individually enter into and negotiate contract terms with different carrying networks.

In 1979, the NCAA started to receive severe criticism from members of the College Football Association (CFA), concerning its football television policy. The CFA, a group of major football conferences and independent schools founded in 1977, was originally organized to lobby for and promote the interests of major football schools within the NCAA. The CFA believed that its members should have a greater voice in establishing NCAA football television policy for two reasons. It contended that major football schools were most likely to benefit from such television contracts, and also argued that since all members of the NCAA, whether or not they actually played

football, had equal voting power concerning football television contracts, this would adversely affect those schools who did play football and wanted to capitalize economically from their programs. As
a result, the CFA began negotiating with NBC for a television contract similar to the one that the NCAA had with ABC.

In response, the NCAA announced that disciplinary action
would be taken against any CFA members who complied with such
a contract. The CFA never went forward with any contract, due to
fear of possible NCAA sanctions. Two members of the CFA, however, the University of Oklahoma and the University of Georgia,
filed a joint antitrust action against the NCAA claiming that the
television policy was an unfair restraint on competition, in violation
of Section 1 of the Sherman Antitrust Act, which ultimately was
heard by the Supreme Court.

The Sherman Antitrust Act prohibits "every contract, in the
form of a trust or otherwise, or conspiracy, that restrains trade or
commerce among the states or with foreign nations." If read liter-
ally, this would outlaw almost every contract, because any agreement between a buyer and a seller restrains trade in some manner.
But the case law evolving from the Act has developed two tests to
judge unreasonable restraints of trade, the *per se* test and the rule of
reason. Under the rule of reason, the court conducts a historical and
market analysis of the particular restraint to determine whether it
results in an unreasonable restraint of trade. Under the *per se* test,
the court recognizes that there are certain situations where the probability that a restraint is anticompetitive is so high that an elaborate
inquiry need not be done. Under either test, the object of the inquiry is the same, that is, to determine whether the challenged restraint curtails competition or not.

Prior to the Oklahoma–Georgia action there were a few other
challenges to the NCAA under the Sherman Antitrust Act in which
the court decisions upheld restrictions designed to carry out the legitimate goals of the NCAA.

In *Jones* v. *NCAA* (1975), for example, the Federal District Court
of Massachusetts held that antitrust law did not reach the actions of
the NCAA in setting eligibility standards for its athletes. The court
upheld as legitimate the NCAA rule prohibiting amateur athletes
from receiving compensation. The court noted that such eligibility

rules were "basic principles of amateurism, principles that have been at the heart of the NCAA since its founding."

Similarly, in *Hennessey* v. *NCAA* (1977), the Fifth Circuit Court of Appeals upheld an NCAA restriction limiting the number of assistant coaches an institution could employ. Because of the nature and purposes of the NCAA, the court refused to apply the traditional *per se* approach as used in other antitrust cases. The court opted for the rule of reason in analyzing the NCAA's justification for the restriction. As its justification, the NCAA said it was to retain a clear line between college athletics and professional sports. Without this restriction, the NCAA claimed, colleges with more successful programs could take advantage of their success by expanding their programs to the ultimate detriment of the whole system of intercollegiate athletics. The *Hennessey* court noted that although some commercial impact was involved, the fundamental objective of the restriction was to preserve and foster competition in intercollegiate athletics while maintaining each school's traditional role as an amateur operating as part of the educational process, and defended the proposition that antitrust laws do not prevent the NCAA from protecting smaller schools and sports from the adverse impact of super-competitive teams.

In *Justice* v. *NCAA* (1983), the Federal District Court of Arizona upheld NCAA sanctions imposed on the University of Arizona football team for its practice of providing its players and recruits compensation and other benefits. The NCAA sanctions prevented Arizona from participating in either post-season competition or television appearances, and were upheld by the court under the rule of reason because they were "reasonably related to the legitimate goals of preserving amateurism and promoting fair competition in intercollegiate athletics."

But the use of the rule of reason in the *Hennessey* and *Justice* cases provided the first breakdown in the defense for the NCAA because the courts examined the *justifications* for the restraint of trade, thereby allowing the court to determine if they truly furthered the goals of the NCAA.

In *NCAA* v. *Board of Regents of the University of Oklahoma*, the NCAA defended its television policy largely in terms of general principles, claiming that it fostered intercollegiate athletics by: maintaining athletics as an essential part of the educational process; preserving the spirit of amateurism both on and off the field; and preventing the balance of competition between colleges from being diluted by professional or commercial considerations. But the Supreme Court held that the NCAA's television policy violated Section 1 of the Sherman Antitrust Act.

The court, in an opinion by Justice Stevens, broke down its holding into three parts. First, the court held that although the NCAA policy appeared to look like price fixing and output limitation, restraints that ordinarily would be held "illegal per se," the court said that it would be inappropriate to apply a *per se* rule in a case where an industry needs some restrictions in order for the product, college football, to be available at all. Thus the court reasoned that a fair evaluation could only be done via the rule of reason; the NCAA, thereby, was allowed an opportunity to justify its television policy. Second, the court concluded that the television policy constituted a restraint on the operation of a free market, since the plan operated to increase prices and reduce output. This result placed a heavy burden on the NCAA to justify its restriction on the free market. Third, the court held that the NCAA failed to meet its burden in justifying the restraints on the free market because the television policy was not reasonably related to the stated goals of the NCAA.

In addressing an argument that the NCAA television policy allowed NCAA football to be marketed more effectively and, therefore, enhanced competition, the Supreme Court adhered to the economic findings of the district court that if member institutions were free to sell television rights, many more games would be shown on television, and that the NCAA's restriction on output had the effect of raising the price the networks pay for television rights. The lower court also found that by fixing a price for television rights to all games, the NCAA created a price structure that was unresponsive to viewer demand. Since the lower court did not find that the NCAA's television plan produced any effects that enhanced competition, the plan only restrained competition. The lower court noted that, if the plan were designed to enhance competition, then there would be a decrease in prices while the output would increase. Since neither of these occurred, the lower court rejected the NCAA's argument.

Another argument advanced by the NCAA dealt with the

organization's interest in protecting live gate attendance from the adverse effects of televised games. Starting in the 1950s, the NCAA was concerned that fan interest in a televised game might lower ticket sales for games not on television. The Supreme Court found that the television policy was not even arguably related to a desire to protect live attendance because it did not ensure that a game was not going to be televised in the area where it was to be played. They reasoned that no cooperative action was necessary for that kind of a "blackout," but rather that a home team could always refuse to sell the right to telecast its game to stations in the immediate area. The district court had found some justification for this argument if the NCAA were appealing to a 1950s market, but the court found no evidence that live attendance would suffer if unlimited television were permitted in the current 1984 market. Further, the court decided that the policy was totally inconsistent with its stated purpose of protecting live attendance because games were already being televised during hours that college football games were being played. Rather, if anything, the plan shows the NCAA's position that ticket sales for college games would not be able to compete in a free market. As a result, the court concluded that the NCAA was trying to insulate live ticket sales from the full spectrum of competition because of the notion that the product, college football, was insufficiently attractive to consumers.

The NCAA's final justification for the television policy was the strong desire to maintain a competitive balance among amateur athletic teams. In its view, the television policy enhanced this desire. The Supreme Court agreed with the desire to maintain a competitive balance among amateur teams but emphatically stated that the television policy, as adopted by the NCAA, was not the proper way to promote this goal. The court noted that there was no attempt by the NCAA to equalize the strength of all members of the NCAA, such as those teams in Division I-A and those in Division I-AA or Division III. What damaged the argument even further was the fact that members of the NCAA who don't have a football team still have an equal voice in the management of revenues generated by football programs at other schools. The court stated that the NCAA's interest in maintaining a competitive balance was neither related to any neutral standard nor to any readily identifiable group of competitors. Since the policy was aimed at the general NCAA member population, it was not even arguably tailored to serve the competitive balance that the NCAA purported that it served. In an emphatic rejection of this final justification, the court held that the NCAA policy simply imposed a restriction on one source of revenue that was more important to some colleges than to others, and concluded that there was no evidence that this restriction produced any greater equality throughout the NCAA than would a restriction on alumni donations, tuition rates, or any other revenue producing activity.

Justice White wrote a dissent arguing that the majority had improperly applied the rule of reason. The dissent claimed that the majority did not give enough attention to the noncommercial goals promoted by the NCAA, namely, amateurism, education, and the competitive balance among all institutions. Justice White contended that if more emphasis had been given to these goals, the court would not have found the television policy had violated the Sherman Antitrust Act. He took offense at the heavy deference the court gave to the economic findings of the district court as well as to the very difficult burden of proof that had to be met by the NCAA in order to sustain the television policy. In essence, Justice White, who was joined by Justice Rehnquist, was unconvinced that the University of Oklahoma and the University of Georgia had shown that there was a real increase in prices or a decrease in output, two of the necessary criteria needed to establish a valid antitrust claim. Justice White noted that the NCAA existed primarily to enhance the contribution made by amateur athletics to the promotion of higher education. Without some regulation, the desire of member institutions to remain athletically competitive would lead them to engage in activities that deny amateurism to the public. As a result, no single institution could confidently enforce its own standards since it could not trust its competitors to do the same. In the end, Justice White believed that the NCAA existed to mitigate "what appears to be a clear failure of the free market to serve the ends and goals of higher education," by ensuring the availability of a unique and valuable product, college football.

What does this all mean in the mid-1990s? There has been a great expansion in the number of intercollegiate football games on television. For example, the CFA entered into a contract with NBC, and as of 1992, the CFA has a contract with CBS. While a game is being broadcast on that network, there often are other games being televised on ABC and ESPN as well. Members of the NCAA are now able to enter into their own television contracts at a price that will best meet the needs of the school without the fear of sanctions. For example, the University of Notre Dame signed a well-publicized contract with NBC for a period of five years in which all Notre Dame home football games will be televised nationally. The free market that was desired by the court back in 1984 has become a reality.

Selected Bibliography

Berry, R. and G. Wong. *Law and Business of the Sports Industries. Volume II: Common Issues in Amateur and Professional Sports.* Dover: Auburn House Publishing Company, 1986.

Jackstadt, R. "*Board of Regents of the University of Oklahoma* v. *The National Collegiate Athletic Association:* Antitrust Violations in College Football." *Saint Louis University Law Journal* 29 (1984): 207–228.

Kirby, R. "Antitrust Law: NCAA Thrown for a Loss by Court's Traditional Antitrust Blitz—*NCAA* v. *Board of Regents of the University of Oklahoma.*" *Creighton Law Review* 18 (1985): 917–952.

Sims, W. "*NCAA* v. *Board of Regents* and a Truncated Rule of Reason: Retaining Flexibility Without Sacrificing Efficiency." *Arizona Law Review* 27 (1985): 193–210.

Books and Bulldogs
Athletes and Academic Standards Abuses

Donald M. McKale

Kemp v. *Ervin*, 651 F.Supp. 495 (1986)

Early in 1986, a jury in the U.S. District Court in Atlanta, Georgia, awarded a staggering $2.58 million to Jan Kemp, a former faculty member at the University of Georgia. Her suit against two university administrators revealed academic abuses involving athletes at the Georgia institution. Kemp, a Phi Beta Kappa with three degrees from the University of Georgia, including a doctorate, had taught in and coordinated the English section of the university's developmental studies department, a remedial program for students. She claimed in her suit that administrators Leroy Ervin and Virginia Trotter had fired her in August 1988 for speaking out against the preferential treatment accorded some university athletes by the developmental studies department.

Kemp challenged her dismissal on the grounds that the university had violated her First Amendment right of free speech. After the university threatened to appeal the huge award to Kemp, she subsequently agreed in May 1986 to an out-of-court settlement that gave her $1.08 million and reinstatement to her job. Her widely publicized case influenced the course of academic reform of intercollegiate athletics, which had begun in 1984 with the formation of the President's Commission of the National Collegiate Athletic Association.

The six-week Kemp trial showed both the ineptness of the university's presentation of its case and the cynical attitude of some of its leading administrators toward Kemp's charges. She accused the University of Georgia of "exploiting" its athletes, particularly African-American athletes, by using the remedial learning program to get them into school and to keep them eligible for sports. In

December 1981, Virginia Trotter, the university's vice president for academic affairs, permitted nine football players to "exit" from the remedial program to the regular university curriculum, despite their having failed a final quarter of English. Vince Dooley, head football coach and athletic director, suited up the nine players for the 1982 Sugar Bowl.

Kemp protested. She argued that the administration had sent the athletes the message that they did not have to work for their promotions, and she was also disturbed by the university's simultaneous dismissal of a failing nonathlete from the remedial program. Trotter admitted in court that athletes received preferential treatment at the university, but defended her action on promoting the students. She testified that "I felt they deserved an opportunity because of the work they had done."

Ervin, the other defendant in the case, served as assistant vice-president for developmental studies. He maintained that Kemp's dismissal resulted from her failure to do scholarly research and from her disruptive influence on the remedial program. During the trial, however, a transcript of a secretly taped meeting of university officials was introduced revealing that Ervin essentially admitted to Kemp's charges. At the meeting, Ervin, an African-American, lamented the poor educational backgrounds of some black athletes in the remedial program, but justified "their utility to the institution" in helping it make millions of dollars a year, mainly at football games. "There is no real sound academic reason for their being here," Ervin said of such athletes, "other than to be utilized to produce income. They are used as a kind of raw material in the production of some good to be sold . . . and they get nothing in return. . . ."

Also, during the trial, the defendants' lawyer and the university's president and football coach, attempted unsuccessfully to defend the school's bending of its standards for academically deficient athletes. According to a January 27, 1986 article in *Sports Illustrated,* attorney Hale Almand startled even his own clients when he declared in his opening argument, "We may not make a university student out of [an athlete]. But if we can teach him to read and write, maybe he can work at the post office rather than as a garbage man when he gets through with his athletic career."

Considering that both University of Georgia President Fred Davison and coach Dooley had played leadership roles in NCAA campaigns to clean up college sports, their testimony left much to be desired. Davison maintained that other universities had lower standards for athletes and "we have to compete [with them] on a level playing field." Dooley, despite strong evidence in the trial that the university had placed eligibility and football ahead of education, contended that the Georgia institution had melded athletics and academics in a "noble and reasonable way."

The trial revealed numerous facts embarrassing to the university. Both former and current faculty members testified that athletes with little hope of graduating were kept eligible in developmental studies, where they did not have to face authentic college-level courses. Athletes comprised 17 percent of the program's enrollment of roughly 335 students. The trial also demonstrated that the state school systems produced talented athletes who graduated from high school barely able to read or write. Also, since 1971, when the University of Georgia had integrated the football team, the school had graduated only sixteen of sixty-six African American players.

According to a story in *Sports Illustrated* published on February 24, 1986, Kemp insisted at the trial's end that she still remained an avid Georgia Bulldog fan, despite the ordeal of her dismissal, which had nearly driven her to suicide. She hoped that her victory and the large award would produce nationwide reforms in the academic preparation of athletes. Indeed, her case captured national attention. Doug Single, athletic director at Northwestern, suggested that universities with high academic standards might schedule games with one another and not worry about playing schools with lower intellectual expectations.

John Weistart, an influential Duke University sports law professor, saw significance in the size of the jury's award to Kemp. "The jury," he commented, "was reacting to the hypocrisy of the Georgia program. They [the University officials] said they were doing something, and in fact they were doing something else." Davison became a major casualty in the Kemp affair. Whereas Kemp received her job back at Georgia, Davison resigned his presidency in March 1986, under heavy pressure from students, faculty, and the University of Georgia System's Board of Regents.

Selected Bibliography

Monaghan, P. "Georgia Teacher Settles with University, Regains Job." *Chronicle of Higher Education.* May 14, 1986: 35.

Nack, W. "This Case Was One for the Books." *Sports Illustrated.* February 24, 1986: 34–36, 41–42.

Neff, C. and R. Sullivan. "Scorecard: On Trial in Georgia: Academic Integrity." *Sports Illustrated.* January 27, 1986: 13.

Switzer, a Sooner Scofflaw?

James W. Hewitt

The year 1989 marked the centennial of the great Oklahoma land rush, when avaricious frontier folk jumped across the border into Indian territory before the starting gun. In their frenzied search for land, promised or otherwise, the overeager entrepreneurs showed they had little regard for rules, and earned for themselves the soubriquet "Sooners," which, in those days, was synonymous with "cheat."

Almost a century later, the football legions of the University of Oklahoma, proudly calling themselves the "Sooners," showed that disregard for law and order in Oklahoma had not vanished with the American frontier. In the span of a long fortnight early in 1989, three Oklahoma University football players were arrested for raping a woman in the athletic dormitory (two were later convicted, one acquitted). In that same dormitory, a corner back shot a lineman (the two had been high school teammates; the lineman survived to play again, while the corner back transferred to Houston, where he successfully closed out his football career). Finally, the Sooners' starting quarterback was arrested for selling cocaine to an FBI plant.

William Shakespeare wrote: "How sharper than a serpent's tooth it is to have a thankless child." Barry Switzer, head of the Oklahoma football enterprise and college football's then most successful active coach, would agree with the Bard's King Lear. His players, whom he recruited zealously and then either ignored or indulged, or enlisted in many of his questionable activities, brought his empire crashing down.

The real tragedy of the breakdown of the Oklahoma gridiron machine was that it was preventable. But Switzer either ignored his prize recruits once he had won them, or took them with him on bibulous forays into the fleshpots of Norman. The players, both African American and white, responded by conclusively demonstrating that over-indulged teenagers, subject to the uncritical adulation of a football-mad populace, simply cannot function effectively without a modicum of oversight and discipline.

Charles Thompson, former Oklahoma high school football star, and then the Sooners' talented quarterback, was the most notable illustration of the lack of discipline. Switzer, learning from a cooperative law enforcement official that the FBI possessed convincing evidence, tipped off his star, thereby earning the enmity of the law enforcement community. To repay Switzer, Thompson aided the same narcotics informer who sprang the trap on him in burglarizing Switzer's home. The FBI informer made off with all of Switzer's championship rings and was later arrested while attempting to peddle them in a Norman tavern.

In February 1989, Thompson's arrest came upon the heels of the two other felonies committed by team members and the National Collegiate Athletic Association's imposition of a three-year probation on the Oklahoma football program in the fall of 1988. David Swank, distinguished legal scholar, dean of the Oklahoma law school, and interim president of the university, had seen enough. According to Switzer, Swank, believing the academic reputation of the university had been compromised, applied unrelenting pressure until Switzer, winner of 157 games, three national titles, and twelve Big Eight Conference titles in sixteen years of coaching, reluctantly resigned.

Both Switzer and Thompson raced into print with "as told to" books, each pointing a finger at the other. Switzer also blamed much of his downfall on Swank, who he said failed to recognize the benefit to the university of having the nation's "winningest" coach on board. Switzer contrasted Swank's attitude with that of former Oklahoma president William Banowsky, who reportedly told Switzer he could openly smoke dope if Oklahoma won the national championship. Apparently not recognizing hyperbole as a figure of speech, Switzer seemed to take Banowsky's permissive exaggeration to heart. In the mid-1980s he was convicted for driving under the influence of alcohol.

Switzer was also sued by the Securities and Exchange Commission in the mid-1980s for violation of its insider trading rules in one of his business ventures, but the case was ultimately dismissed without going to judgment. Whether Switzer needed to fleece anyone is highly conjectural, especially since he boasted of having earned $400,000 per year from his football-related activities at Oklahoma.

Switzer, who grew up in semipoverty as the son of a bootlegger, appeared to have learned little from his father's brushes with the law. Raised in a rural setting, with young African Americans as his primary companions, Switzer seemed proudest of his reputation as college football's leading recruiter of outstanding African American athletes. Paradoxically, all of the players involved in the 1989 scandals that toppled Switzer's regime were African Americans, although Oklahoma and Switzer also suffered the previous year from the bizarre antics of Brian Bosworth, a white linebacker. Bosworth, suspended before the Orange Bowl when traces of steroids appeared in his urine during a drug test, appeared on the Oklahoma sidelines during the game wearing a T-shirt vilifying the NCAA as "National Communists Against Athletes." Perhaps someone from the NCAA remembered that incident when imposing the football program's three-year probation the following fall.

Switzer also contended that he and his staff spent a great deal of time teaching and counseling his aggressive adolescents. He made the point that football coaching staffs spend infinitely more time with student-athletes than do classroom professors. On this issue, he may well be right, but the Oklahoma staff can take little pride in the expenditure of all those long hours if the events of 1989 are at all indicative of the results.

Thompson's book portrays him as a quite unpleasant young man, egotistical to a fault, consumed by carnal desire, and living in a fog of alcohol and cocaine. In the book he admits that what he did was wrong, but blames Switzer for leading him to believe he could do anything he wanted and get away with it. He recounts, in considerable detail, drinking bouts with Switzer and trysts with Switzer's secretaries.

Written while he was in federal prison, Thompson's book ends without describing his conviction, sentence, or subsequent career at Central State of Ohio, at Wilberforce, where he played small-college football. Thompson signed with the Sacramento Gold Miners, the only United States entry in the Canadian Football League, in the spring of 1993, hoping for a career as a running back or wide receiver.

Both Switzer and Thompson were superbly talented, Switzer as a coach and motivator, Thompson as an athlete. Yet apparently neither recognized the role of football in college life, nor had even a vague awareness of appropriate behavior. In this regard, Switzer must bear most of the blame. A coach's job is to guide and educate his team, and to serve as a role model. In drinking and partying with his stars, and ignoring his other charges, Switzer violated the basic tenets of the coaching role. As a result, considerable damage had been done to the gridiron program and the reputation of the University of Oklahoma.

After several years away from the sidelines, Switzer accepted the offer of Jerry Jones, Dallas Cowboys owner, to succeed Jimmy Johnson as coach of the team in 1994.

Selected Bibliography

Jenkins, S. "Barry's Back." *Sports Illustrated.* April 11, 1994: 32–34.

Kreidler, M. "Charles Thompson's Incredible Journey." *Sacramento Bee.* July 4, 1993: Sports, C1.

Switzer, B. and B. Shrake. *Bootlegger's Boy.* New York: William Morrow & Co., Inc., 1990.

Telander, R. and R. Sullivan. "You Reap What You Sow." *Sports Illustrated.* February 27, 1989: 20–26.

Thompson, C. and A. Sonnenschein. *Down and Dirty: The Life and Crimes of Oklahoma Football.* New York: Carroll & Graf, Publishers, Inc., 1990.

The Win at Any Price Syndrome
Steroids in Athletics

Heather M. Feuerhelm

Athletes dream of the opportunity to receive a gold medal. The world watches in awe as athletes are praised for their athletic prowess. To win the gold is to achieve greatness. The biggest nightmare for an athlete, therefore, is to have that medal stripped away.

Ben Johnson, once hailed as the world's fastest man, experienced that nightmare. In 1988, Johnson sprinted to a world-record finish in the 100-yard dash in an amazing 9.79 seconds. The next day, the shock came; Johnson had tested positive for anabolic steroid use. His medal was taken away and the gold was awarded to Johnson's longtime rival, Carl Lewis.

At first glance, it is easy to blame Johnson for trying to cheat his way to the gold. Johnson's coach, Charlie Francis, declares that most Olympic athletes and professional athletes today are guilty of the same training methods: using steroids to enhance performance. The history of steroid use, however, began long before Johnson entered into the sporting world. Since the introduction of steroids to the athletic world, the ethical and legal problems have grown. In fact, according to most experts, use of the drug has become an epidemic in the amateur and professional sporting worlds, and is spreading into the high schools.

Steroid use originally began in the 1930s to treat conditions such as anemia, malnutrition, and skeletal dysfunction. It was a humane treatment meant to help ailing people. During World War II, the ethics were overlooked. Nazi troops were given steroids in the hopes of building a superpower army. Steroid use in the athletic world began in the 1950s, when Soviet and East European athletes used steroids to improve their performance in competition and dominated in strength events due to this drug enhancement. In the 1954 world weight lifting championships, a Russian physician told Dr. John Ziegler, a United States team physician, that the Russian athletes were taking the male hormone testosterone, a steroid, to enhance their performances. Ziegler was impressed and began his own experiments with steroids in 1959.

Ziegler's experiments led him into discoveries beyond what he originally set out to find. The Russian steroid-enhanced female athletes that Ziegler had observed tended to look overly masculine, and Ziegler hoped to find a synthetic version of testosterone that would minimize this effect. By the 1960s, American weight lifters were using steroids. Many athletes who began using steroids had obsessive personalities and tended to believe that if a little helped, a lot would help even more. They began taking more than the recommended doses, sometimes over twenty times more. Ziegler stopped his testing when he discovered that some athletes who were taking steroids had developed liver problems. Later, Ziegler regretted introducing steroids to athletes. In Silverstein's book, Ziegler is quoted as saying, "I wish I had never heard the word 'steroid.' These kids don't realize the terrible price they are going to pay."

Even though Ziegler stopped testing, the world of sports continued to use and experiment with steroids. Athletes in amateur sports such as track and field were already using the drugs to enhance performance. Professional athletes in football found that steroid use built bigger, stronger bodies that could work out longer without depleting energy. *Sports Illustrated* estimated in 1992 that up to 80 percent of NFL linemen and 50 percent of the linebackers have used steroids. Even more staggering are the reports that show large numbers of amateur athletes in colleges and high schools using steroids.

In addition to the growth in the numbers of steroid users, the problems of steroid use have multiplied. Because so many athletes who use steroids believe that more is better, problems have arisen with "stacking," which is taking more than one kind of steroid at a time. The doses have also increased drastically. When Ben Johnson's coach Charlie Francis was researching steroids to determine how his athletes were going to use the enhancement, he discovered how far "stacking" for some athletes had gone. He said, "One power lifter known to us 'stacked' 150 milligrams of Dianabol, 200 milligrams of the particularly toxic Anadrol-50, and 100 milligrams of testosterone—a total of 450 milligrams a day, or about 135,000 milligrams a year."

In contrast, Francis began his own athlete, Angella Taylor, at 5 milligrams of Dianabol a day and in three-week cycles—three weeks on the drug, and three weeks off, to minimize possible side effects. Francis defended his decision to administer steroids by pointing to the safety of his athletes compared to those who overused the drugs. The problem was still evident; steroid use increased because even the most conscientious coaches were beginning to encourage steroid use as a part of training.

As the problems of steroid use have spread, the governing bodies in athletics have begun to set up guidelines regarding drug use. In the 1968 Winter Olympics, drug testing was established in an attempt to keep sports ethical. However, athletes began to look for ways around the rules. Steroids were the ideal choice for improving performance because they built stronger bodies, rather than simply supplying a quick energy burst. In addition, athletes could discontinue their use soon enough before competition to make them become undetectable by testing time, while still maintaining the effects of the drugs. Other performance-enhancing drugs had to be taken right before the competition, but steroids were discovered to be more effective if use was discontinued several weeks before the performance. With all of these factors combined, athletes had found a loophole in the policy. A 1974 Senate subcommittee report concluded that steroids and amphetamines were the most commonly abused drugs in amateur athletics.

In 1975, steroid use was declared illegal by the International Olympic Committee (IOC) because it might give an unfair advantage to the athletes who used performance-enhancing drugs. The list of IOC-banned drugs included anabolic steroids, testosterone, growth hormones, blood doping, and drugs used to hide illegal drugs.

Although the actions taken by the IOC were intended to make competition fair, many athletes and coaches believed it was too late. Competitors all over the world were using steroids, and testing was unreliable, at best. The rules for steroid use were also ignored rather than enforced. The governing bodies who were supposed to enforce the rules actually hid the truth. The combination of unreliable testing and lack of enforcement resulted in athletes continuing to use steroids. Athletes felt this was the only way they could keep up with the competition. The problems continued to multiply.

Articles about steroid use began publicly revealing the problem. An issue of *Sports Illustrated* in 1990 carried an article from the German magazine *Stern* which cited documents from Dr. Manfred Hoppner, deputy director of East Germany's Sports Medical Service, as proof that many of the top athletes from East Germany had used anabolic steroids. According to these documents, athletes such as long jumper Heike Drechsler, Olympic shot put champion Ulf Timmermann, and swimming champion Kristin Otto, had all taken steroids. One revelation was that a routine precompetition drug test ten days before her first event in the 1989 European swimming championships revealed that Otto's testosterone level was three times the acceptable amount. She was nevertheless allowed to compete on the assumption that her testosterone would decrease to an acceptable level by competition time. She won the 100-meter backstroke at the championships and passed the drug test. The ethical concerns were overlooked.

In addition to the German release, other countries reported similar news. A Vienna newspaper reported that twenty-four Austrian athletes had tested positive for steroids in one year. In addition, a sports official from the then U.S.S.R. reported that forty-nine Soviet athletes had tested positive for banned substances in 1990. There were many others who tested positive, including American record holders Randy Barnes, a shot putter, and Butch Reynolds, a 400-meter runner.

The problems spread to high schools as well. The July 22, 1991, issue of *Sports Illustrated* revealed what was known as "Operation 'Roid Raid." In Phoenix, representatives from eight law-enforcement agencies arrested thirty-five people and seized forty thousand bottles of anabolic steroids. They also seized cash and weapons. The raid was the result of an investigation that began after parents of a local high school went to the police because of a concern that their children were using anabolic steroids. This raid came shortly after the announcement that Lyle Alzado, an NFL star, had been using steroids.

Alzado was just one professional athlete who stepped forward and announced his history of drug use. He reported that he had taken anabolic steroids since 1969, and never stopped. He also announced that he had a brain lymphoma, a terminal cancer that he and his doctor were sure was a result of his steroid use. A *Sports Illustrated* article of July 8, 1991, quoted Alzado, "Ninety percent of the athletes I know are on the stuff. We're not born to be 280 or 300 pounds or jump 30 feet. Some people are born that way, but not many, and there are some 1,400 guys in the NFL."

Another NFL player, Steve Courson, recounted his own story of steroid use. According to *Sports Illustrated*'s January 27, 1992, issue, Courson reported that he had gotten sick from steroid use. At one point, his resting pulse was measured at more than 150 beats per minute. His steroid use had gone out of control, but he continued to play football and use the drugs. Three months after he first got sick, he was diagnosed with dilated cardiomyopathy, an enlarged heart that could not pump normally because of lost muscle fibers. He reported, "There's no glory dying for a sport."

In spite of these cases, many athletes simply do not see the dangers that accompany steroid use. The most widely publicized steroid user, Ben Johnson, was suspended from track after testing positive in the 1988 Summer Olympics, and it was hoped that Johnson would serve as an example for other athletes. Johnson vowed he would make a clean comeback. In a July 22, 1991, article *Sports Illustrated* declared that he was "clean and slower," but in 1993 he tested positive for steroid use. This second offense would have resulted in a lifetime suspension from track, but Johnson retired from the sport before he received his penalty.

Amidst all of the ethical controversy, athletes are now arguing that drug testing is not constitutional. In 1987, Santa Clara County Superior Court Judge Peter Stone granted an order and injunction for Stanford University diver Simone LeVant, allowing her to compete in the NCAA, sanctioned competitions. LeVant had refused to sign a form that would obligate her to submit to urine testing for various substances at the NCAA championships. A *Sports Illustrated* commentary noted that the case could lead other courts to similar conclusions: that the NCAA drug testing program violates constitutional privacy protections and is unreasonable.

According to Philip Samuel Sloan's book, *The Athlete and the Law*:

Rules which prohibit the use of drugs in amateur athletics are within the proper authority of athletic organizations in that they protect the health and well-being of the athletes subject to their control and prevent the administering of drugs to increase athletic performance. The constitutional rights guaranteed in the Fourth and Fifth Amendments are questionable when athletes must submit to blood, urine, or saliva testing.

Since the LeVant case, the legality of testing athletes for drug use continues to change. Students are declaring that drug testing programs violate the Fourth Amendment on the basis that such programs constitute unreasonable searches.

In *Hill* v. *NCAA* (1990), new plaintiffs substituted for diver Simone LeVant because she had since graduated. A California court of appeals held that the NCAA program was unreasonable and involved an unconstitutional invasion of privacy. In 1994 the Supreme Court of California reversed the decision of the lower court and directed a final judgment favoring the NCAA.

The problems widen when international sports are involved. The International Amateur Athletic Federation (IAAF), the world governing body for track and field, believes that it should answer to no higher authority, according to a *Sports Illustrated*, December 14, 1992, article. U.S. District Judge Joseph Kinneary in Columbus, Ohio, ordered the IAAF to pay U.S. runner Butch Reynolds $27.3 million for lost income and punitive damages due to his suspension in November 1990 because of a positive test for anabolic steroids. The IAAF argues that it cannot submit to all of its 200-odd member nations as individual judicial systems. They believe they should not answer to other courts.

The debate still continues: Whose ethics and whose laws should be followed? In Sloan's preface, he argued that the history of sports ties the ethical concerns in with the legal issues. Since the beginning of athletic competition, the central concept has been that participants must follow certain prescribed rules of legitimate play. These rules preserve the integrity of the game. To the Greeks, athletic proficiency symbolized the purity of internal balance. Today, those same issues of ethics and true physical achievement without illegal aid are the goal, but too many athletes are breaking the rules and looking for shortcuts.

Ben Johnson stood in the winner's circle at the 1988 Olympics and accepted an award, a gold medal, designating him as the world's fastest man. He accepted the award, in spite of his steroid enhancement. Johnson's lack of ethics eventually cost him his running career. He was also the victim of a sports establishment that tolerates, if not encourages, steroid use.

Mistaken attitudes toward steroid use remain, regardless of all of the problems. Athletes are destroying their bodies, overloading on drugs, and doing anything to win—and then denying that anyone has the right to test them. The viewpoint is one that shocks those who believe in ethical competition. Johnson's coach, Charlie Francis, epitomized the viewpoint that remains the central problem when he said in a *Sports Illustrated*, December 17, 1990, article "I don't call it cheating. My definition of cheating is doing something that nobody else is doing."

Selected Bibliography

Alzado, L. as told to S. "I'm Sick and I'm Scared." *Sports Illustrated.* July 8, 1991: 20ff.

Ferber, A. "Diver Just Says No." *Women's Sports and Fitness* 9 (May 1987): 25.

Francis, C. and J. Coplon. *Speed Trap.* New York: St. Martin's Press, 1990.

Moore, K. "Clean and Slower." *Sports Illustrated.* July 22, 1991: 26–29.

Newman, B. "Another NCAA Fumble." *Sports Illustrated.* December 7, 1987: 100.

O'Neal, Ted. "The Constitutionality of NCAA Drug Testing: A Fine Specimen for Examination." *Southern Methodist Law Review* 4 (Fall 1992): 513–554.

"Scorecard: A Dirty System." *Sports Illustrated.* December 7, 1990: 27.

"Scorecard: Eye Openers." *Sports Illustrated.* July 22, 1991: 10.

"Scorecard: Positively Negative." *Sports Illustrated.* November 19, 1990: 29.

Silverstein, A. *Steroids: Big Muscles, Big Problems.* Hillside: Enslow Publishers, Inc., 1992.

Sloan, P. *The Athlete and the Law.* New York: Oceana Publications, Inc., 1993.

Telander, Rick. "Books: In the Aftermath of Steroids." *Sports Illustrated.* January 27, 1992: 103.

To Play or Not to Play
Substance Abuse Policies of Three Major Sports
Leagues

David Sitz

Drug abuse has become a dominant issue in our society and within
professional sports industries as a whole. Statistics vary on the magnitude of the problem in professional sports. Some say that anywhere between 50 percent and 70 percent of professional athletes
occasionally use illicit drugs and that 20 percent of those are actually suffering from drug addiction. Regardless of the numbers, it has
been recognized that a serious problem exists. In an effort to solve
the problem, virtually all professional sports leagues have implemented their own substance-abuse policies.

In September 1983, for example, the National Basketball Association (NBA) and the National Basketball Players' Association
(NBPA) instituted a comprehensive plan designed to eliminate the
use of drugs in the NBA. Experts recognized it as the pioneering
program in professional sports. The program sets out several goals:
first, prevention and education; second, detection and discipline;
and third, treatment. The NBA's program continues to develop newer
and better techniques to achieve these goals.

Prevention of drug use necessarily entails education about the
drugs themselves and of the catastrophic effects they can have on an
individual's health and professional career. Education plays a major
role in the NBA's program. Each team must attend two antidrug
seminars during its season. The first is held before the league's annual all-star game with a follow-up several weeks later. The seminars
cover the dangers of drug abuse and also teach the players how to
detect a problem in teammates or themselves and how to approach
counselors if they or others have a problem. Sessions are also held
for coaches and general managers to help them deal with players
who have drug-related difficulties.

The NBA also conducts a special orientation program in which each rookie has to attend a two-day seminar before the season starts. Others attending are trained counselors, former and current players, and the previous season's rookies. Issues address the new lifestyle associated with entry into professional basketball. Most players have more money and leisure after signing their professional contracts, factors which can possibly lead to drug use.

Even with these concerted efforts at education and prevention, the use of drugs still becomes a problem for some players. The detection and treatment aspect of the program gives the players the opportunity to seek help for their problem. A player who comes forward to seek treatment is given counseling and treatment at the expense of the club, and the player continues to be paid. If, after treatment, the player lapses but voluntarily comes forward again, he is suspended without pay and undergoes additional treatment. If this occurs a third time, the player is banned from the league and can seek readmittance after a two-year leave, and then only with the approval of the NBA commissioner and the Players Association. These procedures effectively provide a great incentive for players to voluntarily seek assistance.

The program also calls for a two-year dismissal for any player convicted of, pleading guilty to, or testing positive for cocaine or heroin, the only two drugs tested through agreed-upon testing procedures. This aspect of the program is administered by an independent expert in drug abuse detection who decides whether the information received by the NBA or the NBPA constitutes sufficient evidence to test a player for drugs. If the expert deems so, the player is tested without prior knowledge. If the results are positive, he is subject to the penalty prescribed.

Once the existence of a drug problem has been determined, the player embarks on a substantive treatment program. The first stage begins with the player undergoing intensive counseling involving a wide variety of techniques. When a player completes his treatment, an aftercare plan is set up that requires him to attend self-help groups such as Alcoholics Anonymous. Additionally, there is a network in each NBA city which the player can contact while on the road if any problems arise. If a player fails to abide by his treatment plan or aftercare, he is immediately suspended without pay.

While the NBA's drug policy is hailed as the model program among the four major sports leagues, the other major leagues have their own policies. Each has virtually the same goals in mind, but attacks the problem slightly differently.

The National Football League's drug-abuse policy is broken into two distinct parts; one addresses the use of anabolic steroids and the second deals with other drugs. Like the NBA, the NFL allows players to come forward voluntarily to seek treatment, with no disciplinary action, while the player continues to receive his salary. Players are also allowed to come forward without receiving discipline even if they have been in violation or tested positive previously.

The policy on anabolic steroids begins with preseason testing for all players. Throughout the season, weekly regular season and post-season tests are conducted with players randomly selected by computer. Additionally, reasonable cause testing is conducted for players who have tested positive previously. A player testing positive for steroids for the first time is subject to a four-game suspension and if the testing took place during preseason, the suspension is for two weeks. A player testing positive for the second time will be suspended for at least six regular season or post-season games. A player testing positive on a third occasion is suspended for at least one year and can only seek reinstatement after the suspension.

The NFL policy on other drugs is more inclusive than the NBA's with regard to the drugs covered; however, it is not as extensive educationally as the NBA's program. Under the NFL policy, players are prohibited from using, possessing, purchasing, selling, and/or participating in the illegal distribution of drugs. Players who have had prior positive tests or have known prior drug use or substance abuse treatment are subjected to year-round reasonable cause testing. The league has appointed a drug advisor similar to one employed by the NBA to determine the necessity and frequency of the testing procedures. After consultation with the team physician, a decision is made that determines whether further action is needed.

A player testing positive for the first time is subject to a medical evaluation and placed into an appropriate treatment program. A second positive testing results in the player's removal from the roster for six games and further treatment as directed by doctors. For a player who tests positive on a third occasion, a suspension is incurred for at least one year with the right to seek reinstatement after that year. Additionally, if such a player refuses to take a reasonable-cause test, it will be deemed a positive test and the player can be subject to disciplinary action.

The NFL's policy, while fairly extensive, has been criticized in the past for being little more than a drug-testing policy because of its apparent lack of concern over anything but the testing aspect of the program. The NFL's policy does contain all of the same elements the NBA policy has, but critics say that if the NFL really wishes to combat the problem of drugs effectively, the prevention and education aspects of the program could receive more emphasis, and the treatment program might be adapted to resemble the NBA's, where a drug abuser can contact someone at any time to assist in the recovery process. Orientation drug seminars for rookies also seem needed.

The primary objectives of Major League Baseball's (MLB) drug policy are preserving the health and welfare of those who work in baseball and protecting the integrity of the game. As with the previous two league policies, the sale or use of any illegal drug by players or personnel is strictly prohibited. A violation of this sort can be subject to discipline by the commissioner as well as action, under the Uniform Player Contract, by the team. MLB's drug policy includes all illegal drugs.

MLB's drug policy begins much like the NBA policy in that each club establishes an Employee Assistance Program (EAP) for its major and minor league players to provide basic education to players about the dangers of drug abuse, to offer confidential and expert counseling, and if needed, to give rehabilitative assistance. MLB also implements its own drug testing program and procedures directed by a program coordinator appointed by the commissioner, much like the ones existing in the NFL and the NBA. For admitted or detected drug users, drug testing is part of that player's aftercare program throughout the rest of his career in baseball.

The testing procedure for major league players is different than that used for minor league players. Major league players are not subject to unannounced testing for illegal drugs. However, once a player has tested positive or admitted to drug use, the player is subject to mandatory testing throughout the remainder of his career. Minor league players are subjected to random, unannounced testing and are selected by computer. Testing occurs no more than four times per season for anyone covered by the program. Individuals who have had prior dependency problems are subject to more than four tests per season, and, if necessary, off-season testing occurs.

Once the illegal use of a drug has been detected, the disciplinary stage of the program is initiated much like the other programs. The initial positive test does not immediately result in discipline but rather subjects the player to the EAP treatment program. While in the program the player does not lose any pay. Discipline is imposed on players who refuse to enter or comply with the program, violate the drug policy a second time, or refuse to take a test.

The major criticism of MLB's drug policy points to its lack of specific guidelines with respect to the discipline that is to be imposed. Both the NBA and the NFL have distinct penalties for the violation of their respective drug policies. While MLB seems to go further than the NFL with respect to the deterrence and educational aspects of its program, the actual disciplinary aspect of the program lacks the NFL program's bite, and therefore, its effectiveness as a deterrent. Critics of the MLB model for drug prevention seek more concrete penalties for multiple offenders, such as those the NBA and NFL impose. For the time being, however, MLB continues to allow repeat offenders to come back repeatedly.

Two prime examples of the effects of drugs on a professional athlete's career are basketball forward Roy Tarpley, and baseball relief pitcher Steve Howe. Both have had extensive drug-related problems, but while Howe became a millionaire once again, the other is struggling just to make a living playing the game he loves.

Roy Tarpley is six feet ten inches tall, strong, agile, and a former superstar for the Wolverines of the University of Michigan. He was drafted by the Dallas Mavericks and was an immediate success. Tarpley made the All-Rookie team for the 1986–87 season. But he encountered substance abuse problems in 1987 and 1989. In 1991 the NBA banned Tarpley for violating its antidrug policy. Following his suspension, Tarpley played in the Continental Basketball Association and then the Greek League. The NBA reinstated Tarpley who rejoined the Mavericks for the 1994–95 season.

Even with the extensive program provided by the NBA, players like Tarpley have slipped through the safety net, illustrating the awesome power that drugs can have over a person. Players like Michael Ray Richardson and Mitchell Wiggins have essentially thrown their careers away and along with them, considerable prestige and wealth. While there have been success stories, like that of John Lucas recovering from cocaine addiction, and Chris Mullin recovering from alcohol addiction, these seem relatively rare.

In December 1992 Steve Howe signed a two-year deal for over $4 million, and even after previously being run out of the game of baseball seven times, Howe accumulated impressive numbers and honors during his suspension-littered career. A stellar left-handed relief pitcher, Howe received Rookie of the Year recognition as a member of the Los Angeles Dodgers in 1980. But after four standout seasons with the Dodgers, his career disintegrated in failed comeback attempts due to drug use. Because of the ambiguous discipline standards of baseball, Howe was allowed by an arbitrator to return to the major leagues.

In June 1992, Fay Vincent, then the commissioner of baseball, banned Howe for life. This came as a result of Howe's guilty plea to a charge of attempted possession of cocaine in Montana. He was sentenced to three years' probation, a $1,000 fine, and 100 hours of community service. This was the eighth time that Howe had either been caught or had admitted to the use or possession of an illegal substance. A grievance was brought by the Major League Players' Association against Commissioner Vincent and the arbitrator overruled Vincent's ban because of evidence that Howe suffered from hyperactivity, a condition that contributed to his cocaine dependency. The arbitrator ruled that if Howe were caught again, he would be out of baseball permanently, but he did not explain why a medical condition would entitle a chronic drug abuser to exactly eight chances, but no more than that. This incident is evidence of the lack of strict guidelines within the MLB drug program and the need for change.

While none of the programs are perfect, each have been at least fairly effective. There may be no way to completely eradicate the drug problem in professional sports, but these programs are definitely on the right track as they all have the interests of the athlete and the sport in mind. With these two ultimate goals and better overall antidrug education, perhaps one day Americans will see totally drug-free professional sports.

Selected Bibliography

Sisson, D. and B. Trexell. "The National Football League's Substance Abuse Policy: Is Further Conflict Between Players and Management Inevitable?" *Marquette Sports Law Journal* 2 (Fall 1991): 1–38.

"Strike Three: NBA Bans Tarpley for Life." *Chicago Tribune*. October 17, 1991: Sports, 3.

York, M. "Eight Lives Maybe for Howe, But He Isn't Counting on Nine." *St. Louis Post-Dispatch*. March 14, 1993: Sports, 2.

Two All-Pros Collide with the Football Commissioner

Terry Radtke

Alvin "Pete" Rozelle encountered one of his major challenges during the opening years of his reign as commissioner of the National Football League. Born in Southgate, California, in 1926, Rozelle graduated from the University of San Francisco twenty-four years later. He worked as general manager of the Los Angeles Rams immediately prior to his selection in 1960 to succeed Bert Bell as NFL commissioner. During the first few years of his tenure, Rozelle expanded the NFL from twelve to fourteen teams, More significantly, he negotiated the NFL's first one-network television contract.

Rumors of gambling by NFL players provided Rozelle with an opportunity to continue to take decisive measures to promote the interests of the league. Since the early 1920s, professional football had a rule prohibiting players from betting on a game. Questionable relationships with gamblers, however, existed from the 1940s onward. Commissioner Bert Bell indefinitely suspended two members of the New York Giants, Merle Harper and Frank Filchock. The players apparently did not accept a bribe offered them to fix the 1946 championship game against the Chicago Bears, but they failed to report the incident. Even some NFL owners were suspected of connections with bookmakers.

Two NFL All-Pros posed a challenge to Commissioner Rozelle in 1963. Paul Hornung of the Green Bay Packers and Alex Karras of the Detroit Lions became the subjects of an official investigation into their alleged betting on football games. Hornung came to the NFL following stellar careers in Louisville high school sports and in collegiate football at Notre Dame. At the South Bend, Indiana institution, Hornung won All-American honors for two seasons and received the prestigious Heisman Trophy following his senior year.

The first player chosen in the 1957 draft, the "Golden Boy" flourished as a halfback for Vince Lombardi's Green Bay squad, winning All-Pro recognition in 1960 and 1961.

The other All-Pro suspected of gambling on football games carried several nicknames, including "Mad Duck" and "Tippy Toes." Alex Karras played high school football so well in Gary, Indiana, that over one hundred colleges sought his talents. Karras chose the University of Iowa, where he twice earned All-American honors and helped lead the Hawkeyes to a Big Ten championship and a Rose Bowl victory. In 1958 the Detroit Lions selected Karras in the first round of the NFL draft. Although relatively small by today's standards, at 6'2" and 220 pounds, Karras became a premier defensive lineman. Especially adept at the outside pass rush, he won All-Pro Honors in 1960 and 1962.

Commissioner Rozelle appointed NFL Treasurer Austin Gunsell to investigate stories that circulated in 1962 about NFL players associating with known gamblers and hoodlums. In April 1963, Rozelle issued a report summarizing the results of the formal investigation. He fined five players from the Lions for betting on the 1962 NFL championship game. The Detroit team also received a fine because Coach George Wilson ignored a tip from police that some players had been seen with undesirable characters. As for the two All-Pros, Rozelle suspended them indefinitely for betting on football games. The Packer running back reportedly placed bets ranging from $100 to $500 on football games dating back to 1958. From 1959 to 1961, Karras made bets from $50 to $100 on NFL games. Rozelle noted that no evidence existed that any player ever bet against his own team or provided information to gamblers.

The players responded to the suspension in different ways. Hornung cooperated with league officials and with federal investigators examining his relationship to Bernard Shapiro, a licensed gambling operator in Nevada. In contrast, Karras and the Lions initially sought to contest Rozelle's ruling and protested the harsh fines and suspensions, but to no avail. Hornung returned to business activities in Louisville and Karras worked as a professional wrestler and tended bar in Detroit. For his actions in preserving the integrity of the NFL, Rozelle received a "Sportsman of the Year" designation by *Sports Illustrated.*

Almost a year after his ruling, Rozelle reinstated the two stars. Hornung returned to the Packers and played on the NFL championship team of 1965. After retirement in 1967, he flourished as a sports commentator and real estate developer. Hornung's football exploits were recognized by his induction into three Halls of Fame: Packers, College, and Pro. Karras played with the Lions for several years after his suspension. Following retirement, he enjoyed success as a sports writer, television commentator, and actor.

Rozelle's handling of the gambling crisis of the early 1960s earned plaudits from professional football owners and fans. In the years immediately following, Commissioner Rozelle played a major role in the merger of the NFL and the AFL and in the promotion of the Super Bowl, both of which have proved highly successful.

Selected Bibliography

Harris, D. *The League: The Rise and Decline of the NFL.* New York: Bantam Books, 1986.

Plimpton, G. *Mad Ducks and Bears: Football Revisited.* New York: Lyons and Burford, 1973.

Porter, D., ed. *Biographical Dictionary of American Sports: Football.* Westport: Greenwood Press, Inc., 1987.

Commissioner Kuhn Victorious over Owner Finley

M. Philip Lucas

Charles O. Finley & Co., Inc. v. Kuhn, 569 F.2d 527 (7th Cir. 1978)

According to Charlie Finley, owner of the Oakland Athletics, Commissioner of Baseball Bowie Kuhn was "the village idiot." In his autobiography Kuhn remembered Finley as "a bully and cheapskate by nature" with "few redeeming virtues." From the time of his accession to baseball's top position in 1969, Kuhn's contacts with the Athletics owner were generally unpleasant. In 1970 Kuhn forbade Finley to seek revenge on former holdout Reggie Jackson. Finley intended to send the slumping outfielder to the minor leagues. Two years later Kuhn interceded in the contract impasse between Finley and star pitcher, Vida Blue, and, during the 1973 World Series he criticized Finley's treatment of Oakland second baseman, Mike Andrews. In 1975 Finley aggressively sought to replace Kuhn when his first term expired. These incidents were pale preludes to a much greater confrontation.

On June 15, 1976, hours before the midyear trading deadline, Finley disposed of three star players in the largest sale in baseball history. The New York Yankees agreed to pay $1.5 million for Vida Blue while the Boston Red Sox purchased relief pitcher Rollie Fingers and outfielder Joe Rudi for one million dollars apiece. The Yankees and Red Sox were locked in a heated pennant race and both teams thought that these players would provide the edge they needed. Finley saw this as an opportunity to unload three players who planned to become free agents at the end of the season. None of the three wished to resign with Oakland. Blue signed a contract with the understanding that a trade with the Yankees would materialize.

Kuhn, like many in the baseball world, was stunned by the enormity and the salary consequences of the sales. After conferring with Finley twice and with representatives of the Red Sox, Yankees, and Players Association, Kuhn disallowed the transactions. To Finley, this extraordinary action represented a continuation of a personal vendetta. The alleged malice of the commissioner formed the basis of Finley's publicity blitz and multimillion-dollar suit for damages. When Judge Frank McGarr of the U.S. District Court of the Northern District of Illinois ruled against him on March 17, 1977, Finley appealed his case to the Seventh Circuit of the U.S. Court of Appeals.

Other team owners were appalled, first, by the financial and salary implications of Finley's sales, and then by Kuhn's assertion of unprecedented authority. Kuhn argued that, as commissioner, he possessed the right to review all player transactions and that he could disallow these sales if he found them "not in the best interests of baseball." This became the basis of Kuhn's defense, and it was an argument that the District Court and the Court of Appeals found persuasive. The issues raised in both courts were crucial to the confirmation of the power of the commissioner during a time of great change in management–player relations brought about by the advent of free agency.

Finley's case before the U.S. Court of Appeals revolved around four issues. First, the owner of the Athletics alleged that Kuhn had acted arbitrarily and with malice toward his team. Second, he contended that the commissioner simply did not have the power to prohibit the sale of Blue, Fingers, and Rudi. Third, he claimed that the commissioner's decision sought to demolish the Oakland franchise in violation of federal antitrust laws. Finley argued that baseball's exemption from the antitrust laws did not extend to this situation. Finally, Finley disputed District Judge McGarr's view of the Major League Agreement that club owners were forbidden from suing the commissioner.

In the appellate court Finley suffered a shutout. Relying heavily on McGarr's earlier decision, the court accepted Kuhn's interpretation of his powers, the Major League Agreement, and precedents in baseball's history.

As to Finley's accusation of malice, the appellate court found Kuhn's earlier testimony compelling. Kuhn emphasized the troublesome advent of free agency in baseball and the demise of the reserve system which "bound a player to a team perpetually." Team owners had bought and sold players in the past, but free agency promised to accelerate player movements. Since Kuhn feared the rapid accumulation of talent by the wealthiest teams, he claimed he had to reexamine an old policy in order to maintain competitive balance. Wise or foolish, Kuhn's decision was a reasonable response to the new labor system. The appellate court, in fact, quoted Kuhn's justification in its decision.

The appellate court was, thus, free to examine the nature of the commissioner's authority and specifically whether he was "contractually authorized to disapprove player assignments which he finds to be 'not in the best interests of baseball' where neither moral turpitude nor violation of a Major League Rule is involved." Baseball history supported Kuhn's position that the commissioner had broad, "awesome powers." Journalist and sports historian Fred Lieb, who knew first commissioner Judge Kenesaw Mountain Landis, testified that Landis assumed the role of a "czar . . . a monarch . . . [who] had life and death power over everyone from club owner to batboy." Landis had exercised broad powers under the "best interests" clause. After Landis's death in 1944, the major league owners reduced the power of the commissioner, but upon Commissioner Ford Frick's retirement in 1964 those powers were fully restored by the owners.

Particularly damning to Finley's case was that one of the signatories to that agreement was Charles O. Finley himself. The testimony of twenty-one owners supported Kuhn's description of his powers although many disagreed with his policy. The appellate court found this interpretation of history compelling and understood the language of the Major League Agreement in the same way as Kuhn.

Upon examination of several previous cases that challenged baseball's antitrust exemption, the Court of Appeals declined either to reverse that opinion or to limit the exemption. Finley, therefore, could not enlist the federal antitrust laws to his aid.

In the Major League Agreement team owners specifically waived their right to sue the commissioner over his decisions. Under Illinois law (the original Agreement was drawn up in Chicago in 1921), such waivers were binding for voluntary associations, particularly if the rules of the association had been obeyed. When asked about the rationale and origin of this policy, Chicago Cubs owner Phil Wrigley testified in District Court that without the waiver "we would never get out of court. . . . Judge Landis put it in, and . . . as things turned out, I would agree with him."

Finley threatened to appeal the decision of the Court of Appeals to the Supreme Court, but never followed through. In 1980 he sold the Oakland Athletics and, to the relief of many, left baseball. Kuhn paid a price as well. He had preserved the "awesome power" of the commissioner, but Kuhn's policies alienated too many owners. Although he only meant to "protect the clubs from themselves," by 1983 Kuhn accepted the inevitable and withdrew his name for reelection as commissioner. With the forced resignation of Commissioner Fay Vincent in 1992 it is unlikely that baseball will soon see the return of a commissioner with the authority that Landis and Kuhn once enjoyed.

Selected Bibliography

"Appeals Court Ruled on Baseball History in Upholding Lower Court in Finley Case." *Sports Law Reporter* 1 (June 1978): 4.

Durney, J. "Fair or Foul? The Commissioner and Major League Baseball's Disciplinary Power." *Emory Law Journal* 41 (Spring, 1992): 581–631.

Kuhn, B. *Hardball: The Education of a Baseball Commissioner.* New York: Times Books, 1987.

George Steinbrenner's Bronx Zoo

David F. Dolan

In 1989 and again in 1990 baseball commissioners exercised their powers to act in the "best interests" of baseball. A. Bartlett Giamatti banished Pete Rose for life because of Rose's alleged betting on baseball games in the former year. The following year witnessed Fay Vincent removing George Steinbrenner from the game because of his dealing with a gambler. Rose, the former superstar on the diamond but manager at the time of his banishment, and Steinbrenner, the controversial owner of the New York Yankees, both fell victim to the "best interests" authority.

In neither situation was a legal precedent established. Since both Rose and Steinbrenner played prominent roles in baseball, however, the actions of the commissioners came under careful scrutiny. In an *Emory Law Journal* article Jeffrey A. Durney contended that ". . . there is some question about the propriety of one man, in a judicially sanctioned monopoly, wielding unrestricted power over parties forced to submit to his jurisdiction without recourse to the courts."

Marvin Miller, author of the informative *A Whole Different Ballgame*, examined many aspects of the role of the commissioner and the power to make judgments in the "best interests" of the game. Miller, the first executive director of the Major League Players' Association, correctly noted that the owners selected the commissioner to serve their own interests. Occasionally the best interests of the power elite of owners led to disciplinary action against maverick owners such as Charles Finley, George Steinbrenner, and Marge Schott.

Miller suggested that various actions by Steinbrenner led to Commissioner Vincent's judgment against the Yankees' owner. In addition to providing a payoff to a gambler for information about one of his players, Steinbrenner also behaved in ways other owners found unacceptable. In the late 1970s, Steinbrenner spoke out vigorously about limiting the free-agency rights of players. At the same time he provided lucrative contracts to high-profile players such as Catfish Hunter, Reggie Jackson, Goose Gossage, and Tommy John. Steinbrenner's team also featured a revolving door for players, managers, and front office personnel. When the news of Steinbrenner's removal from baseball was reported, fans in Yankee stadium responded with a standing ovation and chanted "No more George! No More George!" The crowd's sentiments were echoed across the nation by Yankee enthusiasts and general baseball fans alike. Clearly, Commissioner Vincent had ejected a very unpopular owner from baseball.

Ironically, former commissioner Bowie Kuhn had welcomed Steinbrenner's purchase of the Yankees. Kuhn had hoped that Steinbrenner could return the Yankees to their proud winning tradition. But in the nearly two decades that Steinbrenner controlled the New Yorkers, he hired and fired nineteen managers, thirteen general managers, and ten team presidents. The Yankees gradually lost the designation of the "Bronx Bombers" and were called the "Bronx Zoo" instead.

Steinbrenner's first major conflict with baseball's commissioner came in 1974, shortly after he bought the Yankees during Kuhn's reign as the czar of the game. A federal grand jury indicted Steinbrenner on fourteen felony counts of illegal contribution to Richard Nixon's reelection campaign and obstruction of justice. In a plea bargain, Steinbrenner admitted guilt to one felony count. The court fined the Yankee owner $15,000 and his company, AmShip, $20,000. Had the court imposed a jail sentence, Steinbrenner would have probably followed the same path as Fred Saigh, convicted owner of the St. Louis Cardinals who was banished from baseball in 1953. Instead, Kuhn gave Steinbrenner a two-year suspension from any dealings with his team and baseball. In addition to Saigh, the only other team owner to receive serious punishment from a commissioner was William Cox of the Philadelphia Phillies. Cox was permanently suspended from baseball for betting on his team.

Notwithstanding the suspension, Steinbrenner probably participated in the decisions on hiring the players that would lead to Yankee successes in the mid-1970s. His strategy called for paying whatever was needed to place the best players available into Yankee uniforms. In retrospect, this game plan indirectly led Steinbrenner into his next major confrontation with a baseball commissioner. In 1980 Steinbrenner acquired Dave Winfield for a $20-million, ten-year contract. The owner hoped that Winfield would replace Reggie Jackson, the famous slugger who earned the moniker of "Mr. October." Steinbrenner eventually referred to Winfield as his "Mr. May," because of Winfield's early-season achievements and weak play in the post-season. As part of Winfield's signing agreement with the Yankees, Steinbrenner agreed to donate $300,000 annually to the David M. Winfield Foundation, an organization intended to help underprivileged children. During Winfield's time with the Yankees, he sued Steinbrenner three times to force $450,000 in back payments to the foundation. In turn, Steinbrenner sued Winfield, contending that the Winfield organization misused funds and that Winfield had not made his own contributions. In a settlement, Winfield admitted that some money had been inappropriately used and paid almost $230,000 of his own delinquent payments.

In 1986, Howard Spira, an employee of the Winfield organization in the early 1980s, contacted Steinbrenner. Spira's relationship with Winfield allowed him access to the Yankee clubhouse and to all personnel. A known gambler with connections to organized crime, Spira informed Steinbrenner that he possessed information that incriminated Winfield. The information was that the Winfield Foundation had misused funds. He also claimed that Winfield and his agent, Al Frohman, had contrived phony death threats during the 1981 World Series as an explanation for Winfield's poor performance. In addition, Spira said Winfield threatened to kill him if Spira didn't repay a $15,000 loan. For the information, Steinbrenner paid Spira $40,000.

Spira's greed, however, led to an extortion conviction for trying to collect additional money from Steinbrenner. Spira's demand for more funds led Steinbrenner to the authorities. In the ensuing investigation of Spira by the Federal Bureau of Investigation, tapes of conversations with Steinbrenner were found, along with a copy of the $40,000 check that the Yankees owner had written to the informant. Steinbrenner's excuses for the payoff ranged from "out of the goodness of his heart" to preventing Spira from revealing information about Yankee employees, specifically manager Lou Pinella's gambling habits. The payoff to a gambler violated baseball's rule 21 (f), which forbids activities against the best interests of baseball.

From Commissioner Vincent's perspective, Steinbrenner deserved suspension from baseball. Initially, the commissioner offered the Yankee owner a two-year suspension. The deal was presumably similar to the suspension that Steinbrenner had received from Kuhn in 1974. Steinbrenner and his lawyers fought the idea of suspension. Curiously, however, they accepted Vincent's second option, which seemed more severe than the first. Now Steinbrenner would give up his majority ownership of the team, acknowledge wrongdoing, not fight Vincent's ruling in court, and accept a lifetime restriction against communicating with the new majority owner about the Yankees. Steinbrenner did not want the words "banned" and "suspension" included in the punishment. Originally, Steinbrenner stipulated that his son would become the new majority owner, but his son refused the position.

Vincent, therefore, removed Steinbrenner from the daily operations of the Yankees for acting in a manner contrary to the best interests of baseball, specifically his dealings with Spira. Commissioner Vincent clearly acted within the scope of his position, but did he act in a judicious manner for all the persons involved? Steinbrenner certainly received what he deserved, but an investigation by *Sports Illustrated* in 1990 suggested that Vincent and his staff were less than thorough or even-handed in their preparation of the case.

Several allegations surfaced that placed others in precarious positions similar to Steinbrenner's. A secretary of the Winfield Foundation, Kim Slamka, reported that Spira had placed bets on sporting events for Winfield and his agent, Al Frohman. The latter's widow contended that when Winfield loaned Spira $15,000, the player knew that it was for gambling debts. One of the reasons Steinbrenner claimed for giving Spira $40,000 was to prevent Spira from going public about Pinella's gambling habits. Spira claimed that Pinella bet on football games and horse races.

The reasons for Vincent's apparent lack of effort to properly investigate more thoroughly may lie in broader issues. From the time that Steinbrenner obtained free agent Hunter in 1975, he incurred the hostility of the other team owners. Some students of baseball believe that this incident began the escalation of player salaries, leading to financial problems and loss of competitiveness for many franchises. In 1990, Steinbrenner's Yankees received large amounts of television money to broadcast games. The owners clearly feared that once again Steinbrenner would loosen the purse strings and buy another winning team. The owners wanted Steinbrenner forced out of baseball and Vincent, their employee, enforced their wishes.

Before he was forced to resign by disgruntled owners two years later, Vincent lifted the "lifetime ban" on Steinbrenner. The Yankee owner triumphantly returned to baseball in March 1993. Not long thereafter Steinbrenner talked about moving the team to nearby New Jersey. Rather than playing in "the house that Ruth built," the Yankees could then perform before larger crowds in a ball park constructed by Steinbrenner.

So long as the courts continue to find that the best approach for the self-governance of Major League Baseball is through the enormous powers granted to the commissioner, the "best interests of" will translate into the best interests of the powerful owners.

Selected Bibliography

Durney, J. "Comments: Fair or Foul? The Commissioner and Major League Baseball's Disciplinary Process." *Emory Law Journal* 41 (Spring 1992): 581–631.
Gutman, D. *Baseball Babylon: From the Black Sox to Pete Rose, the Real Stories Behind the Scandals that Rocked the Game.* New York: Viking Penguin, 1992.
Kuhn, B. *Hardball.* New York: McGraw-Hill, Inc., 1988.
Miller, M. *A Whole Different Ball Game: The Sport and Business of Baseball.* Secaucus: Carol Publishing Group, 1991.

In the Groove?

The Legal War over Golf Clubs

John W. Johnson

Bob Gilder, Ken Green, John Inman, Rafe Botts, et al., v. PGA Tour, Inc., 936 F.2d 417 (9th Cir. 1991). [U.S. Court of Appeals, 9th Circuit]

It is commonplace to observe that technology has changed the face of sport. In just the last generation tennis players have moved almost exclusively to oversized racquets; baseball (except in the major leagues) has been won over by metal bats; football at all levels has gone to expensive body-protecting (and, regrettably, body-injuring) uniforms; basketball players sport pump-up shoes; and skiing has resorted to all manner of space-age compositions. But, a strong case can be made that no sport has been affected more by technological change in the last quarter-century than the "royal and ancient" game of golf.

As even the most casual frequenter of the links knows, the well-equipped golf bag now contains graphite or titanium-shafted irons, metal-headed, over-sized "woods" (the first metal woods were marketed as "Pittsburgh persimmons"), a Gore-Tex rain suit, a putter balanced with the precision of a surgical instrument, and balls with more dimples than all the babies in a large hospital nursery.

The United States Golf Association (USGA) tests each new or modified piece of equipment to determine if it conforms to the Association's strict—some would say "arbitrary"—standards of fairness and performance capabilities. The philosophy of the USGA is that a golfer should achieve a score based primarily upon ability, not through souped-up equipment. For example, a few years ago the USGA banned the Weight-Rite golf shoe because its tests found that the shoes provided artificial balancing aids during a golfer's swing. More commonly, the USGA is called upon to test new clubs and balls for their adherence to Association standards. The machine used by the USGA for such tests has been dubbed "Iron Byron," because the programmed swing of the machine is patterned after the swing of Byron Nelson, one of the best golfers of all time. Amateurs may occasionally play an illegal or "hot ball," but it would be against the rules of golf to play a banned ball in a tournament.

Given the revolutionary changes in golf equipment in the 1970s and 1980s—the oversized heads on metal woods, cavity-backed heads for irons, shafts made out of rare metallic elements, and computer-configured dimple patterns on golf balls—it is ironic that the most momentous equipment controversy in the history of golf has involved something that most golfers thought little about until recently: the minuscule grooves on the face of golf irons.

The face of each iron contains about twelve to fourteen very shallow lined indentations, or grooves. For years all clubs were manufactured with grooves that were V-shaped, with the point of the "V" imbedded about 1/32 of an inch into the club face. On January 1, 1984, in a largely unnoticed action, the USGA put into effect a rule permitting U-grooves (also known as "square grooves" or "box grooves") on golf club faces. Shortly after this rule change, Karsten Manufacturing Corporation of Phoenix, Arizona, became the first golf equipment manufacturer to make irons with U-grooves. And therein lies one of the strangest tales in the legal/economic history of American sport.

The founder and still CEO of Karsten Manufacturing Corporation is Karsten Solheim, a stubborn octogenarian engineer/inventer/ entrepreneur/multimillionaire. Solheim, the son of a Norwegian shoemaker, arrived in this country in 1913 at the age of two. As an engineer for General Electric in the 1950s he took up golf and discovered just how tough the game could be. Especially difficult for him was putting. So he applied his engineering talents to club construction, building what he felt was a better putter than the conventional "flat stick." For over a decade he sold or gave away his heel-toe balanced putters to friends and golf pros while continuing to work for GE, now at one of its Phoenix plants. In 1967 he refused a transfer to Oklahoma City, quit GE, invested his savings in a small building, and went full-time into the golf manufacturing business. His lines of putters and irons quickly became some of the hottest clubs in golf. Solheim and his sons became millionaires and local heroes in Phoenix. Today Solheim's company is one of the largest sports manufacturing enterprises in the world; it employs over two thousand workers; and it annually sells about a quarter of all the golf clubs marketed worldwide. In 1992 *Forbes* magazine estimated Karsten Solheim's personal net worth at $450 million.

Solheim's trademark is the Ping line of golf equipment—named for the characteristic sound made when one of his putters strikes a golf ball. In 1982 Ping introduced the Eye2 set of irons. Initially the Eye2 clubs had conventional V-grooves. Following the USGA's 1984 rule revision, the Eye2 was redesigned with U-grooves. Besides the U-grooves, the Eye2s sported cavity backs and perimeter weighting, technological advances that help golfers achieve good results from off-center hits. But it was the U-grooves that created the most interest and controversy.

All grooves on club faces promote spin. Just as a spinning bullet from the barrel of a weapon that is rifled will fly straighter than a non-spinning bullet, so too will a golf ball that is spinning fly straighter than one that is not. But it is backspin, not just any spin, that the best golfers covet: backspin allows them to hit balls to greens and have the balls stop quickly or even back up when they hit the surface of the greens. Backspin is particularly desirable for shots struck from the "rough," the higher grass that grows beyond the edges of the preferred fairways. The long grass of the rough usually intrudes between the club face and the ball at impact, thus diminishing backspin and making a ball tougher to keep on the green after it lands. Hence, a club that can generate a high degree of backspin from a lie in the rough has great appeal.

Allegedly the Ping Eye2 was the club that produced the most backspin from a lie in the rough. When that word began to circulate, the Eye2 became increasingly popular among players on the men's and women's professional golf tours. The conventional wisdom of those who claimed to know golf equipment was that it was the U-groove feature of the Eye2 that was responsible for the increased backspin. In 1987 in a televised golf tournament in Florida, Mark Calcavecchia, then a virtually unknown touring pro, hit a spectacular shot with incredible backspin from deep rough. His shot, made by an Eye2 iron, was replayed many times, adding to the legend of the Eye2. When Calcavecchia later won the British Open by hitting several shots with high backspin from the thick British rough, amateur golfers' appetites for the already hot Ping irons became almost insatiable, and Karsten Manufacturing raked in greater and greater revenues.

There was, however, a dark cloud hanging over the Eye2s. The edges of the U-grooves were so sharp that they badly scratched golf balls. This was not a concern for the typical touring professional who changed balls every few holes. But for the amateur golfer accustomed to playing a single hard-covered ball for one or more eighteen-hole rounds, the scarring was a major drawback. To satisfy the typical golfer, Karsten Manufacturing rounded the edges of the grooves. This took care of the scuffing problem, but the rounding reduced the USGA's required distance between grooves on the face of irons.

When informed in 1986 that his irons might not conform to USGA standards, Solheim disagreed and refused to change the design of the Eye2s. This led the USGA in June 1987 to announce a ban on all U-groove clubs, effective in 1990 for Association competitions and in 1996 for all events conducted under the rules of golf. This angered many of the thousands of golfers who had purchased the Eye2s; they did not relish the choice of playing with illegal equipment or being forced to abandon their Pings and spend hundreds of dollars for acceptable substitutes.

The USGA continued its tests on the Eye2s through 1987. Although the Association found that the Ping irons did not satisfy the letter of Association regulations for distance between grooves, it also concluded that the U-grooves themselves did not significantly enhance the performance of golfers, even highly skilled professionals. As a result, the USGA abandoned its plan to ban U-grooved clubs in the 1990s. But the Eye2 was far from being out of the woods.

Enter the Professional Golfer's Association (PGA) Tour. The PGA Tour sponsors the major professional golf tournaments for men: in 1993 there were forty-five tournaments on the regular PGA Tour, forty-one on the Senior Tour (for male professionals over the age of fifty), and thirty on the Nike Tour (a "minor league" tour, formerly the Ben Hogan Tour). Shortly after the Ping Eye2 line was introduced, several male professional golfers on the PGA Tour complained that the U-grooves on irons offered an unfair advantage to the Eye2-wielding golfers. They argued that clubs with U-grooves reduced the premium on skill in striking a golf ball. They maintained that such clubs, with their propensity to generate high backspin from the rough, took away the traditional advantage of hitting the ball in the fairway.

Even more than any of the pros on the PGA Tour, the tour's commissioner, Deane Beman, took up the crusade against the Ping Eye2. Starting at about the time that the USGA settled its differences with Karsten Manufacturing over the Eye2 clubs, Beman began a campaign to have them banned from the PGA Tour. Beman himself was an outstanding golfer in the 1960s and 1970s, twice winning the U.S. Amateur championship and later making a good living for several years on the professional circuit. The PGA Tour's policy board, perhaps impressed by Beman's success as an insurance broker as well as his knowledge of golf, appointed him as the Tour commissioner in 1974. He has served in that capacity ever since, making him the longest reigning commissioner in recent professional sports history. In early 1994 Beman announced his retirement as commissioner, effective in 1995.

No one has done more for the financial side of professional golf than Deane Beman. When he took over as commissioner in 1974, total PGA tournament purses were $8.2 million. In 1993 the figure was almost $100 million. The leading money winner on the PGA tour in 1974 was Johnny Miller; he earned $353,000. In 1992 the tour's leading money winner, Fred Couples, made $1,300,000 in official earnings. In 1974 the average of the top 125 money winners on the tour made about $60,000; in 1992 the average was $348,000—about the same amount that Miller made eighteen years earlier when he led the tour. Besides increasing tour purses, Beman successfully negotiated lucrative television contracts and secured corporate cosponsorships for most PGA events. He has also brought the tour into successful golf course design and merchandising operations. The Senior Tour, which did not even exist in 1974, now rivals the Ladies PGA Tour in total revenue. In short, the PGA Tour under Beman's leadership has prospered during the recessions of the seventies and eighties, helped to popularize the sport of golf, and made a small number of tan men in long pants very wealthy.

In the process of building up the tour to one of the most financially successful operations in the world of sport, Beman has made his share of enemies. He is regarded by his antagonists as arrogant and sometimes testy. He has also been criticized for involving the PGA Tour in at least one financial partnership in the U.S. with the Yakuza, the Japanese Mafia. And Beman has been very hesitant to divulge details of his personal—reportedly munificent—compensation package from the PGA Tour. What has caused Beman more grief of late than anything mentioned so far has been his dispute with Karsten Solheim over the legality of playing Ping Eye2 irons on the PGA Tour.

The clash that developed in the late 1980s and still persists between Solheim and Beman—arguably the two most powerful men on the current golf scene—has been one of epic proportions. On the one hand is Karsten Solheim, the inventor and wildly successful businessman with a great product. On the other hand is Deane Beman, the dapper Czar of professional golf, haughty but out to preserve the game from what he sees as technology run rampant. This clash would ultimately lead to a legal climax in the case of *Gilder* v. *PGA Tour, Inc.*

The action that precipitated the case was the PGA Tour policy board's May 1988 vote to ban all U-grooved clubs from tour competition in 1989. The tour took this position, apparently, because it had little faith that the USGA would be able to force Solheim to withdraw or modify his U-grooved irons. From this point on the dispute was essentially Beman versus Solheim, with various golfers on the tour playing supporting roles on both sides. Some commentators saw this as just a feud about equipment for golf's elite. But the consensus of golf experts was that the dispute still held wide-ranging consequences for millions of golfers worldwide. If the PGA Tour could come between equipment manufacturers and the USGA on this issue, the position of the PGA Tour commissioner would be strengthened and the USGA's rule-making power would be diminished. Also, since many amateurs want to play the "same clubs the pros play," if the PGA Tour prevailed in the legal dispute the general impact on the retail golf equipment market would be substantial.

In August 1988 the USGA formally requested that the tour policy board reconsider its banning of U-grooves. The policy board refused. Both organizations, nevertheless, continued to conduct tests on the controversial clubs. The resulting tests by the tour and the USGA revealed that top players hitting U-grooved wedges from the rough were able to impart more backspin and, thus, stop the ball more quickly on the green than top players using conventional V-grooved clubs from similar lies. However, the tests did not show that the balls hit with the U-grooved clubs finished any closer to the holes than those struck with V-grooved clubs.

On February 28, 1989, the PGA Tour's policy board acted unilaterally, voting to ban all U-grooved clubs in PGA-sponsored events. Only three members of the ten-member board voted, however. The other seven (four tour pros and three club professionals) abstained because of conflicts of interest, that is, because they represented golf equipment firms that competed with Solheim's Eye2s. The PGA Tour's own rules stipulate that a majority of the player members of the board must be present and voting on rule changes for those changes to be put into effect. Nevertheless, the board permitted its 3–0 vote to stand and ordered the ban on U-grooved clubs to take effect on January 1, 1990. Beman followed this up a few months later with a memorandum to PGA players threatening to sue any player who joined Solheim's legal actions against the PGA Tour.

On December 1, 1989, just a month before the PGA's threatened ban on U-grooved clubs was scheduled to go into effect, Solheim's Karsten Manufacturing Corporation filed a complaint against the tour's intended U-groove ban, citing as illegal the tour policy board's February 28, 1989, vote. In defiance of Beman's threat to bring legal action against players siding with Solheim, seven professionals (Bob Gilder, Ken Green, and John Inman on the regular tour; Rafe Botts, Bob Erickson, Daniel M. Morgan, and Walter Zembriski on the Senior Tour) joined Karsten Manufacturing in the action. Solheim later agreed to pay all the legal expenses of these golf professionals.

Solheim and the seven pros asked the federal courts to move quickly and impose an injunction on the PGA Tour, preventing the ban on U-grooved clubs from taking effect on January 1, 1990. Fearing that such an injunction might well be ordered due to the unusual policy board vote of February 28, 1989, the tour convened a special policy board meeting on December 5, 1989. During that meeting the tour policy board passed an amendment to its bylaws which removed the requirement that votes on rule changes must be accomplished by a majority of the player members of the board. The tour's policy board apparently sought to provide an *ex post facto* imprimatur for its decree at the February 28, 1989 meeting and, thus, hoped to prevent the federal courts from issuing a preliminary injunction against the soon-to-go-into-effect ban on U-grooved clubs.

Also in the busy month of December 1989, a Chicago golfer filed a class action lawsuit against Karsten Manufacturing and the USGA on behalf of himself and all golfers owning Ping Eye2 irons. The complaint alleged that the golfers had purchased Ping clubs believing them to be in every way in accord with USGA rules. Had they known about the U-groove problem, the complaint maintained, they would not have purchased the clubs.

A hearing on Karsten Manufacturing's request for injunctive relief was held in mid-December 1989 before Federal District Judge Paul G. Rosenblatt for the District of Arizona. Solheim based his petition for an injunction on his belief that the tour's ban on U-grooved irons would violate the federal government's Sherman Antitrust Act and various Arizona antitrust legislation. It also charged that the Tour's ban would interfere with Solheim's business generally and that the PGA policy board members had breached their fiduciary duties to their membership by playing fast and loose with the PGA Tour's bylaws. (Considering the talk about conflicts of interest in the lawsuit, it is ironic that none of the parties were bothered when, at the beginning of the hearing, Judge Rosenblatt revealed that he was a golfer and that he used Ping clubs.)

Testifying at the hearing, an Arizona State University economist contended that the U-grooved clubs did not adversely affect the tour because the percentage of tour prize money won by players using Eye2 clubs was less than the percentage of tour players not using the Eye2s. In addition, he testified that Karsten Manufacturing had experienced a decline in its market share of golf club sales and other golf products since news of the possible ban on Eye2s was made public. Also at the hearing, tour player Bob Gilder testified that switching clubs would impair his performance in PGA events and adversely affect his endorsement income. Gilder, who had used Ping clubs since 1970, testified that he liked "the design and dynamics" of the Eye2s but that he did not find anything special about the U-grooves. Another tour player, left-handed George Lanning, testified that, in his opinion, Karsten Manufacturing produced the only quality left-handed club on the market and that he feared he might lose his tour exempt status were he forced to switch to another set of irons.

In support of the tour's position, Tom Kite, professional golf's all-time leading money winner, testified that, in his expert judgment, the Eye2 irons produced so much backspin from lies in the rough that they unfairly negated the benefits of hitting the ball in the fairway. As one of golf's straightest drivers, Kite hits fewer shots from the rough than most other professionals. This, in addition to the fact that he plays V-grooved clubs manufactured by the rival Ben Hogan Company, made it less than surprising that Kite would testify in favor of the ban on Karsten Solheim's irons. Commissioner Beman acted as a witness in his own behalf, arguing that the issuance of an injunction blocking the tour's ban on U-grooved clubs would undercut the PGA's ability to regulate the golf tournaments that it conducts.

On Christmas Eve 1989, Judge Rosenblatt issued a preliminary injunction against the PGA Tour, stopping it temporarily from implementing the ban on U-grooved clubs. Judge Rosenblatt ruled that the complaint of the seven golf professional plaintiffs had raised significant questions for litigation and that the plaintiffs would have a reasonable chance to win a trial on the merits of their complaint against the PGA tour. In his view, the plaintiffs also demonstrated that they would incur serious financial burdens should the injunction not be levied. Almost immediately, the PGA Tour announced its determination to appeal.

While awaiting review by the Circuit Court of Appeals, Solheim settled his suit with the USGA. No money changed hands, but Solheim agreed to henceforth manufacture clubs that comply with USGA standards. In consideration, the USGA agreed to grandfather in all previously made Ping irons. To those knowledgeable about golf and the antitrust law, it appeared likely that this settlement may have been hastened by the PGA Tour's filing of its class action suit against Ping and the USGA. In April 1991 Karsten Manufacturing and the PGA Tour argued their positions before the Ninth Circuit Court of Appeals. Beman, confident as ever, stated that the player plaintiffs would have only a week to change their clubs if and when the injunction was lifted.

On June 12, 1991, a three-judge Court of Appeals for the Ninth Circuit filed a nine-page unanimous opinion upholding District Judge Rosenblatt's injunction. The appellate judges concluded that the harm suffered by Solheim's company and the player plaintiffs was greater than that suffered by the PGA Tour. The appeals court determined that Judge Rosenblatt correctly found that the player plaintiffs would suffer more harm from the U-groove ban than would the PGA Tour from the imposition of the injunction preventing the ban. The court supported Rosenblatt's finding that Karsten Manufacturer would be harmed by the ban on U-grooved clubs because the company "would be required to redesign its clubs, retool its manufacturing process, and abandon its well-established U-groove market." In addition, the appeals court noted that it found compelling Solheim's evidence that his reputation as a club manufacturer was being harmed by the threat of the ban on the Eye2 irons. By contrast, the appeals court accepted the finding of the district court to the effect that the granting of an injunction would lead to no monetary harms to the tour. The only harm to the tour's reputation, the court stated, was brought on by the tour's own attempt to ban U-groove clubs.

The appeals court, thus, left the injunction against the tour's U-groove ban in place, agreed with Judge Rosenblatt that the "balance of hardships tips sharply in favor of the plaintiffs," and held that the "district court did not abuse its discretion in determining that this case raises serious questions that must be resolved at trial." Hence, the case was returned to Judge Rosenblatt's court for a full-dress civil trial. Despite this clear victory for Karsten Manufacturing and the player plaintiffs on the injunction issue, Beman referred to the appeals court decision as "merely procedural."

The appeals court also upheld the district court finding that "serious questions exist which should be resolved in a hearing on the merits." In particular, the appeals court agreed with the district court's analysis of the highly irregular activities of the tour's policy board in changing its bylaws so as to legitimate rulings on rule changes with only nonplayer members of the board voting. This, the appeals court concluded, constituted an abuse of the policy board's fiduciary duty to the plaintiff players and the PGA organization generally.

To compound the PGA Tour's legal problems on the groove issue, Solheim followed up his victory in the appellate court with an amended complaint. His new complaint added to the targets of his antitrust accusations the Ben Hogan Company and two "experts" hired by the tour to test U-groove clubs. The tour fought back by filing a $100-million counterclaim against Solheim, contending that he had been manufacturing illegal clubs for fifteen years. Solheim almost immediately moved to dismiss the counterclaim and, near the end of 1991, filed for economic sanctions against the tour for its "frivolous" counterclaim. He also demanded attorneys' fees and costs in order to oppose the tour's suit. In February 1992, Solheim moved to dismiss the counterclaim, but his motion was denied by a federal judge in Florida. Hence, the tour's $100 million counterclaim was referred to an arbitration panel.

Throughout 1991 and 1992 the lawyers for Karsten Manufacturing, the player plaintiffs, Deane Beman, and the PGA Tour conducted "discovery" in preparation for the trial on the original suit before Judge Rosenblatt and the counterclaim by the PGA Tour before the arbitration panel. Scores of witnesses were deposed, and more than sixty thousand pages of documents were exchanged among the parties. Several times during 1991 and 1992 the tour proposed settlement, but Solheim rebuffed these efforts, claiming they did not constitute serious offers. Efforts by the tour's insurance carrier to settle the case also failed. The trial before Judge Rosenblatt was originally scheduled for January 11, 1993 but it was postponed until April 20, 1993. In March the judge denied a long series of tour motions to dismiss the case and held that Solheim could even seek punitive damages at the trial.

Finally, on April 14, 1993, having traveled to the brink of a full-blown trial, the PGA Tour and Karsten Manufacturing arrived at a settlement. The clear winner was Karsten Solheim. Under the terms of the settlement the tour agreed to lift its ban on U-groove clubs and not to attempt to ban U-groove clubs in the future unless the USGA did so first. The PGA Tour also agreed to dismiss its counterclaim against Karsten Manufacturing. Finally, the tour consented to have its insurance carrier pay Solheim about $5 million in attorneys' fees. In return, all that was required of Solheim was for him to drop his sanctions suit against the tour for frivolous counterclaims.

Another important element of the settlement was the creation of an "equipment advisory committee" to the PGA Tour. This committee, because it will not include PGA players or tour staff, will not fall prey to the conflicts of interest that so confounded the PGA's policy board in the U-groove dispute and placed the tour in a weakened legal position vis-à-vis Karsten Manufacturing. The committee is empowered to choose a staff, conduct independent testing, and operate in a generally open manner. The hope is that this independent committee will protect equipment manufacturers from arbitrary actions of the tour staff and, at the same time, provide the PGA Tour with even-handed, expert advice on equipment matters. Under this arrangement, the PGA Tour may still propose equipment rule changes, but the advisory committee is authorized to "verify that . . . a final tour rule is consistent with the committee's recommendation."

The suit between Karsten Manufacturing and the PGA Tour had dragged on for four years. The parties had taken over one hundred depositions, compiled thousands of exhibits, and prepared countless expert witnesses for testimony in court. All the while the meters of at least six outside law firms had been expensively ticking away. Added to the money recompensed by the tour to Solheim for his attorneys' fees, the tour's deputy commissioner Tim Finchem estimated that the tour had spent about $9 million for its own legal representation in the U-groove litigation—only about half of which will ultimately be reimbursed by insurance.

The one clear benefit of the settlement to Beman was that he and the PGA Tour avoided a potential financial and public relations disaster. Given Judge Rosenblatt's rulings on the injunction and various motions, the tour was at risk not just of losing, but of losing big. Solheim's claim against the PGA was $200 million. Were even a small portion of that amount to be awarded by a court—for example 10 percent—that would be $20 million. That figure would then be tripled under antitrust law, resulting in a hypothetical loss of $60 million. And then there are the punitive damages that Judge Rosenblatt hinted might be assessed in this case. Since the PGA Tour's liability insurance is capped at $10 million, a loss to Karsten Manufacturing at trial could have been catastrophic to the tour. In addition, a loss in a publicized trial might have undercut the PGA Tour's history of successful marketing campaigns during Beman's twenty-year tenure. As a consequence, his reputation as one of the best commissioners in twentieth-century American sport would have been besmirched. In the editorial opinion of *Golf Digest,* the settlement allowed Beman to turn "a potential disaster into a mere defeat."

Through all the legal skirmishing over the U-groove issue, the PGA Tour maintained that it would prevail in the end. Thus several tour players were shocked when Beman announced that the tour had agreed to settle the case. They were even more shocked when they heard the specific terms of the settlement. Peter Jacobsen, a player member of the policy board, struggled to come to terms with the out-of-court resolution in the language of the sport itself: "It felt to me like we had a three-shot lead with six holes to play and we turned to our opponent and said, 'Let's call it a tie.'" In attempting to put the best face on the settlement, Deane Beman argued that the creation of the equipment advisory committee was what he and the PGA Tour had wanted all along. In a confidential memorandum to tour players, Beman bravely asserted that the new advisory committee might even reconsider the U-groove issue. If this happens the tour may once again have to contend with Solheim's attorneys.

If the settlement holds, the sport of golf will breathe a collective sigh of relief. Players of U-groove clubs will feel vindicated that they are employing legal equipment. Any golfer, if he or she is willing to spend the money, will still be able to play "the same clubs the pros play." Golf will also be spared the ignominy of two competing sets of rules: one for elite professionals and one for everyone else. Finally, the establishment of an independent advisory committee to the PGA Tour should promote a fairer testing procedure to address the continuing technological changes in the "royal and ancient game."

There is a brief epilogue to the war over golf clubs. In early 1994 Deane Beman announced his decision to resign as PGA commissioner. This announcement came just a few months after the legal settlement between the PGA and Karsten Manufacturing. Most golf commentators saw Beman's retirement as motivated, at least in part, by the PGA's less than satisfactory resolution of its legal difficulties with Karsten Solheim. At about the same time that Beman was announcing his resignation, Solheim released his long-awaited line of Ping "metal woods." However, the golf club-buying public, to date, has not flocked to Solheim's metal woods with anywhere near the passion it has long expressed for his irons.

Selected Bibliography

Brennan, J. "The Ping Heard Round the World." *Forbes* (October 26, 1992): 248–249.

Chambers, M. "My Kingdom for a Groove!" *Golf Digest* 43 (November 1992): 90–103.

Chambers, M. "News Analysis: Groove Settlement Leaves Golf Better Off." *Golf Digest* 44 (July 1993): 48–53.

Hershey, S. "PGA Tour's Success Has Boss Beamin'." *USA Today* (January 13, 1993): 1C–2C.

Baseball's Big Inning
The Sacrifice of the 1919 Black Sox

Wayne S. Quirk

The summer of 1919 represents an important period in the history of the United States in general, and in organized baseball in particular. Employment lines swelled with returning Great War veterans in the city of Chicago, as well as in the rest of the country. Although Chicago strikes by workers reached resolution, over one million American workers remained on strike. Uneasy racial and social tensions in Chicago culminated in a July race riot. Prohibition loomed on the horizon. Major league baseball reigned as one of the few sources of pride and optimism for the country during the hot summer. The game of baseball held a devout place in the hearts of many Americans, and was favored with a near reverent quality.

Chicagoans were treated to an uplifting August when the South Side White Sox returned from a road trip with the American League flag. Only a few months later, however, rumors of a potential fix of the 1919 World Series shocked the American public. Americans reeled with the possibility that their sacred game was also subject to the corrupt dealings then evident in international politics, government, and industry.

Historical analysis of the 1919 World Series for suspicious play proves challenging. Performance subtleties, inherent to baseball, permeated the games. The puzzling behavior of players, owners, gamblers, and administrators further contribute to difficulties of analysis, and many of the suspected participants in the fix took their stories to the grave. Ultimately, the fifteen-day trial of eight White Sox players, dubbed the Black Sox, proved as meaningless as a March exhibition game. The center of the scandal, at first glance, included a profane alliance of eight White Sox players and an assortment of gamblers and mobsters. Suspicions focused first on the players, and fans questioned how these baseball players could do the unconscionable and tarnish the hallowed American game. The answers, now more apparent, are that the Black Sox and the gamblers were not alone in shameful behavior. In fact, the Black Sox turned out to be the ones "double-crossed" by their sacrifice to the public by these same gamblers, baseball owners, and Commissioner Judge Kenesaw Mountain Landis.

Contemporary misconceptions concerning the Black Sox scandal stem from confusion about the climate of professional baseball during the early years of the organized game, particularly in regard to baseball's administrative echelon and the inexorable tangle of professional sports and professional gambling.

Baseball ownership provided fertile grounds for player displeasure, and White Sox ownership is widely recognized by historians as a major factor in the scandal. Charles Comiskey, known to his friends as "The Old Roman," presided as sole owner of the South Side ball club. A solid baseball man who earned credit for innovations both on the field and in baseball ownership, Comiskey also earned a reputation as a contemptible and miserly taskmaster. The Sox players were remarkably underpaid compared to their Series opponents, as well as to ballplayers of lesser talent on second division teams. Comiskey's closefisted approach to player management extended beyond salary to include low-budget practices with meal and laundry money. Even more deplorable, Comiskey's unfulfilled promises to the team and to star pitcher Eddie Cicotte shamefully obscured the 1917 World Championship. The Old Roman promised Cicotte a $10,000 bonus following his thirtieth victory during the regular season of the championship year. Mysteriously benched for the remainder of the regular season following his early August twenty-eighth victory, Cicotte missed at least five starts. Hauntingly, the amount of the unfulfilled bonus equalled the soiled amount Cicotte reportedly accepted from the gamblers prior to the first game of the 1919 Series.

The critical power of Comiskey and baseball owners rested in the reserve clause, which prohibited players from signing with other teams. This clause created the predicament for players of either accepting a low salary offer or leaving professional baseball. This perpetual reserve clause was aggressively guarded and exercised by owners until 1975, when ballplayers finally gained free agency. Organized baseball's system of control over players explains the players' summers of financial discontent and certainly cultivated the field for the unthinkable. Clearly, however, the alliance of baseball with organized gambling brought the conspiracy to fruition.

In the early days of baseball, open gambling was as common as a well-executed sacrifice bunt. Gamblers filled the stands and bet on everything, including individual at bats. As the game evolved, so did gambling, and the interaction took more sophisticated forms. Gamblers openly boasted about having key players on salary. Most fans could not detect suspicious play and ballplayers made an art of chicanery with such practices as short-legging fly balls and taking a little off critical pitches. Gamblers moved into social circles with both the owners and the players intending to gain a betting edge. Inside information on starting pitchers (which was not provided in advance, as it is today), social entanglements, and nagging injuries easily disturbed the probabilities in a game with a small scoring variance. Evidence indicates that these practices by ballplayers and gamblers were both accepted and common knowledge. So pervasive was gambling in the game that it probably never crossed the minds of the conspirators that they would be caught, much less punished.

The roots of the conspiracy unquestionably took hold with player–gambler interaction. It is also clear that discussions of the plot to fix the 1919 Series originated with Sox first baseman Arnold "Chick" Gandil and gambler Joseph "Sport" Sullivan. Historians report that Gandil and Sullivan met in a pool hall in 1916. The aptly named gambler quickly profited from inside information. Several weeks prior to the 1919 Series, these confederates discussed the possibility of throwing the Series, and the key player in the scheme was Sox pitcher Cicotte. The financial details of the conspiracy are vague. Circumstances suggest that Sullivan approached notorious big-time gangster and gambler, Arnold Rothstein, for financial backing. Rothstein and his constituents, most notably former featherweight boxing champion and Rothstein's middleman, Abe "Little Champ" Attel, entered into the plan and essentially degraded the fix from piker control to control by organized gangsters. The involvement of these big-league gangsters determined the outcome of the 1919 World Series before Cicotte threw the first pitch.

As the Rothstein mob took control, word of the fix spread to former big-league pitcher "Sleepy" Bill Burns and his friend, Billy Maharg. Following a brief major league career, Burns amassed a small fortune in the Texas oil business and seized the opportunity for quick profits by joining the conspiracy. Reportedly, the involved players readily let these two in on the fix, apparently welcoming the chance to add to their spoils. The entry of Burns and Maharg signaled the confusion that came to characterize the fix. Neither the players nor the gamblers knew which games would be fixed and it was not clear which players were involved after the first two games. These two gamblers also symbolize the many ironies that plagued the coming months. Burns lost his winnings on the first two games due to an apparent breakdown in communication regarding the fix of the third game. He subsequently became the key witness for the State of Illinois. Moreover, Maharg accurately foreshadowed the scandal when he announced to an Illinois Grand Jury, "The whole upshot of the matter was that Attel and his gang cleaned up and the Sox players were double crossed."

The 1919 White Sox typified a team divided. Second baseman Eddie Collins and catcher Ray Schalk led a group that included pitchers Urban "Red" Faber and Dickie Kerr. Gandil and Charles "Swede" Risberg headed the other circle. The groups rarely interacted and, according to rumor, the double-play combination of Risberg and Collins never spoke to each other on or off the field. The Gandil-Risberg group comprised the suspected eight players and may be distinguished fairly easily in terms of the depth of involvement in the fix. Pitchers Cicotte and Claude "Lefty" Williams, Gandil, and outfielder Oscar "Happy" Felsch clearly participated in throwing ballgames. Gandil, a fourteen-year veteran, both participated and acted as liaison between the players and the gamblers.

The White Sox pitching rotation called for Cicotte to throw in three of the potential nine Series games. A fix in baseball must include a pitcher, since he has the most control of the outcome while other players may not be involved in critical win-lose situations. An advance of $10,000 readily secured Cicotte's participation, considering both his well-known gripe with Comiskey and the fact that he faced the twilight of his career. Williams, a lanky southpaw renowned for his control, contributed three losses to the plot, thanks to a sudden loss of accuracy. The rangy shortstop, Risberg, hit a pathetic .080 in the Series and played miserable defense. Outfielder "Happy" Felsch turned in such a dismal performance that Sox Manager William "Kid" Gleason moved him out of center field after the seventh game.

"Shoeless" Joe Jackson is the most recognizable of the Sox on the fringe of the fix. The ubiquitous left fielder, who haunts contemporary culture in song, cinema, and opera, is remembered as one of the finest left-handed hitters of all time. Jackson's career ended with a Hall-of-Fame-worthy .356 batting average. Although his twelve hits established a Series record and he did not commit an error, his defensive play proved suspicious and evidence supports his alignment with Gandil, Cicotte, and Williams.

But while the Jackson story is timeless, the individual tragedy of the blackballed eight belongs to third baseman Buck Weaver. Weaver worked endlessly with Gleason to become the finest third baseman in the league. His defensive skills were so superior that Detroit Tiger great Ty Cobb refused to bunt down the third baseline against the Sox. Weaver's stellar play in the Series angered the conspirators and confused those suspicious of the fix. It appears Weaver's error consisted of attending a shady meeting with his teammates and several gamblers. He spent the remainder of his life unsuccessfully appealing to a series of baseball commissioners attempting to clear his name of the scandal. Utility man Fred McMullin played sparingly and is implicated only by his alliance with the Gandil-Risberg clique.

The Series was scheduled to open in Cincinnati with Cicotte on the mound for the heavily favored Sox and Dutch Reuther on the hill for the Reds. Word of the fix spread so rapidly that the odds on the game and the Series dramatically shifted. Panicked, yet resourceful Chicago gamblers, initiated a counterfix by drinking with Reuther, a celebrated imbiber, late into the night before the opening game. Meanwhile, Cicotte explained to his co-conspirators the art of throwing ballgames. The next day, Cicotte executed his plan by crossing up his catcher's signals and letting up on critical pitches. His art, coupled with a less subtle blown double-play opportunity, led to a 9–1 loss in the Series opener. William's famed control disappeared in the second game and the southpaw artfully lost the second game by the score of 4–2. Suspicions grew among astute baseball men. Comiskey and Gleason dragged National League commissioner John Heydler into a frantic midnight meeting to express their concerns. At the same time, the $10,000 Cicotte accepted accounted for the only money received from the gamblers and the players probably suspected the double cross. The thought of winning for rookie Kerr disgusted the conspirators, but somehow the "busher" led them to their first victory, 3–0. Oddly enough, Gandil's run-producing single in the second inning proved to be the game winning run.

Cicotte's paradoxical mastery on the mound and dubious play in the field accented the fourth game and the Sox stumbled to a 2–0 loss. A rain day punctuated the confusion prior to the next game scheduled for Comiskey Park. Impotent Sox batting against Cincinnati shine ball pitcher, Hod Eller, and defensive misplays by Felsch, "lowlighted" the ensuing ball game. The ninth inning left the sellout crowd disheartened as Williams absorbed his second loss of the Series, 4–0.

Kerr notched a second Series victory in game six when Gandil again drove in the game-winning run in the top of the 10th inning. The Reds' fans did not show excitement at the prospect of a World Championship by going out to the old ball game for game seven. Cicotte treated a sparse crowd of 13,923 to a superb pitching performance and a 4–1 victory. The Reds' play appeared suspicious in Kerr's victory, and if attendance is an indicator, the small crowd at the potentially deciding game seemed to send a message to baseball.

With the fix in peril, Rothstein insured a return on his investment by strong arming Williams prior to the eighth game. Fearing for his wife's safety, the southpaw obliged the gangsters in the first inning and the Sox lost the game 10–5. The Reds won the tainted series five games to three and held a locker-room celebration. Rothstein and the owners celebrated in private in the real winning locker rooms—their estates and board rooms.

Several circumstances suggested a potential end of the scandal following the eighth game. The owners quadrupled their split from the previous year and doubled earnings from the 1917 Series. With the onset of Prohibition, Rothstein surreptitiously anticipated America's thirst for whiskey, and the rest of the gamblers fled the country. Many of the suspected players enjoyed career years in the summer of 1920. Several forces, however, converged to prompt formal investigation. Most notably, the chronic suspicious play of many major league teams during the season provoked movement for official inquiry. A Phillies-Cubs series proved so dubious that the Cook County Grand Jury initiated an investigation into baseball. The relentless work of newspapermen Hugh Fullerton and Jim Cruisenberry chronicled the persistent errant play and may have prompted the investigation. Cruisenberry penned a pivotal open letter expressing public dissatisfaction with baseball. The letter, signed by prominent Chicagoan Fred Loomis, appeared in the September 19, 1920 issue of the *Chicago Tribune.*

The grand jury investigation quickly became a forum for the internal squabbles and grudges of organized baseball. The most evident infighting involved American League President Ban Johnson, and his longtime adversary, Comiskey. The feud proved so potent that Gleason and Comiskey approached John Heydler, president of the National League, with their suspicions after the second game of the Series. Comiskey's million-dollar business balanced precariously as Johnson waged an attack on his club and several of his players began a succession of curiously induced confessions. As his alternatives disappeared, Comiskey decided to suspend eight of his key players in the heat of a pennant race with Cleveland. News of the fix littered the headlines of major newspapers across the country and stunned the naive public. The sacred game quickly lost its purity and baseball teetered so perilously on the edge of ruin that the 1920 Series faced cancellation.

The momentum of the grand jury investigation and public unrest reached full swing that fall. In a desperate maneuver, the owners anointed Judge Kenesaw Mountain Landis as the first commissioner of baseball. Despite the distinguished judge's inability to solve a seemingly simple labor dispute at the time, he ably negotiated with the owners for both a healthy salary and unchecked power for himself.

Concomitantly, the grand jury indicted the eight Sox players and five gamblers, with the notable exception of Rothstein and the inclusion of Hal Chase, a blackballed New York player. The disappearance of key documents marred the arraignment. Johnson became so frustrated by the sluggish proceedings that he personally

supplied a key witness for the state from the other side of the Mexican border—"Sleepy" Burns.

Following a lengthy jury selection, the trial began on July 18,
1921. A former congressman, George Gorman, led a team of two
Illinois assistant state's attorneys and two special prosecutors representing the state. A group of eight seasoned legal veterans, with unknown financial backing, represented the players. Conspicuously
absent from the defense table were all of the indicted gamblers.

The testimony of Burns opened the trial, after which Gorman
apprised the Court that the written confessions of Cicotte, Jackson,
and Williams were among the missing documents. While it is not
clear exactly what happened to the documents, circumstances again
point to the foul play of Rothstein, who forged an irreverent trinity
with Comiskey and his legal counsel, Alfred Austrian. Interestingly,
Jackson's signed testimony resurfaced in Austrian's possession during a
subsequent conflict between Comiskey and Jackson over lost wages.
Just as Rothstein's entry into the fix doomed the outcome of the Series, his subterranean pass through the investigation determined the
outcome of the trial. The lineup of eight attorneys and the Rothstein-
Comiskey axis easily outmanned Gorman's team and acquittal seemed
assured. The proceedings continued, however, and featured a show of
support for the defendants by several of the "clean" Sox, Gleason, and
Comiskey. On the evening of August 2, 1921, the jury found the
players not guilty. The overflow crowd cheered as the players briskly
left the Criminal Courts Building. The eight reconvened in a private
room at a local restaurant that curiously adjoined a room housing a
party for the jurors. Not surprisingly the parties soon coalesced.

Judge Landis sobered the celebration as he concurrently proclaimed to the press, "Regardless of the verdict of juries, no player
that throws a game, no player that entertains proposals or promises
to throw a game, no player that sits in a conference with a bunch of
crooked gamblers, where the ways and means of throwing games are
discussed, and does not promptly tell his club about it, will ever play
professional baseball."

In retrospect, the iron-handed banishment of the eight Black
Sox players by Judge Landis served organized baseball well. The exile of the Black Sox restored public confidence in the game. Organized baseball returned to handling subsequent delicate matters, in-

volving such notable players as Tris Speaker and Ty Cobb, behind closed doors. Organized gambling was chased from the game. The exile of the Black Sox sufficed to keep baseball alive for a decade of unprecedented and unequalled offensive excitement. The new style of play, created by an assortment of rule adjustments and the great Babe Ruth, put to rest an era of low-scoring strategic baseball, characterized by subtleties such as advancing runners with bunts, turning singles into doubles, and making defensive adjustments for individual batters and ball-strike counts. The sacrifice of the Black Sox saved organized baseball from a precarious future. The players, on the other hand, were left to bear the double cross of the gamblers and organized baseball.

It is peculiar that the organization of baseball departs so significantly from the game of baseball. The game is a hallowed American tradition embodied by an elegant harmony of symmetry and asymmetry. The dimensions of the game are so precise that a perfect sacrifice bunt is nearly indefensible. The power of organized baseball has chosen not to recognize the significance of the sacrifice of the Black Sox. The actions of the Black Sox were consistent with their times, and the players, in fact, received acquittal in the 1921 American judicial system.

Currently, American society recognizes unusual circumstances and conditions leading to foul play. This is certainly evident in the political arena where the courts recently decided former President Richard Nixon should be paid for transcripts of his corrupt political dealings. On their own ball field, organized baseball reinstated New York Yankee pitcher, Steve Howe, following his seventh substance-abuse suspension. It seems an appropriate time for organized baseball to actively and publicly acknowledge the conditions leading to the Black Sox players' actions, as well as the intent of their punishment. Two runners can easily be advanced into scoring position by clearing the name of Buck Weaver, and enshrining Shoeless Joe with his peers in the Hall of Fame. It could turn out to be a winning strategy at a time when baseball is in need of another big inning.

Selected Bibliography

Asinof, E. *Eight Men Out: The Black Sox and the 1919 World Series*. New York: Holt and Company, Inc., 1987.

Boyer, A. "The Great Gatsby, the Black Sox, High Finance, and American Law." *Michi-*

gan Law Review 88 (November 1989): 328–342.

Cruisenberry, J. "Coverage of the Trial of the Black Sox." *Chicago Tribune.* September 28–30, 1921.

———. "Open Letter Signed by Fred Loomis." *Chicago Tribune.* September 19, 1930.

———. "A Newsman's Biggest Story." *Sports Illustrated.* September 17, 1956: 69–71.

Durney, J. "Fair or Foul? The Commissioner and Major League Baseball's Disciplinary Process." *Emery Law Journal* 41 (Spring 1992): 581–631.

Gandil, A. "This Is My Story of the Black Sox Series." *Sports Illustrated.* September 17, 1956: 69–71.

Kirby, J. "The Year They Fixed the World Series." *American Bar Association Journal* 792 (1988): 54–59.

Beating the Spread
College Basketball Point Shaving

Ted Hovet Jr. and Scott McEthron

While modern college basketball has weathered a seemingly endless stream of rules violations, recruiting scandals, and academic imbroglios, its *bête noire,* the one activity that has seemed to hold the potential to irrevocably damage the sport, has always been point shaving. Point shaving is both illustrative and symptomatic of the proliferation of money and gambling in the world of amateur athletics. College basketball now commands television and merchandising revenues well in excess of a billion dollars, and it is responsible for a significant portion of the estimated seventy billion dollars wagered on sports annually. From the time that the college game first reached national prominence in the 1940s, gamblers, aware of its ever-expanding financial success and equally aware of the relative poverty of college players, have discovered in point shaving a means of ensuring that everyone can get a piece of the action.

The process of point shaving and the reasons basketball is especially susceptible to such manipulations emerge from the system of "point spreads," a handicapping mechanism common since the 1940s that establishes both the favored team and the number of points by which that team is expected to win a particular game. Printed every day in the sports pages of newspapers across the country, point spreads are for many fans an entertaining sidelight to the games themselves, a hypothetical numerical evaluation of the relative strengths and weaknesses of various teams.

In reality point spreads are a means for the gambling industry to intensify betting interest in even potentially lopsided matchups. If, for example, the point spread for an upcoming basketball game favors Syracuse by fourteen points over Pittsburgh, a bet on Syracuse will pay off only if it wins by fifteen points or more, while money on Pitt will return for either a Pitt victory or a Pitt loss by no more than 13 points. The spread, then, functions not as a prediction of a game's outcome but as a means of inducing equal numbers of wagers for both teams; if bets come in on both sides, bookmakers, who always collect a percentage of the money they handle, are guaranteed a profit.

For the gambler who wishes to influence the outcome of a game by bribing a player to play poorly, the point spread offers an enticing opportunity: its "cushion" of points means that a team can win its game but "lose" versus the spread. "Successful" point shaving might be seen as the best of all possible worlds for the participants: the favored team wins; school pride is maintained; and the level of play by the players involved need not be suspiciously awful. Indeed, City College of New York (CCNY) and Kentucky, two teams implicated in the widespread 1951 point-shaving scandals which covered activity from 1947 to 1951, actually won national championships while some of their players were actively point shaving.

The history of college basketball point shaving involves four major cases: the 1951 incident, centered primarily around four New York City schools (CCNY, Long Island University, Manhattan College, New York University) and Kentucky; a 1961 scandal, which implicated twenty-four universities from across the country; a 1981 Boston College case; and the 1985 Tulane case.

Point shaving cases have proved remarkably difficult to prosecute. Participants in the 1951 and 1961 cases were charged under state laws with either conspiracy or the more serious charge of sports bribery. Most of the laws had been written in the aftermath of the 1919 Black Sox scandal. According to Charles Rosen, however, some states had no gambling laws directly applicable to college basketball. The 1951 scandal involved at least thirty-three players from seven schools and the attempted fixing of at least forty-nine games in nineteen states, yet even with this massive involvement (which most commentators attribute to the players' belief that it was a widespread occurrence that would go unpunished), only four players from the New York City schools ever spent time in jail. Indeed, the ineffectiveness of laws as a deterrent seemed apparent when, only ten years later, a new series of incidents resulted in the arrest of fifty players and the fixing of games in twenty-two states.

The prosecution of the 1981 Boston College case represented a concerted federal effort. It was the first attempted use of RICO (Racketeer Influenced and Corrupt Organizations) federal statutes in conjunction with sports bribery statutes. The point shaving involved several organized crime figures, including self-professed fixer Henry Hill, who only days before initiating talks with Boston College player Rick Kuhn took part in the Lufthansa Airlines heist at Kennedy Airport. Despite Hill's lengthy pretrial "confession" in an article in the February 16, 1981 issue of *Sports Illustrated* in which he implicated three Boston College players, only Kuhn spent time in jail. Hill himself, admittedly a partner in a wide range of crimes, was granted immunity as part of the Federal Witness Protection Program.

In the 1985 Tulane case, which resulted in the university's in-house decision to shut down its basketball program entirely for a period of three years, a series of plea bargains and grants of immunity resulted in the effective dissolution of the most serious charges. The two attempts to try star player John "Hot Rod" Williams under Louisiana's sports bribery laws ended first in a mistrial and then in Williams's acquittal.

Currently, Federal Sports Bribery Laws, found in Title 18, section 224 of the U.S. Code, carry a penalty of up to five years imprisonment and/or fines of up to $10,000, but evaluating either the past and/or the present effectiveness of the various laws used to prosecute point shaving is difficult. As Philip A. Stelly, Christopher McIntire, and Charles Rosen chronicle, each of the major trials has been distinguished by the presence of peculiar and idiosyncratic circumstances that made the prosecution's job difficult. Evaluation is also perplexing because of the relative scarcity of cases brought to trial, although the very fact that so few cases have ever been prosecuted strongly suggests that current laws are inadequate. In attempting to assess the scope of the problem, it should also be noted that over the years many unsubstantiated allegations about other point shaving cases have been made. While it is fruitless to speculate about the veracity of those allegations, given the atmosphere of big money surrounding the game, it is, if anything, surprising that point shaving has not been an even more visible problem for college basketball.

Selected Bibliography

Anderson, S. "Sports of The Times: Something Better Than a Sermon." *The New York Times.* November 29, 1981: Section 5, 3.

Hill, H. with D. Looney. "How I Put the Fix In." *Sports Illustrated.* February 16, 1981, 14–19.

McIntire, C. "RICO, Reporter's Privilege and the Boston College Point-Shaving Scandal." *Loyola Entertainment Law Journal Annual* 5 (1985): 269–281.

Rosen, C. *Scandals of '51.* New York: Holt, Rinehart, and Winston, 1978.

Stelly, P. "Jurors in La. Put 'Hot Rod' in High Gear." *National Law Journal* 8 (June 30, 1986): 6.

Jack Molinas
A Basketball Player with Great but Unclean Hands

Charles E. Quirk

Molinas v. Podoloff, 133 N.Y.S. 2d 743(1954)

Molinas v. National Basketball Association, 190 F. Supp. 241 S.D.N.Y. (1961)

In the sport of basketball, a small percentage of the millions of women and men who play the game possess "great hands." The select group of players given great hands display their talent in a variety of ways: a soft touch when releasing the ball toward the basket, strength to rip away rebounds from opponents, quickness to flick the ball away from a player seeking to penetrate the paint, and accuracy when threading the ball through a maze of defenders to a teammate streaking for a lay up.

Jack Molinas belongs in the group of players blessed with great hands. A playground legend in New York City, Molinas starred in both high school and later at Columbia University. At 6'6" and 210 pounds, Molinas scored inside with an almost unstoppable hook shot and outside with a deadly long shot. Upon his graduation from Columbia in 1953, the Fort Wayne Pistons made Molinas their first draft pick. In his first and only season in the National Basketball Association, Molinas played in twenty-nine games of the schedule. He averaged twelve points a game, shooting at a respectable 39 percent from the field and 76 percent from the free throw line. Molinas showed potential for ascending to the upper echelon of professional basketball players in the 1950s.

Professional basketball in the years immediately following World War II bore little resemblance to the sport of the past few decades. The Basketball Association of America (BAA) was formed by a small group of investors in June 1946. Most of the founders were involved in hockey and arena businesses. They believed that basketball fans who flocked to college games would also turn out to watch professional basketball. The founders chose Maurice Podoloff to serve as president of the BAA. Podoloff's family operated an arena in New Haven, Connecticut, and he presided over the American Hockey League. Born in 1890, in Russia, Podoloff earned both a bachelor of arts and a law degree from Yale University. Standing only 5'2", Podoloff came to the presidency of the BAA with little knowledge of basketball but with a keen mind and a gift for innovations. During his tenure as president, first of the BAA, then of the NBA, which resulted from a 1949 merger of the BAA and the National Basketball League, professional basketball took on features now taken for granted: large crowds watching a fast-paced game, thanks to the use of the twenty-four-second shot clock; television and radio coverage; and highly talented offensive players showcased by their respective teams, due in part to the restriction against employing zone defenses.

Podoloff cut short Molinas's NBA career in January 1954. Following several weeks of investigation, Podoloff suspended Molinas from his $9,600-a-year position with the Fort Wayne Pistons because the star forward had bet on his own team. Molinas voluntarily signed a statement admitting betting about ten times. Podoloff's action was based on an NBA rule forbidding players from betting on any games in which they played.

Molinas brought legal action against Podoloff in an effort to overturn the suspension and to receive a hearing in addition to receiving damages. In *Molinas* v. *Podoloff* (1954), Judge Samuel Joseph, a Bronx County judge serving temporarily in the New York Supreme Court, denied all of Molinas's requests. Judge Joseph stressed that Molinas had voluntarily signed a written statement admitting that he had wagered on the Pistons. Acknowledging that Molinas had not been given notice and a hearing, Judge Joseph sided with defendant Podoloff's contention that the voluntarily admission by Molinas represented a waiver of his rights provided in his team contract and the NBA Constitution. The judge invoked the "clean hands doctrine," which requires that someone seeking a remedy from the judicial system must come to the court with clean hands; that is, the plaintiff must not have violated conscience or good faith in prior conduct. Molinas clearly possessed soiled hands. Judge Joseph correctly noted that the basketball player who bets on games is not merely wagering on the team to win, but is working the point spread. Speaking directly about Molinas, Judge Joseph declared that "the position of the plaintiff, in reality, seems to be one of asserting that he wagered on games, he breached his contract, he violated the constitution of the NBA and was morally dishonest." Earlier in his opinion, Judge Joseph remarked that "in light of his knowledge of the basketball scandals, the express prohibitions in wagering and the manner of his betting, I am constrained to say plaintiff's conduct was reprehensible."

In the early part of 1954, Molinas entered Brooklyn Law School and for several years combined his legal education with serving as player-coach of the Williamsport, Pennsylvania, Billies in the Eastern Basketball League. During his dual career as a law student and player-coach, Molinas found time to bribe college players to fix games. After graduating from law school, Molinas filed a $3 million damage suit in federal court. He named Podoloff, the NBA, and the owners of its eight teams as defendants.

In *Molinas* v. *National Basketball Association* (1961), the basketball player-lawyer alleged violations of antitrust laws, sought an injunction against supposed conspiracies, and demanded reinstatement into the NBA. Federal District Judge Irving R. Kaufman heard the case and ruled against Molinas in every particular. He rejected the plaintiff's claim that antitrust laws had been violated by conspiring to restrain trade. Molinas called into question the allocation of players under the reserve system, his own suspension and unsuccessful attempts to win reinstatement into the NBA, and the refusal of NBA teams to play in exhibition games in which he participated. According to Judge Kaufman, Molinas failed to establish ". . . clear causal connections between violations alleged and injuries suffered." Although highly successful on the basketball court in college, in the NBA, and in the Eastern circuit, Molinas could not rise to meet the burden of proof requirement in the courtroom.

Two years following his second loss in court, Molinas was convicted as a co-conspirator in the college point shaving scandals of the late 1950s and early 1960s. Molinas served five years of a ten- to fifteen-year sentence, then moved his operation to California. In the Golden State, Molinas sought fortune in a variety of enterprises including the pornographic film industry and the fur business. He continued his gambling habits, revealing a penchant for collecting his winnings but welshing on his loans and betting losses. On August 3, 1975, Molinas was shot and killed in the back yard of his Los Angeles home. The murder displayed a style that suggested a connection to organized crime.

Although the on-court talents of Jack Molinas are well known to historians of basketball, and sports law experts understand his two unsuccessful suits in court, it is the fictional accounts by writers Neil Isaacs and Phil Berger that ultimately may attract the widest public attention to the bizarre life of one of basketball's most notorious players, Jack Molinas, a basketball player with great but unclean hands.

Selected Bibliography

Berger, P. *Big Time*. Roanoke: Jefferson Street Press, 1990.

Hollander, A., ed. *The NBA's Official Encyclopedia of Pro Basketball*. New York: New American Library, 1981.

Isaacs, N. *The Great Molinas*. Bethesda: WID Publishing Group and Johnson City: Sports Literature Association, 1992.

Norman, G. "After the Fall." *Sports Illustrated*. May 20, 1991: 72–89.

Sobel, L. *Professional Sports and the Law*. New York: Law-Arts Publishers, Inc., 1977.

Fast Balls and Fast Bucks Don't Mix

Jack Kolbe

The history of professional baseball is littered with scandals, from the Black Sox fixing of the 1919 World Series to the Pete Rose debacle of 1989, but probably none seem more bizarre than the one involving Dennis Dale McLain of the Detroit Tigers.

On the pitching mound, Denny McLain displayed an extraordinary talent, one that a fan witnesses perhaps only once in a lifetime. In five full seasons with Detroit, 1965 through 1969, he won 108 games while losing 51, an enviable record for a young man of twenty-five years. He was voted the American League's Most Valuable Player in 1968, the same year he became the first pitcher since Dizzy Dean in 1934 to win 30 games in one season, with a record of 31 and 6. When McLain was presented his second consecutive Cy Young award in 1969, an award given to the league's best pitcher, baseball's world seemed to be at his fingertips with his trademark pitch, a high, hard fastball. McLain, however, would not reach the brilliant future envisioned for him.

The first hint of trouble came in January 1970 when McLain was summoned to testify before a closed federal grand jury investigating interstate gambling. One month later the bomb that was to rock professional baseball came in a copyrighted article entitled "Downfall of a Hero," in the February 23, 1970 issue of *Sports Illustrated.* The article alleged first, that McLain was a partner in a bookmaking operation in 1967; second, that the bookmaking operation went sour when McLain and his partners were not able to pay a $46,000 gambling debt; third, that Cosa Nostra enforcer Tony Giacalone encouraged McLain to pay the debt by stomping his heel into the pitcher's left foot, dislocating the toes, causing McLain to miss two or three pitching starts during the September pennant race with Boston; fourth, that the gambler who was owed the debt died in a mysterious auto accident; and, fifth, that Giacalone's brother, Vito, a Mafioso, bet heavily against Detroit in the pennant race as well as in the final crucial game of 1967. The Tigers lost that final game, a game in which McLain was ineffective as a pitcher, and Detroit finished the season one game behind pennant-winning Boston. The question that still haunts the sports world is: did McLain's 1967 off-field and on-field activities cost Detroit the pennant?

Baseball commissioner Bowie Kuhn, while admitting that McLain had been involved in a bookmaking scheme, stated that: "There is no evidence to indicate that McLain ever bet on a baseball game involving the Detroit Tigers or any other team. There is no evidence to indicate that McLain gave less than his best effort at any time while performing for the Detroit Tigers."

In the only known case in sports law, Commissioner Kuhn received a presidential blessing on an athlete's punishment: Richard Nixon pronounced Kuhn's proposed sentence of suspending McLain from baseball for half the 1970 season to be "fair," leaving Kuhn with some assurance that the Justice Department would not pursue an indictment. When the penalty was publicly announced by Kuhn on April 1, 1970, many within the sports world cried "bad call." If McLain were innocent as Kuhn claimed, why punish him, and three years after the fact? But if McLain knowingly and willingly engaged in bookmaking activities, violating some of the strictest laws of sports, why such a lenient sentence? Alex Karras of the Detroit Lions, who had been suspended for one year for betting on football games, remarked that, "Maybe if a guy wins forty baseball games in a season he can get away with murder." McLain's troubles did not end with the gambling-related suspension. In June 1970, he filed for bankruptcy, claiming $400,000 in debts and no assets. When he returned to the mound in July, much of the magic had disappeared from his pitches; the high, hard fast ball that had confounded hitters was gone. That August he was suspended for one week by the team's management for dumping buckets of water on the heads of two sportswriters. Then the final blow of the year came in September when Commissioner Kuhn suspended him for the remainder of the season for carrying a concealed, unlicensed gun.

Ordinarily, when a sports hero falls from grace, he soon disappears from the public eye. Not so with McLain. In 1985, seventeen years following his Most Valuable Player award, McLain was convicted in federal court of racketeering and narcotics violations and sentenced to twenty-three years in prison. According to the prosecutors, McLain had found new partners, associates who were in the business of bookmaking, accepting illegal kickbacks on loans, and charging usurious rates on debts. When the State of Florida closed down that operation in 1983, McLain had then ventured into the cocaine trade which, although lucrative, led to his arrest.

After serving twenty-nine months in federal prisons, McLain's conviction was overturned by an appeals court based on errors committed by the trial judge and prosecution. Scheduled for a retrial in October, 1988, McLain pleaded guilty to all charges and was sentenced to time served and probation. As a condition of his probation, the judge ordered McLain to revise his second autobiography, *Strikeout*, published earlier in 1988, in which he had denied all of the charges against him. Said the judge: "It's about time you start getting things truthfully in order."

Since release from prison, McLain's life seemed to turn in positive directions. He credited his family, especially his wife Sharyn, with providing support for his rehabilitation. In 1992 an automobile accident took the life of their twenty-six-year-old daughter Kristin McLain Sutherland. McLain regarded this blow as more difficult to bear than the prison sentence. The former Tiger pitcher became a prominent figure in the Detroit area. He hosted both a highly rated early-morning radio call-in show and a popular weekly television sports show. In mid-1993 he purchased a meat-packing plant. A portion of the funds went to a foundation he established in Kristin's name to fly needy children with major illnesses to the University of Michigan Medical Center. McLain, a portly three-hundred-pounder, frequently serves as pilot.

But the ex-fastball pitcher's fortunes reversed in 1994 and 1995. He left the radio and television circuits. McLain and his partner, Roger Smiegel, took charge of the Peet Packing Company in January 1994. Quickly their financial dealings came under criticism. In the fall McLain departed from the Peer operation, and Smiegel resigned his leadership position in April 1995. Federal investigators questioned whether the McLain-Smiegel team raided an employee pension fund for about $2.5 million.

McLain also encountered serious problems with his Great Lakes Media Group. Smiegel and McLain bought the network in August 1994 as part of the Peet Packing Company empire. Several creditors filed lawsuits in order to collect reimbursement for a wide variety of services, including remodeling, equipment, rent, and consulting. McLain blamed the former management for the debts and proclaimed that the network is "fine and dandy."

Selected Bibliography

Freehan, B. *Behind the Mask*. New York: Maddick Manuscripts, Inc., 1970.

McLain, D. with D. Diles. *Nobody's Perfect*. New York: Dial Press, 1975.

McLain, D. with M. Nahrstedt. *Strikeout*. St. Louis: The Sporting News Publishing Company, 1988.

Pitoniak, S. "McLain Still Makes His Pitch; Former Tiger Gets Life Back Together as On-Air Personality." *Chicago Sun-Times*. November 21, 1993: Sports, 19.

Rushin, S. "The Season of High Heat." *Sports Illustrated*. July 19, 1993: 30–37.

Sharnik, M. "Downfall of a Hero." *Sports Illustrated*. February 23, 1970, 16–21.

Sinclair, N. "Peet Packing President Steps Down." *The Detroit News*. April 10, 1995: B4.

Sinclair, N. and A. Lengel. "McLain Finds Himself in Another Jam. *The Detroit News*. June 4, 1995: C1.

A Gridiron Hero Self-Destructs

Jack Kolbe

The prologue to Art Schlichter's 1981 biography, *Straight Arrow,* contains an almost prophetic insight into the personalities of two sports heroes of the day: "He [Schlichter] functions as if driven by a deep inner well of energy. Pete Rose is fueled by a similar drive that makes him a human whirlwind all the time." Within the decade, both men, compulsively driven, were to be consumed and disgraced in a whirlwind of gambling.

In 1982 Art Schlichter was considered the nation's top college quarterback. Professional football scouts compared him to Terry Bradshaw and Roger Staubach, quarterbacks who could make the big play. All-American at Ohio State, and a Heisman trophy candidate, Schlichter was the 1982 first-round draft pick of the National Football League Baltimore Colts who awarded him a three-year, $830,000 contract. Baltimore fans were ecstatic; here was the man who could lead their beleaguered Colts out of the doldrums of mediocrity.

Unfortunately for Baltimore enthusiasts, their hopes came up empty. Schlichter came into the Colts' 1982 summer training camp mentally unprepared and physically out of condition. He lost the starting quarterback job to another rookie, a fourth-round pick, and found himself relegated to the bench during the strike-shortened 1982 season. What was afflicting the gifted young man who had performed so brilliantly at Ohio State?

Schlichter had simply, and disastrously, shifted the focus of his attentions and energies from football to gambling. In March, 1983, Schlichter himself broke the story when he sought FBI protection from Baltimore bookmakers who were allegedly threatening to collect, one way or another, on a $159,000 gambling debt. A month later Schlichter's attorney revealed that his client had amassed an incredible $750,000 in gambling debts. Gaming of such magnitude had never before, or since, been heard of within the ranks of NFL players.

When Schlichter appeared before NFL Commissioner Pete Rozelle for a hearing on his gambling activity, he knew he was playing the most important game of his life. His career was on the line. Schlichter brought along his team: Dr. Robert Custer, an expert in pathological gambling, and attorney John J. Chester, a special counsel to President Richard Nixon during the Watergate proceedings. The game plan was to convince Rozelle that the young quarterback had acknowledged that his gambling was an illness, but one susceptible to treatment and control, and then to persuade Rozelle to handle the case as he would treat drug cases, which was to allow a player to rejoin his team as soon as he had successfully completed treatment.

The game plan failed. On May 20, 1983, nine days following the hearing, Rozelle released his ruling: Schlichter was guilty of betting substantial amounts of money on at least ten NFL games and of associating with illegal bookmakers and, therefore, was under indefinite suspension. Schlicter's lawyer Chester said, following the ruling, "An indefinite suspension has you out there hanging in the wind until they decide what they want to do with you." Unlike termination, which releases a player from contractual obligations, suspension denies the player not only of his salary, but also of his property right to sell his skills to another team. The player, under suspension, remains the property right of the club, bound by the terms of an exclusive employment contract. (Suspensions have been challenged in the courts, with mixed results by athletes and coaches, on grounds that their "due process" right had been denied them; most notably in the 1988 case of *NCAA* v. *Tarkanian*. The courts have yet to consider the antitrust implications of the penalty.)

The authority Rozelle used for Schlichter's indefinite suspension is contained in paragraphs 14 and 15 of the NFL's standard player contract. Here the player consents to be subject to both club and league disciplinary rules, granting the club and the league discretionary power not only to define the rules, but to administer the discipline as well, an arrangement unique to sports. Paragraph 15 cites a broad range of penalties the league commissioner can impose on a player who "knowingly associates with gamblers or engages in gambling activity." The NFL's interpretation of this clause has been rather narrow; penalize players only for betting on National Football League games, as in the Alex Karras and Paul Hornung suspensions of 1963. The amount of money wagered has been decisive in determining the punishment. Karras bet $100 on NFL games while five of his teammates bet lesser amounts and were fined $2,000 but not suspended. Quarterback Tommy Kramer received a mere reprimand for wagering $25 with a bartender on an NFL game.

As for associating with gamblers, there appears to be considerable inconsistency in the league's enforcement of paragraph 15. In 1982, NFL security personnel reported to league headquarters possible links between Cleveland Brown players and a drug dealer, who was also a known gambler, but no apparent action was taken. Similarly, no action was taken amid allegations that Ken Stabler of the Houston Oilers had a longtime association with a convicted bookmaker. In 1981, however, John Unitas was forced out of the Colts organization because he had lent his name to a football touting service. Twelve years earlier, New York Jet Joe Namath had been forced to sell his interest in a cocktail lounge that was frequented by persons of questionable background.

Whither Art Schlichter? In June, 1984, following a favorable report on Schlichter by NFL security personnel, Commissioner Rozelle lifted the suspension. Schlichter rejoined the Colts, who had become the Indianapolis Colts following their "infamous" midnight ride out of Baltimore, and he struggled through the 1984 season. The following year Schlichter won the job of starting quarterback but hurt his knee in the opening game against Pittsburgh. The day he was reactivated from the injured reserve list, October 17, 1985, the Colts announced, amid rumors of continued gambling activity, that Schlichter had been cut from the team and his contract terminated. As a free agent, Schlichter was signed by the NFL Buffalo Bills in 1986, but released in the preseason when the Bills acquired Jim Kelly, the top quarterback from the defunct United States Football League. Then, in January of 1987, the death knell sounded; Schlichter had been arrested by Indianapolis police for illegal gambling. The specific charge was that he had wagered $232,000 over a seventy-day period in late 1986 with a sports betting operation which had alleged links to organized crime. League headquarters announced that there would be no reentry into the NFL for Schlichter because of his history of gambling.

Although ineligible to play again in the NFL, Schlichter experienced a resurrection on and off the field. In the early 1990s, he played quarterback for the Detroit Drive of the Arena Football League. He once again displayed the ability to scramble which characterized his style at Ohio State University. Under his leadership, the Detroit Drive won the Arena championship in 1990 and Schlichter received Most Valuable Player honors. More importantly, Schlichter seemed to find fulfillment with his wife and daughter. He enjoyed a personal-services arrangement with Mike Ilitch, owner of the Drive, which provided year-round employment. He also regularly attended meetings of Gamblers Anonymous.

Schlichter, however, reverted to his self-destructive behavior. In 1994 he moved to Las Vegas where he worked as an afternoon talk show host for a local radio station. Schlichter conned relatives, friends, and even people who called in to his show out of an estimated $500,000 in order to support his gambling addiction. In January 1995 he received a two-year sentence to Federal Prison in Terre Haute, Indiana, for committing bank fraud.

One curious question remains: why does the NFL place players who gamble on a different level than players who are drug users? Certainly players who gamble and associate with gamblers create a clear and present danger of deals to fix games, particularly when substantial sums are wagered. On the other hand, one may ask: is it beyond probability that a drug supplier would suggest a deal to fix a game in exchange for a steady supply of high-quality, high-priced merchandise?

Selected Bibliography

Collett, R. *Straight Arrow: The Art Schlichter Story*. Dayton: Landfall Press, 1981.
Hudson, M. "Schlichter Is Sacked for a Two-Year Loss." *Los Angeles Times*. January 28, 1995, Sports 1.
"Schlichter: Only Gamble He'll Take Is to Play in NFL." *St. Louis Post-Dispatch*. July 14, 1991: Sports 12F.
Sloan, P. *The Athlete and the Law*. New York: Oceana Publications, Inc., 1983.

Charlie the Hustler and the Hall of Saints

David Rodgers

The life and fate of Peter Edward Rose is a story that would have been worthy subject matter for the best of the classical Greek tragedians. He came from humble origins but was gifted with athletic skills. Through unremitting tenacity and drive, he pushed himself to the pinnacle of the game of baseball. Then, after carving out a niche for himself beside the few true legendary names of the game, he was brought to his knees by a fatal flaw of character.

A Cincinnati kid from the word "go," Rose was born, bred, and had his greatest glory with the hometown Reds, baseball's oldest franchise and one of its most storied. With the Reds, Rose broke the immortal Ty Cobb's hit record of 4,191, ending his career with a staggering 4,256 hits. He "owned" the summer of 1978 when he set the National League consecutive-game hitting streak at forty-four games, falling twelve games short of Joe DiMaggio's all-time major league mark. A perennial All-Star and three-time member of world championship teams, he was Rookie of the Year in 1963, Most Valuable Player in 1973, and won three batting titles.

The great achievements on the field are only half of Rose's legend. The rest came from his great charisma and hard-driving approach to the game. From his earliest days he captivated the fans with his hustle, his headfirst dives, his sprinting down the line after drawing walks, his crouched steely-eyed batting stance, and his battling spirit. He commanded attention both on and off the diamond. A player of his appeal demanded a nickname and his was bestowed early in his first season, "Charlie Hustle." The media fell in love with Rose, finding him to be as great and willing an interview subject as he was a ballplayer. They fired the furnace of his legend with adoring broadcast soliloquies and page after page of glowing prose.

By the end of the 1988 season, Rose was a "lock" to gain election to the Hall of Fame on the first ballot and perhaps even to become the first unanimously elected candidate. He also seemed to be on the verge of managing a young Reds team to the top of the game. By the end of the 1989 season, however, he was banned from baseball for life, faced the possibility of imprisonment for tax offenses, and watched his popularity fall to new depths by the day. No careful observer of the game could guess at what point his fall would end.

Rose was banished for life from any association with baseball on August 24, 1989. The heart of the matter was that Commissioner of Baseball A. Bartlett Giamatti believed that Rose had gambled on baseball. The document that supported this belief was the Dowd Report. John M. Dowd, a Washington lawyer with a background in government criminal investigations, was hired by the commissioner's office on February 23, 1989. The results of Dowd's investigation were turned over to Giamatti on May 9. The report made a compelling case against Rose. A key part of the evidence consisted of information about phone calls made from Rose's home and Reds' clubhouses to known bookmakers and bookmaking intermediaries. The calls were of one to two minutes in length and at the appropriate time to make, and to check on, bets. Two associates of Rose, Ron Peters, convicted of drug and tax offenses, and Paul Janszen, convicted of tax fraud, both testified that they had handled bets by Rose on baseball games.

Most damning, and interestingly enough, inadmissible in a court of law, were handwritten "betting slips" that Janszen admitted stealing from Rose's home. An expert called in by the commissioner's office verified that the slips were in Rose's handwriting. Written on one of the slips are the entries "CINCY W" and "CIN W" under what appear to be the dates 4/10/87 and 4/11/87. Based on this evidence, it appeared that Rose bet on baseball but he bet to win on a team for which he served as manager. In Rose's favor, there was no evidence in Dowd's report pointing to him betting on his team to lose. In addition, as Roger Kahn pointed out in a 1989 book, "[Dowd] denied Rose the right of cross-examination and the right to confront his accusers." Also, the major accusers in the report were both convicted felons with reasons for wanting to get even with Rose.

Along with the gambling issue, Rose also had serious tax problems. He had substantially underreported his income in the mid-eighties, a mistake that he would find himself paying for soon after his battle with the commissioner over gambling.

While the case against Rose was compelling, the way in which it was handled by Commissioner Giamatti left much to be desired. During his investigation, Dowd obtained Commissioner Giamatti's promise to provide a letter on behalf of witness Ron Peters, who was awaiting sentencing on drug and tax offenses, by showing him worthy of leniency due to his conscientious help with major league baseball's investigation of Rose. While the reasoning behind this request was flawed, it was disastrous considering that the judge who was to receive the letter was Cincinnati resident and Reds fan, District Judge Carl Rubin. The key to the blunder on Giamatti's part is that the letter was sent two weeks *before* the commissioner received Dowd's report.

The letter contained the statement that Giamatti found the testimony of one of Rose's prime accusers "candid, forthright and truthful." Judge Rubin quickly contacted Rose's agent, Reuven J. Katz. Their feeling, as expressed by them in later public statements, was that the commissioner was clearly biased and had prejudged Rose. Rubin even went so far as to announce in a presentencing conference that Giamatti was involved in "a vendetta against Pete Rose."

Until this letter was sent, Rose's fate was totally in the commissioner's hands. Giamatti was empowered by the rules of office to take any action that he deemed in the best interests of baseball. The only tangible checks on the office were the censure of public opinion and opposition by club owners. Armed with Giamatti's letter to Judge Rubin and with the advantage of bringing action in Cincinnati venues, Rose's lawyers worked on a series of legal actions meant both to delay and, hopefully, overturn Giamatti's right to judge Rose.

On June 19, 1989, Rose's lawyers filed suit against Giamatti in Cincinnati's Hamilton County Common Pleas Court, in hopes of having Giamatti removed from making any judgment concerning Rose, claiming that the commissioner had "displayed bias and outrageous conduct" that would cause "irreparable harm to [Rose's] reputation." On June 26 the presiding judge, Norbert A. Nadel, issued a restraining order on the grounds that Giamatti had "prejudged Rose."

There then followed a battle between the Rose and Giamatti forces concerning the venue for the trial. Rose's legal team wanted the advantage of a trial in Hamilton County Court, the Reds' heartland. Giamatti managed to have the case moved to United States District Court in Columbus on July 3rd. On July 5th, in the Sixth District Court of Appeals, lawyers for Rose attempted to have the case moved back to Hamilton County on grounds of lack of diversity of citizenship. This motion was rejected on July 31. Not long afterward, Giamatti set August 17, 1989, as the date for his hearing with Rose. One more appeal by Rose was refused by the United States Court of Appeals on this same day. Rose's back was to the wall, not only due to the damaging evidence of Dowd's report, but also because his tax-fraud case was going poorly. He was fighting a costly two-front legal war and he needed to make the best deal available as quickly as possible.

Surprisingly, Giamatti also had good reason to seek a deal. The length of the proceedings against Rose was distracting from, and some said ruining, the 1989 season. Also, Giamatti showed himself to be a potentially damaging witness for his own side while giving his deposition to Rose's legal team on July 29, during which he pontificated disjointedly, chain-smoked, showed radical mood swings, and was clearly in declining health. In *Collision at the Plate,* James Reston, Jr. observed, "In the days that followed the deposition, the strategists for major league baseball became profoundly worried, both for their case and for their commissioner's personal welfare." Fay Vincent, then deputy commissioner, tried to reach an agreement with Rose's legal team. Vincent was willing to commit to a finite but lengthy ban, but wanted definite language in the agreement that the cause of banishment was for gambling. Rose's lawyers wanted no language to this effect and in the end settled for a lifetime ban to avoid having to admit to gambling.

Rose agreed to sign a document that waived his right to continue legal action. While it banned him from the game for life, it did state that "Peter Edward Rose will conclude these proceedings before the commissioner without a hearing and the commissioner will not make any formal findings or determinations on any matter without limitation on the allegation that Peter Edward Rose bet on any

Major League Baseball game" and that "Nothing in this agreement shall be deemed either an admission or a denial by Peter Edward Rose of the allegation that he bet on any Major League Baseball game." Rose understood that he had little chance at reinstatement and election into the Hall of Fame if he admitted to baseball's biggest offense.

Much has been written and said about a possible under-the-table deal between the parties. It is highly unlikely that this took place, because the commissioner had too many cards in his hand. But it is clear by how the negotiation proceeded that Rose had a justified expectation that once the document was signed, Giamatti would, for the best interest of all involved, let the matter go. Rose would be suspended, he would do his time, and the matter would fall into the background.

Giamatti did not let the matter drop, which proved to be his final mistake in the affair. During the press conference at which the suspension was announced, Giamatti stated, "I have concluded that he bet on baseball." This was an unconscionable comment considering that his office had just arranged a deal with Rose's lawyers in which it was agreed that this was the worst possible statement that Giamatti could make. Certainly Rose's side would have been better off to fight it out in court than to have the matter end with such a definitive statement from the commissioner of the game. Giamatti's action, at a time so close to a peaceful resolution of the matter, so close to a process of negotiation where the obfuscation of the gambling allegations was key, is compelling evidence supporting those who hold that Giamatti had a vendetta against Rose.

Rose's fortunes did not improve even after baseball's ultimate censure. He pleaded guilty in his tax fraud case, and plea-bargained to have a charge of misreporting dropped in exchange for a guilty plea on two other years of underreporting of income, and was sentenced to five months in federal prison followed by three months in a halfway house. His behavior after banishment was uneven, at times unrepentant and at others contritely admitting a gambling addiction. Rose made frequent appearances at sports memorabilia shows, including one on television soon after his banishment. By the time he entered federal prison in Marion, Illinois, his standing with the league office and with baseball fans was extremely low.

Rose would have been eligible for the Baseball Hall of Fame in 1992. But before sportswriters could vote on the issue of his worthiness, organized baseball made one more blunder in the Rose case. The Board of Directors of the Hall of Fame decided that Rose's name could not be voted on for admission. This decision was aimed at sparing organized baseball the perceived embarrassment of having a banned player so enshrined. The decision was abhorrent to many on two counts; first, it was a vote of no confidence in the baseball press; and second, and more importantly, it eliminated a clear path to a clean ending to the Rose controversy. A vote by the press to admit Rose, either in 1992 or years later, would give the proper perspective to his legendary accomplishments as a player, while the ban from participation could live on as a stern example against flaunting the gambling rules.

Interestingly, Rose's legend may benefit more from a long ban from the game and exclusion from the Hall of Fame. Both provide the romance and tragedy necessary for a legend to grow even larger. As it stands, Rose must first be reinstated to be considered for the Hall of Fame. To be reinstated, Rose certainly will have to show contrition and rehabilitation, and while he has made progress in this area, Rose is too much of an iconoclast to live the "monkish" life that would likely be required for reinstatement. Thus Rose stands a fair chance of ending his days banned from the game he mastered.

But the day may well come when it will be a good public-relations move for organized baseball to pardon Rose. One clear statement on the Hall of Fame issue is a line heard repeatedly over the last few years which will soon become a cliché, if it is not already, though like many clichés it may become overused due to the obvious truth at its core: "Heaven is for saints. The Hall of Fame is for great ball players."

Selected Bibliography

Durney, J. "Fair or Foul? The Commissioner and Major League Baseball's Disciplinary Process." *Emery Law Journal* 41 (Spring 1992): 581–631.

Gutman, D. *Baseball Babylon.* Harmondsworth: Penguin Books, 1992.

Miller, M. *A Whole Different Game: The Sport and Business of Baseball.* New York: Birch Lane Press, 1991.

Neiman, P. "'Root, Root, Root for the Home Team': Pete Rose, Nominal Parties, and Diversity Jurisdictions." *New York University Law Review* 66 (April 1991): 148–188.

Fantasy Sports and the Law

William L. Wegman

Montana Code Annotated, 23-5-801-810 (1993)

Fantasy or "rotisserie" sports leagues attract the avid participation of millions of Americans. Thousands of leagues operate across the nation. Statistical services, newsletters, and books provide eagerly sought information and guidance for novices and veterans alike. Rotisserie baseball is the most widely played, but the action also includes football and basketball. After paying an entry fee, "team owners," either through an auction or a draft, select real players to fill the requisite positions. Accumulated seasonal production for each of the players and the team are totaled. The fantasy team with the most points wins the league and, in most operations, a significant portion of the entry fees.

Some rotisserie players received more than they expected from taking part in the popular pastime. Mick Lura, Executive Director of the Iowa Racing and Gaming Commission was given a one-week suspension in 1990 for his participation in a rotisserie baseball league. An investigation revealed that Lura used an office copying machine and computer, and played fantasy baseball during working hours. He lost about $1,600 in pay and decided to withdraw from the league.

A more significant episode involved Randy Bramos, a firefighter in North Lauderdale, Florida. Early in 1991, the Florida state attorney general issued an opinion that the prize money won by rotisserie leaguers represented illegal gambling. Players faced a misdemeanor charge, time in jail, and a fine. Bramos served as commissioner of a twelve-team league at the time of his arrest. Fantasy enthusiasts throughout the nation followed the case closely. They saw the Florida prosecution of Bramos as leading to a likely legal resolution of the central question of whether or not prize money constituted illegal gambling. Their expectation failed to materialize. The charges were dismissed after a Broward County judge determined the state had engaged in an illegal search of Bramos's property and that the evidence seized, primarily the notebook containing information about the "Fan-Addicts League," required suppression. Without the evidence, prosecutors decided to withdraw charges of second-degree gambling. Bramos, however, not only lost his thirteen-year job as a fire department lieutenant, but also faced about $30,000 in legal fees. Ironically, Florida allows betting on golf and bowling tournaments. It also permits the awarding of prizes in these two activities. The Sunshine State also permits gambling in various card games such as poker and bridge, so long as no single hand exceeds ten dollars in value.

Early in the 1990s, Montana passed the first law in the nation permitting gambling on fantasy sports if organized via a formal fantasy league. The law defined a fantasy sports league as consisting "of a limited number of persons or groups of persons who pay an entrance fee for membership in the league." The legislation provided for members' eligibility to "receive a payout based on the number of points accumulated." It also allowed the payout to take the form of cash or prizes.

Many states make the determination of whether or not the activity is illegal gambling by placing a daily limit on the amount that one can win or lose. If, however, one participates in a fantasy sports league, which occurs over an entire sports season and in which one might win several hundred dollars at the conclusion of the season, the issue becomes more complicated. Did the person in first place win the prize money only at the conclusion of the season or over the entire season? A league whose season runs for a period of 180 days, at $50 per day, would be able to legally award up to $9,000, if it were determined that the money was won over the entire season. Inasmuch as statistics are accumulated over all the days that make up the season, it can be reasonably argued that the money awarded was earned not on the final day but over the entire 180 days. Montana decided to exempt bona-fide leagues and the players from subjection to the state's gambling laws.

Another issue is whether winning in a fantasy sports league represents merely luck or a reasonable amount of skill. Unlike playing a slot machine, successful fantasy team owners must demonstrate considerable expertise. They decide on complicated questions such as the amount to offer for an established player, the length of contract extension, replacements for injured players, and trades. To remain competitive, the rotisserie executive must demonstrate preparedness and knowledge. One can argue that success in a fantasy sports league is no more a case of gambling than investing wisely in the stock market.

Most team owners seem more concerned with a high position in the final standings than with the money they might win. Perhaps the best solution is to legalize the concept of fantasy leagues but to limit the maximum amount earned to a figure acceptable to the entire community. A person might participate avidly in a rotisserie league that only awards a trophy to the season winner. Other money remaining from the entry fees could go to providing a mid-winter trading session banquet.

Fantasy sports leagues represent an area demanding legislation. Millions of Americans play fantasy sports and most do not regard themselves as criminals. Unless the concepts contained in the Montana law are duplicated, however, many otherwise law-abiding citizens may find themselves in the same situation as former firefighter Bramos.

Selected Bibliography

Cobb, N. "Rotiss: The Greatest Game for Baseball Fans Since Baseball." *Smithsonian* 21 (June 1990): 100–112.

USA Today, August 21, 1991.

Walsh, M. "In New York: Major League Fantasies." *Time.* May 4, 1987: 10–11.

Part Three

Sports Law: The Rights of Players and Owners

Many people participate in the games we call sports for the sheer pleasure they provide. But for professional athletes and franchise owners, the *sine qua non* for playing the game is money. Players demand compensation, the freedom to market their services, and fair treatment in disciplinary cases. Owners require a return on their investments and also some ancillary perquisites (such as a percentage of concessions sold at the games). The essays in Part III probe cases that concern the legal rights of players and owners, almost all of which come down to dollars and cents.

The first three essays on the rights of players deal with baseball. "When a Professional Sport Is Not a Business" offers a detailed analysis of legal cases, especially the landmark 1922 United States Supreme Court decision concerning the question of whether baseball is a game rather than a business. The next essay, "Let the Bidding Begin: Free Agency Comes to Baseball," describes court decisions in the mid-1970s that gave a great deal of freedom to players. "Baseball Owners Called 'Out' for Collusion" reveals the unsuccessful tactics employed by owners in attempting to circumvent free agency.

Three essays treat developments in professional football. "Joe Kapp's Fight for Free Agency" examines an effort in the 1970s to achieve free agent status. The next article, "Tight End Mackey Blocks Commissoner Rozelle," explains the legal battle against the so-called Rozelle Rule. Rounding out the football cases, "These People Just Plain Don't Like Each Other," brings the story into the 1990s with the *McNeil* v. *National Football League* decision.

"Oscar Robertson: The Player and the Case" continues the topic of the rights of players, focusing on the "Big O" and his effort to achieve freedom to negotiate for professional basketball players. The next essay, "The Letter of Intent and Collegiate Athletes," explores the experiences of two student athletes after they signed letters of intent. In "Agents, Athletes, and Academics," the reader will find a discussion of the limitations placed upon agents seeking to represent college players. The final essay, "Minnesota Gopher Basketball: Problems on the Court and in the Courts," investigates the rights to due process in two University of Minnesota cases in the 1970s.

Opening up the the topic of the rights of owners, "Sports Broadcasting: Who Owns the Property Rights?" examines legal cases stretching from the late 1930s through the early 1990s. The next essay, "The Land of the Free Disputes Homes for the Braves," examines the legal conflicts surrounding the movement of the Milwaukee Braves major league baseball team to Atlanta in the mid-1960s. "Fear, Attack, and Pressure: The Relocation of the Raiders" probes into the complicated lawsuits related to the Oakland Raiders National Football League team and their aggressive managing partner, Al Davis. The following essay, "Colts Gallop to Indianapolis," discusses the way in which football team owner Robert Irsay took his Colts out of Baltimore and into Hoosier land. The final essay on the rights of owners, "The NFL-AFL Merger: Law, Politics, and the Power of Money," offers a detailed investigation of a crucial development in professional football in the 1960s.

When a Professional Sport Is Not a Business

Baseball's Infamous Antitrust Exemption

John W. Johnson

Federal Baseball Club of Baltimore, Inc. v. National League of Professional Baseball Clubs, et al., 259 U.S. 200 (1922).

Toolson v. New York Yankees, Inc. et al., 346 U.S. (1953).

Flood v. Kuhn et al., 407 U.S. 258 (1972).

It begins:

It is a century and a quarter since the New York Nine defeated the Knickerbockers 23 to 1 on Hoboken's Elysian Fields June 19, 1846, with Alexander Jay Cartwright as the instigator and the umpire. The teams were amateur, but the contest marked a significant date in baseball's beginnings.

And it continues:

Then there are the many names, celebrated for one reason or another, that have sparked the diamond and its environs and that have provided tinder for recaptured thrills, for reminiscence and comparisons, and for conversation and anticipation in-season and off-season: Ty Cobb, Babe Ruth, Tris Speaker, Walter Johnson, Henry Chadwick, Eddie Collins, Lou Gehrig, Grover Cleveland Alexander, Rogers Hornsby, Harry Hooper, Goose Goslin, Jackie Robinson, Honus Wagner. . . . The list seems endless.

No, these quotations are not from a pedantic history of baseball or from a formalistic address by a baseball commissioner. Rather, they appear at the beginning of one of the most unusual United

States Supreme Court opinions in the more than two hundred-year history of the nation's highest court. The case was *Flood* v. *Kuhn*, decided in 1972. The author of the majority opinion from which the quotations are drawn was Associate Justice Harry Blackmun, best known for his still controversial majority opinion in the 1973 abortion case, *Roe* v. *Wade*.

Blackmun's paean to baseball in *Flood* v. *Kuhn* was written from the unabashed perspective of a dedicated fan. The specific question in the case was whether Curt Flood, a fine major league ball player of the 1960s, would have to accept a management-authorized trade from the St. Louis Cardinals to a rival National League club, the Philadelphia Phillies, or whether he could refuse the trade and proceed to market his services to a higher bidder or a team otherwise more to his liking than the Phillies.

The larger issue in the *Flood* case was whether baseball was a business or a game. As a business it would be subject to federal antitrust legislation, but as a game it could continue to be controlled by the team owners. Millions of dollars in salaries and other financial considerations were riding on Curt Flood's aversion to Philadelphia. Moreover, bringing baseball within the gambit of antitrust legislation could alter the very basis by which the game had operated for almost a century.

Flood v. *Kuhn* did not mark the first time that the nation's highest court had considered whether baseball should be subject to antitrust regulation. Twice before in the twentieth century the Supreme Court had directly faced this question. And both times it held that baseball was a game, not a business. In *Flood* v. *Kuhn* the Supreme Court took this position yet a third time. To understand fully what many commentators have found to be the tortured logic underpinning baseball's antitrust exemption, it is helpful to review each of the three Supreme Court decisions on the subject.

The first case was a 1922 decision, *Federal Baseball Club of Baltimore, Inc.* v. *National League of Professional Baseball Clubs, et al.* This case involved a suit by a "base ball" club incorporated in Maryland against the American and National Baseball leagues and various officials of major league baseball. The Federal Baseball Club of Baltimore had, prior to the suit, been a member of the Federal League of Professional Base Ball Clubs. The Federal League, founded in

1914, had attempted to become the third major league. The American and National leagues responded to this threat by blacklisting all players who had the temerity to play for a Federal League team. It was also alleged that the older leagues had effectively destroyed the Federal League by buying some of the clubs in that league or otherwise persuading clubs to abandon the league. By 1920, the Baltimore Federal Baseball Club was the only viable Federal League team that had not been absorbed by either the National or American League.

The Maryland club received an award of $80,000 in damages from a federal court in the District of Columbia. Under the terms of federal antitrust laws that figure was tripled to $240,000. On appeal to an intermediate appellate court, the award was reversed. Hence the Maryland club sought to exhaust its final opportunity for relief by appeal to the U.S. Supreme Court.

Article I, section 8 of the United States Constitution gives Congress the right to "regulate Commerce . . . among the several States." The Sherman Antitrust Act of 1890 granted Congress, pursuant to the constitutional language just quoted, the right to outlaw every "contract, combination . . . or conspiracy in restraint of trade or commerce." The Maryland club argued, in what appeared to be common sense fashion, that the activities of the National and American leagues effectively destroyed the Federal Baseball League and, thus, constituted a combination or conspiracy in restraint of trade. In a terse unanimous opinion, the revered Associate Justice Oliver Wendell Holmes saw things differently.

Holmes's opinion upheld the intermediate appeals court's decision to throw out the lower court verdict. The "Yankee from Olympus" stated that "the business is giving exhibitions of baseball, which are purely state affairs." Holmes acknowledged that teams had to travel across state lines routinely for these "exhibitions" but that "the transport is a mere incident, not the essential thing." What Holmes was saying was that the commerce that made the game possible—that is, interstate travel and financial transactions—was not determinate of the legal status of the game. The effect of the decision was to bolster the power of the two "major" leagues and the newly appointed baseball commissioner, Judge Kenesaw Mountain Landis.

Critics of the decision claimed that Holmes's narrow reading of the commerce clause was a throwback to such museum piece decisions as *U.S.* v. *E.C. Knight* (1890) in which the Court refused to break up a trust responsible for 95 percent of the sugar refining in the United States by blithely positing that "manufacturing is not commerce." Supporters of the *Federal Baseball Club* decision, on the other hand, said that Holmes's unanimous opinion helped to stabilize major league baseball at a perilous time in its history. When the decision was argued before the Supreme Court in 1922, baseball was still suffering from image problems as a result of the "Black Sox" World Series fixing scandal. In return for payoffs from gamblers, eight members of the Chicago White Sox team had allegedly thrown the 1919 World Series to the Cincinnati Redlegs. All the accused ballplayers were eventually found not guilty by a trial jury, but Commissioner Landis attempted to strike a blow for the integrity of the sport by imposing a lifetime ban against all eight White Sox players. Included among this unfortunate group was "Shoeless" Joe Jackson, one of the great stars of the era who has recently become a posthumous cause célèbre as portrayed in such popular films as "Field of Dreams" and "Eight Men Out."

At the time, it looked to many Court watchers as if the justices had gone out of their way to allow baseball to regulate itself rather than to appear to suggest that baseball was in such sorry ethical shape that it needed government regulation. Many years later, one baseball writer claimed that the decision favorable to the sport's ownership was influenced by the fact that Chief Justice William H. Taft was related to the Chicago Cubs' owner, Philip Wrigley.

The first serious legal criticism of the *Federal Baseball Club* decision came in a concurring opinion by Judge Jerome Frank in a 1949 Second Circuit Court of Appeals case, *Gardella* v. *Chandler*. This case involved a major league player who was blacklisted for signing with the Mexican League. In that case, Frank, an acerbic jurist and brilliant legal writer, referred to Holmes's 1922 decision as an "impotent zombi," submitting that the Supreme Court would certainly find that the Sherman and Clayton acts would apply to baseball if presented with the issue *de novo* (i.e., afresh). The *Gardella* case, however, was ultimately settled out of court, so the *Federal Baseball Club* precedent remained intact.

When another case involving baseball's antitrust exemption did reach the Supreme Court, Judge Frank's prediction as to the demise of Holmes's 1922 decision was proven wrong. In *Toolson* v. *New York Yankees, Inc. et al.* (1953), by a *per curiam* Supreme Court opinion (i.e. a "by the Court" opinion in which no individual justice claimed authorship), the Court reiterated and followed the 1922 *Federal Baseball Club* ruling. The *Toolson* case arose when a pitcher in the New York Yankee organization, George Toolson, refused to report to the Binghamton, New York, farm team to which he had been assigned by the parent team. The Yankee organization maintained that it had exclusive rights to Toolson's services. Under what was then and is still now known as the "reserve clause," each player in organized baseball has a contractual relationship under the current Major-Minor League Agreement which stipulates that the team that first signs a player possesses a "continuing and exclusive right" to the player's services. Similar reserve clauses had been written into baseball player contracts as far back as 1887. Their original purpose was to protect the established baseball leagues from raiding by the "outlaw leagues" that were common a century ago.

Baseball's modern reserve clause provides that, before a certain date each year, a club will "designate a reserve list of active and eligible players which it desires to reserve for the ensuing year. That no player on . . . [the] reserve list may thereafter be eligible to play for any other club until his contract has been assigned or until he has been released."

Toolson was on the Yankee's reserve list in the early 1950s. He refused to report to the Binghamton club to which he had been assigned by the Yankee organization. He also sued for his "freedom" from the Yankees, maintaining that organized baseball's reserve clause violated the Sherman and Clayton Acts since it interfered with the free flow of interstate commerce and denied him the opportunity to attempt to sell his services to other baseball organizations. In what must have seemed to Toolson like a self-fulfilling prediction, the Yankees responded to his recalcitrance to report to the Binghamton club by blacklisting him, effectively preventing his negotiations with any other baseball organizations.

When Toolson's case reached the Supreme Court in 1953 it was joined with two other challenges to baseball's antitrust exemption,

Kowalski v. *Chandler* and *Corbett* v. *Chandler*. In the lead case, Toolson argued that his situation was distinguishable—that is, substantially different—from the 1922 *Federal Baseball Club* precedent because major league baseball in the early fifties was not the same game it had been thirty years before. Regardless of what one might have thought about the alleged commercial status of baseball in the twenties, Toolson submitted that baseball by the fifties was clearly part of interstate commerce, particularly given the revenue generated from radio and television broadcasting and because the sport was marketed aggressively by multistate advertising campaigns.

In an unusual response to the one-paragraph *per curiam* opinion, two justices, Harold Burton and Stanley Reed, filed an eight-page dissent. Their essential point was that baseball was interstate commerce on a grand scale and, thus, should be subject to the strictures of the Sherman and Clayton Acts. They quoted at length from the report of a House of Representatives Subcommittee on Monopoly Power which offered specific documentation of the interstate, commercial character of the national pastime. For example, the report noted that in 1952 there were 380 baseball clubs operating in forty-two states, the District of Columbia, and three foreign countries (Canada, Cuba, and Mexico). These clubs were organized within fifty-two separate leagues, of which thirty-nine conducted competition among teams from two or more states. The dissent also presented data, culled from the House report, on the substantial revenue generated by the then sixteen major league clubs. In 1950, for example, major league baseball's gross receipts—collected from ticket sales, concessions, and radio/television payments—totaled $32 million.

In its short opinion, the Supreme Court emphasized that the game of baseball had been left to develop for a generation since the *Federal Baseball Club* decision without being subject to antitrust legislation. If there is (was) wisdom in changing this policy, the Court said that it should be done so by Congress, and, since Congress had been studying the matter recently and had failed to act, the Court was not willing to impose its own judgment, whatever that might be.

In the two decades following the *per curiam* opinion in *Toolson*, American courts handed down several rulings on the antitrust status of sports other than baseball. Across the board—in sports as diverse as boxing, golf, basketball, hockey, and football—the judiciary ruled that antitrust legislation held sway. Baseball with its antitrust exemption increasingly stood alone. Many legal experts ventured the opinion that the special treatment of baseball was untenable and that it would just be a matter of time before Congress or the federal courts would see fit to subject baseball to the same configuration of legal regulation as other professional sports.

But time continued to pass, and baseball remained—in a legal sense at least—a game and not a business. Between 1953 and 1972 more than fifty bills were introduced in Congress dealing with the question of extending antitrust regulation to baseball. Yet Congress failed to pass any of these measures.

The episode that triggered *Flood* v. *Kuhn,* the third Supreme Court opinion on baseball's exemption from antitrust coverage, was the October 1969 announcement that Curt Flood of the St. Louis Cardinals had been traded to the Philadelphia Phillies as part of a multiplayer deal. At the time of the trade, Flood was thirty-one years old and regarded as one of major league baseball's best players. In twelve seasons as a center fielder with the Cardinals he maintained a career batting average of .293 (with six seasons over .300), received seven Golden Glove awards for his fielding, and was co-captain of the squad from 1965 to 1969. Flood's salary for his 1969 season with the Cardinals was $90,000.

Flood was not consulted about the trade to the Phillies or even advised that one was in the offing. He learned about the trade by phone only after the details had been finalized by the teams involved. Flood protested what he felt was patronizing treatment to Commissioner of Baseball Bowie Kuhn. Flood demanded to be made a "free agent" and to be able to pursue opportunities with teams of his choosing. The commissioner denied his request. So, in January 1970, Flood filed suit in the Southern District of New York against the commissioner, the presidents of the two major leagues, and all twenty-four major league clubs. His complaint alleged that major league baseball had imposed upon him a form of peonage and involuntary servitude contrary to the Thirteenth Amendment and that baseball was in violation of federal antitrust and civil rights statutes, various state laws, and the common law. Flood sought an injunction to prohibit the trade and treble damages.

While his suit proceeded, Flood elected not to play for Philadelphia, despite a $100,000 salary offer for the 1970 season. One legal expert later wrote that Flood's reticence to accept the trade might have been inspired by W. C. Fields's epitaph, "I'd rather be dead than in Philadelphia." At the end of the 1970 season, Philadelphia sold its rights to Flood to the Washington Senators. Flood elected to accept the Senators' offer of $110,000 for the 1971 season, having extracted from the Senators and major league baseball a promise that playing for the Washington club would not prejudice his lawsuit against baseball. Flood started the 1971 season with the Senators but left them on April 27, unhappy with his performance. He did not play professional baseball again.

The defendants in Flood's suit filed various motions to dismiss. The injunction was denied, but a trial was held on the primary causes of action in May and June 1970. Sitting without a jury, the trial judge dismissed the involuntary servitude allegation because there was no "showing of compulsory service." He also threw out Flood's state law and common law allegations. Most importantly, the judge ruled that the *Federal Baseball Club* and *Toolson* decisions were controlling on the antitrust issues and found for the defendants. Flood appealed the judge's ruling. The Second Circuit Court of Appeals acknowledged that *"Federal Baseball Club* was not one of Mr. Justice Holmes' happiest days" but felt bound by the antitrust components of those decisions. The Circuit Court did not find it necessary to address Commissioner Kuhn's additional argument that, because the reserve system was by 1971 subsumed under the general collective bargaining agreement between major league baseball and the players' union, federal labor statutes and not federal antitrust laws were controlling.

Late in 1971 the Supreme Court granted *certiorari* (i.e., agreed to hear the case under its discretionary jurisdiction). The case was argued before the nation's highest court on March 20, 1972. Presenting the case for Flood before the Supreme Court was none other than Arthur Goldberg, a former Supreme Court justice and secretary of labor. Delivering the oral argument for the commissioner was Paul A. Porter, a distinguished Washington attorney from one of Washington, D.C.'s most powerful law firms.

On June 19, 1972, near the end of the Supreme Court's annual term, Justice Blackmun presented the opinion of the five-justice majority (Justice Lewis Powell did not take part in the case). Blackmun's opinion begins, as we have already seen, almost with a secular hymn to baseball. After discoursing reverently about baseball history, Blackmun recounted the facts in the Flood appeal, explained the procedural steps that brought the case to the Supreme Court, and reviewed the legal background of baseball's antitrust exemption, focusing on the *Federal Baseball Club* and *Toolson* decisions.

Finally, in the last four pages of his opinion, Blackmun pronounced the majority's conclusions. Although he acknowledged the interstate commercial character of baseball and the anomalous situation presented in the field of professional sports by having baseball alone stand outside the scope of antitrust legislation, Blackmun still concluded that the antitrust exemption should be maintained and that the reserve clause should be upheld. Notwithstanding the fact that courts had found that federal antitrust legislation applied to other interstate professional sports, Blackmun submitted that baseball's "aberration . . . has been with us now for half a century, one heretofore deemed fully entitled to the benefit of *stare decisis,* and one that has survived the Court's expanding concept of interstate commerce."

Baseball, Blackmun argued, had developed and expanded for half a century "unhindered by federal legislative action." The game, its practitioners, and its patrons had come to rely upon the antitrust exemption. Congress, as the Court had pointed out in the *Toolson* decision, had confronted scores of legislative proposals over many years to place baseball under the sway of the Sherman and Clayton Acts but had chosen not to enact any of these pieces of legislation. Blackmun put the matter simply: "We continue to be loath, 50 years after *Federal Baseball* and almost two decades after *Toolson,* to overturn those cases judicially when Congress, by its positive inaction, has allowed those decisions to stand . . . and, far beyond mere inference and implication, has clearly evinced a desire not to disapprove them legislatively."

If Congress does at some point elect to bring major league baseball under the dominion of federal antitrust legislation, Blackmun maintained that this would be preferable to a judicial overruling of the *Federal Baseball Club* decision because the effect of legislative change is "prospective" (i.e., applying only to the future), but a judicial reversal might be "retrospective" (i.e., applied to situations in the past) and, thus, require an alteration of long held business understandings and practices.

Perhaps in an attempt to confront accusations from the legal community that the Supreme Court was once again being inconsistent in holding baseball to a different standard of competitive regulation than other professional sports, Blackmun insisted: "If there is any inconsistency or illogic in all this, it is an inconsistency and illogic of long standing that is to be remedied by the Congress and not by this Court." Then, on the penultimate page of the majority opinion, Justice Blackmun expressed a sentiment that aptly encapsulated the Court's position that the reserve clause was legally acceptable and that baseball should maintain its antitrust exemption. He observed: "[T]here is merit in consistency even though some might claim that beneath that consistency is a layer of inconsistency." Devotees of Lewis Carroll's *Alice's Adventures in Wonderland* would have more tolerance for this dictum than would the Court's dissenting justices.

Justices William O. Douglas and Thurgood Marshall filed separate dissenting opinions. Justice William Brennan joined both opinions. Douglas referred to Justice Holmes's *Federal Baseball Club* decision as a "derelict in the stream of the law that we, its creator, should remove." He saw that decision as predicated on a "narrow, parochial view of commerce." To Douglas, the beneficiaries of baseball antitrust exemption are not the players, the fans, or the game of baseball generally; those who gain most from the exemption are the owners whose records, Douglas charged, "reveal a proclivity for predatory practices." Furthermore, Douglas expressed no sympathy whatsoever for the majority's claim that Congressional inaction necessarily signalled support of the antitrust exemption. To the contrary, Douglas argued that Congressional unwillingness to extend antitrust exemption to other professional sports should carry more weight than Congressional silence on the special case of baseball. He concluded his short opinion with a simple admonition to his brother justices: "The unbroken silence of Congress should not prevent us from correcting our own mistakes."

Justice Marshall's dissent, while tracking some of Douglas's argumentation on the danger of reading too much into Congressional inaction, took two additional tacks. He emphasized that baseball's reserve clause kept an athlete, even a highly paid one, in involuntary servitude. Marshall quoted with apparent sympathy from a letter that Curt Flood sent to Bowie Kuhn on Christmas Eve 1969 to the effect that he was being treated like "a piece of property to be bought and sold irrespective of my wishes." The other point addressed by Marshall concerned the allegedly disruptive effect that an overruling of the *Federal Baseball Club* decision would have on past business practices in the sport. Marshall's solution here was simple: have the Court announce that the overruling was prospective (i.e., affecting only future activities) and not retrospective.

Since 1972 the American legal community has not shown much sympathy for the three Supreme Court decisions upholding baseball's exemption from federal antitrust regulation. The general line of reasoning has followed that of the Douglas and Marshall dissents: baseball may be a great game, but professional baseball is big business that should be subject to the same antitrust network of regulation as that of other professional sports. The majority of legal experts who have written on the subject acknowledge that the line of Supreme Court opinions maintaining baseball's antitrust exemption may be consistent, but it is consistently wrong and deserves to be reversed by Court decision, if not by legislation. A number of legal-economic analyses have appeared in the last two decades in law reviews and economics journals attesting to the competitive advantage that baseball enjoys over other professional sports due to its independence from antitrust regulation.

The victory of the baseball owners in *Flood* v. *Kuhn* was undercut to a degree by the mid-seventies birth of "free agency." This came about when two pitchers, Andy Messersmith and Dave McNally, played the 1975 season without contracts and claimed that they were then free to negotiate with other teams as well as their current organizations. They took their grievances to arbitration, as permitted by the standard management-players agreement. Their subsequent victory in arbitration was upheld by the Eighth Circuit Court of Appeals in *Kansas City Royal Baseball Corporation* v. *Major League Baseball Players Association* (1976). The arbitrator and the appeals court agreed that the issue in dispute was not a decision for or against the reserve system but that it concerned the Uniform Players Contract and Major League Rules.

One of the reasons that the arbitrator and the appellate court could divorce free agency from the reserve clause is because baseball owners had successfully pushed to modify the collective bargaining agreement while the litigation in *Flood* v. *Kuhn* was still underway. Fearing that the Supreme Court might strike down the reserve system if it found baseball no longer exempt from antitrust regulation, the commissioner's office successfully had written into baseball's Collective Bargaining Agreement the words "this agreement does not deal with the reserve system." When the Supreme Court upheld the reserve system in 1972 this cautionary language struck some as an unnecessary redundancy. But that very language no doubt benefited the owners when the appeals court in the Messersmith-McNally case endorsed free agency but stopped short of compromising the reserve clause.

In the last fifteen years or so, free agency has allowed a few veteran stars to sell their services to the highest bidders—a recent notable case being Barry Bonds, now of the San Francisco Giants, who pursued free agency and ultimately signed a contract for almost $8 million a year for six years. But the persistence of the reserve clause has allowed baseball owners to keep their young marquee players under contract at below-market-level salaries for up to six years. Ken Griffey, Jr. of the Seattle Mariners, for example, could probably more than double his current salary if he were allowed to test the market; however, he does not yet have enough years in the major leagues to declare free agency.

As baseball moves into the last years of the twentieth century, the cry to remove its antitrust exemption is still sounded. For instance, in March 1993 Senator Howard Metzenbaum (Democrat, Ohio), chair of the Antitrust Subcommittee of the Senate Judiciary Committee, introduced legislation to repeal baseball's antitrust exemption. At the time he introduced his bill, Metzenbaum asserted that "giving . . . baseball owners free rein to decide what's in the best interests of the game is like giving the members of OPEC free rein to set world energy policy." Metzenbaum's bill did not come to a vote in 1993, but similar legislation is once again before Congress.

At the end of the 1993–94 term of the Supreme Court, Justice Harry Blackmun, the author of the Court's *Flood* v. *Kuhn* decision which enunciated the Supreme Court's 1972 restatement of baseball's antitrust exemption, resigned. Upon the announcement of his resignation, Blackmun was celebrated as an honorable, common-sense jurist who had the capacity to grow intellectually after putting on his Supreme Court robes.

Regrettably for the legal legacy of Justice Blackmun, the antitrust exemption he grudgingly restated in *Flood* v. *Kuhn* no longer makes common sense, if it ever did. A recent U.S. district court case cogently illustrates this point. In *Vincent M. Piazza* v. *Major League Baseball* (1993), a federal judge in Pennsylvania, John R. Padova, considered the complaint that the major league baseball owners had illegally thwarted the efforts of Piazza and others to purchase the San Francisco Giants and move the team to Tampa Bay, Florida. In the course of a thorough and provocative opinion, Judge Padova declared that baseball's antitrust exemption encompassed only the reserve system and did not extend to the entire business of baseball. In October 1994 the Florida Supreme Court came to a similar conclusion. Since the reserve system had been substantially undercut by free agency, the Pennsylvania and Florida court decisions, if extended or upheld by the U.S. Supreme Court, would leave baseball's antitrust exemption virtually meaningless.

As we have seen, for over seventy years attempts to bring baseball into competitive parity with other professional sports have failed. Given the history of baseball's antitrust exemption recounted above, it is safe to say that future attempts to remove or modify this legal anomaly will be hotly contested by baseball owners because they see the exemption as a key element in their financial control of the game.

Behind the recent efforts to subject major league baseball to antitrust regulation have been a series of publicized occurrences which call into serious question whether professional baseball as it is now structured is acting in the "best interests of the game." One of the most obvious of these was at issue in the *Piazza* case: why should an owner be prevented by a coalition of other owners from selling his team to investors who want to relocate the franchise to an area that has been lusting for a major league franchise for years? Other incidents embarrassing to the game include: the owner of the Cincinnati Reds receiving a slap on the wrist for her documented series of racist comments; major league baseball persisting in the virtual exclusion of racial minorities from management positions, even though a majority of its players are African-American or Latino; and the owners of the twenty-eight major league baseball teams being unwilling or unable (as of May 1994) to hire a commissioner of baseball to replace Fay Vincent, who resigned in anger in 1992.

Despite the protests of baseball purists, the American and National leagues reshuffled their divisional alignment in 1994 and adopted an expanded playoff system that will prolong an already too long season, perhaps even into November. Major league baseball will now approach professional basketball and hockey in terms of the number of teams that have the opportunity to play for a "world championship." Although baseball has attempted to promote the expanded playoff system on the basis that it will increase fan interest in a greater number of cities, the more important impetus for the new format is financial: baseball owners see this as a way to recoup some of the money that will be lost when baseball's new and less munificent television contract goes into effect.

Recent estimates are that a family of four attending a major league baseball game spends between $75–$100 on tickets, parking, ballpark food, and souvenirs. This may seem a steep price to pay for an afternoon at the park, but, compared to attending a National Football League or National Basketball Association game, a major league baseball game is still a bargain. A cheap seat (without brats, programs, and beer) can still be had in several major league parks for five dollars or less. Whether because of low ticket prices, good promotion, or just luck, attendance at major league baseball games was never better than in 1993. For instance, a first-year expansion team, the Colorado Rockies, drew four million fans to its home park in that year. Attractive new parks which opened in the 1990s in Baltimore, Chicago, Cleveland, and Arlington, Texas, also sparked fan interest in major league baseball.

As healthy as major league baseball seemed on the surface, off-the-field bumbling has recently led to the worst crisis in the game's history since the Black Sox Scandal of 1919. In the summer of 1994, while players in both leagues chased time-honored records in several batting categories, an impasse off the field led to a debacle from which the game will not soon recover. Very much a part of this situation is baseball's now doddering antitrust exemption.

The twenty-six major league owners, claiming financial hardship due to escalating player salaries and declining television revenues, sought to institute a "salary cap," that is, a maximum total salary for the players on each team, similar in concept to the team limits currently prevailing in professional football and basketball. Major league baseball players and their union negotiators, however, adamantly refused to accept a salary cap. On August 12, when no compromise seemed possible, the players went on strike. A few weeks later the remainder of the season, including the expanded new playoff scheme and the World Series, was cancelled. Thus, the 1994 season, one of the best in recent memory, came to a screeching halt.

Legal experts and sports journalists conferred most of the blame for the abortive 1994 baseball season upon the owners, suggesting that their financial condition was much healthier than their creative bookkeeping proclaimed. Fans, however, tended to direct their anger at both camps—blasting each group as a bunch of greedy, spoiled millionaires.

Throughout the fall of 1994, instead of reading about the playoffs and the World Series, fans perusing the sports pages were faced with dense, legalistic stories about the likelihood of a Congressional repeal of baseball's antitrust exemption. If baseball were made subject to the same antitrust laws as were other professional sports, the argument went, the players could go to court to keep the owners from imposing a salary cap or other unpopular work rules. Without the antitrust exemption, baseball owners would have to engage in collective bargaining on a more equal footing with the players.

Legislation to repeal the antitrust exemption was proposed in both houses of Congress. One bill even received approval from the Judiciary Committee of the House of Representatives. However, Congress adjourned on October 7 before the repeal legislation could come to the floor of the lower chamber for debate.

During the final third of 1994, representatives of the owners and players met several times with a federal mediator, attempting to hammer out a new labor contract that would allow major league baseball to resurrect itself. Arbitration failed, with both sides sticking to their guns: the owners insisted that a salary cap was necessary to control costs, and the players refused to accept any new bargaining agreement that included a salary cap. Finally, on December 23, 1994, the owners ended any pretense of negotiations by rejecting the players' latest proposal and voted to impose a salary cap. In the words of the chief management negotiator: "due to the continued existense [sic] of this deadlock and the need to prepare for the 1995 season, [the owners' executive council] . . . voted to exercise Major League Baseball's right under federal labor law to implement the clubs' final salary cap proposal." Baseball fans had received a big lump of coal in their Christmas stockings.

In early 1995, instead of talk of spring training, baseball's *opera buffa* continued. The National Labor Relations Board (NLRB) announced that it was considering lodging an unfair labor practices complaint against the owners for, among other things, the imposition of the salary cap. As a result, on February 3 the owners abandoned the salary cap. Talks between the owners and players continued in fits and starts through February and early March, with the owners grooming "replacement players" to begin the 1995 season. Attendance at spring training games was down, with fans exhibiting little enthusiasm for the no-name players.

In late March the NLRB once again threatened to issue an unfair labor practices complaint against the owners—this time for unilaterally eliminating salary arbitration and free-agent bidding. The players' general counsel then sought an injunction to restore the eliminated features of the agreement and allow the players to begin the 1995 season under the old work rules and 1994 salaries. On March 31 U.S. District Judge Sonia Sotomayor granted the players' request for an injunction, thus ordering the owners to restore free-agent bidding, salary arbitration, and the anticollusion provisions of the former players' contract. The players' union immediately announced an end to the strike.

In the wake of Judge Sotomayor's injunction, the owners contemplated, but decided against, a lockout. But they did appeal the injunction. On April 4 the injunction was upheld by a three-judge panel of the Second U.S. Circuit Court of Appeals. The owners elected not to appeal the stay of the injunction to the U.S. Supreme Court, and they quickly delivered walking papers to the replacement players. By mutual agreement, the owners and players announced that Opening Day would be postponed until April 25 and that the 1995 season would take place with about 144 games per team (down from the normal 162).

The end of the 1994–95 baseball strike does not mean that the game is back to normal. The injunction simply delayed the day of reckoning for the salary cap, free agency, and other collective bargaining issues dividing the players and owners. These must be hammered out or another stoppage of the game is possible. In addition, the fate of baseball's antitrust exemption is still up in the air.

Just as the baseball strike was winding down in late March, the U.S. Court of Appeals for the District of Columbia issued a ruling regarding professional football that may have implications for the summer game. In a 2–1 decision in *Brown* v. *Pro Football Inc.,* Chief Judge Harry Edwards wrote for the appeals court majority that "injecting antitrust liability into the system for resolving disputes between unions and employers would both subvert national labor policy and exaggerate federal antitrust concerns." One reading of this decision is that, even if baseball's antitrust exemption is removed, the players' union would have to decertify before it could file suit against the owners on antitrust grounds.

As of this writing (April 1995), there are indications that the new Republican-dominated Congress will give serious consideration to legislation altering baseball's anomalous legal status as a game and not a business. But, until Congress or the Supreme Court acts, Justice Holmes's "impotent zombi"—baseball's more than seventy-year-old antitrust exemption—continues to haunt the diamond.

Selected Bibliography

Balfour, A. and P.K. Porter. "The Reserve Clause in Professional Sports: Legality and Effect on Competitive Balance." *Labor Law Journal* (January 1991): 8–18.

Classen, H.W. "Three Strikes and You're Out: An Investigation of Professional Baseball's Antitrust Exemption." *Akron Law Review* 21 (Spring 1988): 369–390.

Curle, D. "'On Higher Ground': Baseball and the Rule of *Flood* vs. *Kuhn.*" *Legal Reference Services Quarterly* 8 (1988): 29–62.

"Flood in the Land of Antitrust: Another Look at Professional Athletics, the Antitrust Laws and the Labor Law Exemption." *Indiana Law Review* 7 (1974): 541–578.

Holahan, W.L. "The Long-Run Effects of Abolishing the Baseball Player Reserve System." *The Journal of Legal Studies* 7 (January 1978): 129–137.

Jacobs, M.S. and R.K. Winter, Jr. "Antitrust Principles and Collective Bargaining by Athletes: Of Superstars in Peonage." *The Yale Law Journal* 81 (November 1971): 1–29.

Martin, P.L. "The Labor Controversy in Professional Baseball: The *Flood* Case." *Labor Law Journal* (September 1972): 567–571.

Rogers, C.P. III. "Judicial Reinterpretation of Statutes: The Example of Baseball and the Antitrust Laws." *Houston Law Review* 14 (March 1977): 611–634.

Let the Bidding Begin

Free Agency Comes to Baseball

Scott Katz

***Kansas City Royals Baseball Corporation* v. *Major League Baseball Players Association*, 409 F. Supp. 233 (1976)**

***Kansas City Royals Baseball Corporation* v. *Major League Baseball Players Association*, 532 F. 2d 615 (1976)**

***National and American League Professional Baseball Clubs* v. *Major League Baseball Players Association*, 66 Labor Arbitration 101 (1975)**

Forty-seven million dollars for six years' work. Salaries such as this are possible because baseball operates on a free agency system. Free agency allows a player after six years of continuous service to negotiate with any of the major league teams for a contract. If a player is good enough he will probably receive multiple offers.

This system was not always in place. Prior to 1976, under the "reserve clause," teams had exclusive and permanent rights to their players' services, and the only way a player could become a free agent was for his team to release him. If a team released a player, it was unlikely that the player's ability warranted other teams bidding over his contract.

Free agency did not initially come to baseball through any agreement between the club owners (League) and the player's union (Players Association). Instead, it came about through an arbitration decision in 1976 involving pitchers Andy Messersmith and Dave McNally and the Kansas City Royals. A court case between the League and the Players Association that same year made the arbitration decision binding.

Even prior to the Messersmith-McNally decision, the reserve

system had come under attack in an arbitration hearing concerning Jim "Catfish" Hunter. Pitching for the Oakland Athletics, Hunter won 106 games during the 1970–74 seasons. In the last year, Hunter recorded twenty-five victories and received the American League's Cy Young award. Off the field later in 1974, Hunter initiated a grievance against the Athletics' owner, Charles O. Finley, contending that Finley had defaulted in payments. Hunter sought the amounts owed by Finley but, more significantly, also sought free agent status. In December 1974, a three-member arbitration panel, by a two-to-one vote, ordered Finley to pay Hunter the amounts due plus interest, and also ruled Hunter a free agent.

Baseball is subject to the Collective Bargaining Agreement between the Players Association and the League. A collective bargaining agreement is an agreement between management and a union as to wages, benefits, and conditions of employment. The agreement in effect during the Messersmith, McNally, and Hunter controversies covered the period January 1, 1973, to December 31, 1975. Disputed provisions in that agreement were the arbitration of grievances and the reserve system.

When a player joins a team, he signs the Uniform Players Contract, a standard contract between the clubs and individual players containing certain general provisions agreed upon by the League and Players Association that are the same for all players. More specific provisions, such as salary, are decided between individual players and their clubs.

The Major League Rules are also the result of agreements between the League and the Players Association. These rules contain provisions as to what a player or team owner may or may not do. For example, the Major League Rules state that teams may reserve forty players and other teams may not tamper with players who are currently under contract with their teams.

During the time of the Messersmith and McNally dispute, Article XIII of the Collective Bargaining Agreement and Section 9(a) of the Uniform Players Contract incorporated the Major League Rules into the parties' agreements. Thus, there were three agreements acting together. The Collective Bargaining Agreement governed the conditions of employment, the Uniform Players Contract governed specific provisions between the player and the club and, finally, the

Major League Rules governed what the clubs and players could or could not do.

The reserve system functioned via the use of several provisions of the Collective Bargaining Agreement, Uniform Players Contract, and Major League Rules all working in concert. There was no specific provision in any of the agreements that directly mentioned a reserve clause or system. Instead, the reserve system was understood to be, and had functioned as, an integral part of baseball for many years.

Provision 10a of the Uniform Players Contract stated that the team had the right to renew the player's contract for an additional year at the team's discretion. The player did not need to consent or even sign this new contract. Rule 4A(a) of the Major League Rules gave the team the right to reserve forty players until those players' contracts were assigned or released. Rule 3(g) of the Major League Rules, a rule against tampering, stated that once a player was contracted or reserved by a team, no other team could negotiate with that player to get that player under contract. Thus, players reserved under Rule 4A(a), or whose contracts were automatically renewed for another year under Provision 10(a) of the Uniform Players Contract, could not negotiate with other teams via Rule 3(g).

For example, prior to 1976 the New York Yankees could have ensured that star first baseman Don Mattingly would never leave the team. Using Rule 4A(a) they could have reserved Mattingly at the end of his prior contract. Rule 3(g), the no tampering provision, ensured that no other team could negotiate with him. If Mattingly decided not to sign a new contract with the Yankees, they could automatically renew Mattingly's contract for one year using Provision 10(a) of the Uniform Players Contract. The new contract contained the same provisions as the old contract. At the end of the one-year renewal period, the Yankees had the right to renew the contract again, for another one-year period, since the same provisions applied. In effect, the Yankees could perpetually renew Mattingly's contract. Thus, once Mattingly signed onto the Yankees, it would have been within the sole discretion of the Yankees whether he could play for any other major league team during his baseball career.

Article X of the Collective Bargaining Agreement provided that grievances between players and the League would be filed with an arbitration panel containing one arbitrator chosen by the Players Association, one chosen by the League, and a third person agreed upon by the two selected arbitrators. A grievance was defined as "a complaint which involve[d] the interpretation of or compliance with" provisions of the Collective Bargaining Agreement. The arbitration panel could only interpret, apply, or determine compliance with the provisions. The panel did not have the authority or jurisdiction to alter the provisions in any way.

However, the Collective Bargaining Agreement contained a snag in regard to the reserve system. Since it had been possible that the Supreme Court might strike down the reserve system in the *Flood* v. *Kuhn* case in 1972 on the grounds that it violated antitrust laws, the Players Association and the League at that time entered a provision, Article XV, into the Collective Bargaining Agreement stating that "this agreement does not deal with the reserve system." It was thought this would ensure that the entire Collective Bargaining Agreement could not be ruled invalid if the reserve system were found contrary to the antitrust laws. As it happened, in the *Flood* case the Supreme Court ruled that baseball was exempt from antitrust laws, but Article XV was retained in the Collective Bargaining Agreement.

So at the time of the Messersmith-McNally cases there was a reserve system that allowed owners perpetual contract renewal, a collective bargaining agreement that contained a provision for arbitration of grievances, and, at the same time, a statement (Article XV) that the agreement itself did "not deal with the reserve system."

Messersmith was a pitcher for the Los Angeles Dodgers. He played in 1974 under contract for $90,000. After that year, the Dodgers used Provision 10(a) to automatically renew Messersmith's contract, which set the salary at $115,000. But Messersmith refused to sign because the new contract did not contain a no-trade provision. Messersmith pitched the 1975 season without signing a new contract. At the end of the season, Messersmith declared that the contractual relationship between himself and the Los Angeles Dodgers had ended. Since he had played his renewal year, he was a free agent, free to negotiate with all of the clubs.

McNally, a pitcher with the Montreal Expos, like Messersmith played the 1975 season without signing a contract. Midway through the 1975 season McNally decided to retire from baseball and like Messersmith, contended that the contractual relationship between himself and the Expos had expired and that he was a free agent.

On October 7, 1975, a grievance was filed by the Players Association on behalf of Messersmith. Two days later a second grievance was filed on behalf of McNally. These grievances asked that both Messersmith and McNally be declared free of their contractual relationship with their respective teams. Thus, they would achieve free-agent status and be able to negotiate with all the major league teams. Eventually these two grievances were merged because of their similarity. In accordance with Article X (arbitration) of the Collective Bargaining Agreement, these grievances were to be brought before an arbitration panel which would convene beginning November 21, 1975.

On October 28, 1975, the Kansas City Royals brought suit in federal court to obtain a declaratory judgment that these grievances could not be brought before an arbitration panel and sought an injunction to stop the arbitration, invoking Article XV to the effect that since the Collective Bargaining Agreement "[did] not deal with the reserve system," the arbitration panel could not consider the matter. The Players Association responded by asking for an order forcing the League to arbitrate. The court ruled to stay its proceedings until after the arbitration panel had ruled. The arbitration panel was allowed to rule on its own jurisdiction to decide if it could properly hear the matter.

By filing the suit, the League preserved its objection to the panel's jurisdiction. Further, if the panel did not rule in the League's favor, it gave them a "second chance" at arguing the merits of their case. Once losing on the merits of their case at arbitration, however, the League would have to show that the decision was clearly contrary to the Collective Bargaining Agreement in order to win at trial.

The League presented three main contentions to the arbitration panel. First was the jurisdictional argument involving Article XV mentioned earlier. Second, there was an argument on the merits of the case at issue. Here the League argued that during the renewal year the same provisions were included in the new contract as were in the previous one. Provision 10(a) of the Uniform Players Contract stated that the team had the right to renew a player's contract, and when the same contract was renewed, the team once again incurred the right to renew a player's contract for an additional year. This, the League argued, was what a player agreed to by signing the Uniform Players Contract, which was the reserve system in full effect, and which could not be tampered with by arbitration. Further, the League contended that the system had been understood to function in this fashion since the 1890s.

In conjunction with the above argument, the League added that even if the renewal year were not included in the new contract, the club still had the right to reserve the player under Major League Rule 4A(a). This rule gave the club the right to reserve forty players. The Los Angeles Dodgers had filed all the paperwork with the proper authorities and invoked their privilege to reserve Messersmith. Thus, under Rule 3(g), the no-tampering provision, no other club could negotiate with him.

Finally, the League gave a general argument regarding the future status of the sport of baseball if the arbitration panel were to rule against them. The League contended that baseball would suffer irreparable harm if the longstanding reserve system were to be destroyed, because, as free agents, players would have no motivation to stay with their present teams, and the good players would all go to the "big money" teams.

The Players Association replied that the question was properly brought before an arbitration panel. They contended that this dispute did not "deal with the reserve system" but, instead, "involve[d] the interpretation of or compliance with" provisions of the Uniform Players Contract, and the Major League Rules. Thus, the grievances were properly brought before the arbitration panel under Article X of the Collective Bargaining Agreement.

The Players Association also argued that the renewal clause only applied to the first year the player played without signing a new contract. After the end of this renewal year, a player no longer had a contractual relationship with the club because there was no signed contract to renew. Thus, the player was now a free agent and able to negotiate with all the clubs.

Finally, the Players Association contended that in order for the club to invoke Major League Rule 4A(a) and place a player on the reserve list, there had to have been a preexisting contractual relationship. Since Messersmith's and McNally's contractual relationship ended with the completion of their renewal year, the League could not properly invoke Rule 4A(a), and a player was no longer subject to the no-tampering provision in Rule 3(g) as well.

The arbitration panel, in compliance with Article X, consisted of three people, and they were the same people who heard the Hunter grievance: Marvin Miller, the executive director of the Players Association, chosen by his organization; John Gaherin (the dissenter in the Hunter decision), head negotiator for the League, chosen by the League; and Peter Seitz, a New York lawyer and arbitrator, the impartial chairman selected by Miller and Gaherin. Over the course of three days the panel studied 842 pages of testimony and 97 exhibits. On December 23, 1975, Seitz ruled in favor of the Players Association. In a sixty-one-page opinion Seitz supported his decision with a variety of arguments.

First, Seitz ruled that the arbitration panel had jurisdiction over the matter. Seitz pointed out that the League's argument contained a major contradiction. The League reported that Article XV should be interpreted as stating that the Collective Bargaining Agreement had nothing to do with the reserve system. Provisions within that very agreement, however, made up the reserve system. Article XIII of the Collective Bargaining Agreement incorporated the Major League Rules into the Collective Bargaining Agreement. Thus, Rule 4A(a), the right to reserve forty players, and Rule 3(g), the no-tampering provision, were inherently part of the Collective Bargaining Agreement that, purportedly, "[did] not deal with the reserve system."

Seitz also cited the evolution of Article XV's inclusion in the 1973 Collective Bargaining Agreement. This provision originated during the time when *Flood* v. *Kuhn* was still under litigation, a case which was a direct attack on the reserve clause. Using this reasoning Seitz found that Article XV was inserted to prevent a challenge to the reserve system itself. Seitz ruled with the Players Association, stating this dispute did not directly attack the reserve system, but rather it was a case of how to interpret provisions that made up the reserve system.

Seitz also compared Provision 10(a), the renewal clause, to similar provisions that existed in the National Basketball Association's constitution. The NBA's renewal provisions had been brought before courts in both Ohio and California, and in both these cases the courts found that the renewal provision in basketball extended the contract for the renewal year only. Seitz found that the substantially similar provision in baseball's Uniform Players Contract should be construed in the same fashion.

Next, Seitz referred to the language contained within the Major League Rules that purported to make up part of the reserve clause to dismiss the League's contention that Messersmith and McNally were subject to Rule 4A(a). Seitz cited multiple provisions contained within the Collective Bargaining Agreement that presupposed the existence of a player's contract with the club. Even Rule 4A(a) itself used the language "until his contract ha[d] been assigned . . ." In fact, in almost all the rules that contained a reference to the reserve system there was a reference to a preexisting contract between the player and the club. Seitz concluded that once the contract between the club and the player expired so did that club's right to reserve the player and to subject the player to the no-tampering provision. Thus, since Messersmith and McNally had both finished their renewal year and the contractual relationship between them and their teams had expired, they could no longer be on a team's "reserve list."

Finally, Seitz dismissed the League's argument that a ruling against the League would destroy the reserve system and, ultimately, baseball itself. Seitz found that this argument was based on "speculations as to what may ensue." Seitz would not base his decision about the interpretation of these provisions on what might or might not occur in the future.

Throughout his decision Seitz made it clear that this was not a decision for or against the reserve system or its merits. Instead, it was a decision based on "only one aspect of a complicated system." Seitz further emphasized the importance that these disputes be resolved through the formation of the next Collective Bargaining Agreement since the parties are best able to decide exactly what provision would be necessary to ensure an effective and fair reserve system.

Immediately following the decision of the arbitration panel, the League resumed its court battle to have the jurisdiction of the case taken away from the arbitration panel. The League also wanted the court to rule that declaring Messersmith and McNally free agents was a flagrant violation of the arbitrator's power and clearly contrary to the Collective Bargaining Agreement. The League argued that the arbitrators failed to take into account the historical operation of the reserve system, which was always understood to be a perpetual right of renewal.

The district court ruled in favor of the Players Association, finding the panel's jurisdiction proper, and the merits not contrary to the Collective Bargaining Agreement. The League appealed the case to the Federal Court of Appeals (8th Circuit), which upheld the lower court's decision for the Players Association. The appellate court followed the same logic as Seitz, finding that the arbitration panel had jurisdiction. Regarding the historical operation of the reserve system as a perpetual right of renewal, the court stated that there was no express provision that allowed it to interpret the reserve system in this manner. The court expressed no opinion on the merits of the reserve system, suggesting that the League and the Players' Association should draft a comprehensive agreement that would preserve the integrity of baseball.

As a result of the Messersmith-McNally decision, free agency came to baseball. This decision motivated the League to draft into the next collective bargaining agreement provisions specifically addressing free agency. The League feared that allowing free agency, after playing the renewal year, would motivate too many players to avoid signing new contracts and force the clubs to exercise the renewal option. The League did not want to give this option to players.

The League and Players Association agreed that a player would not be eligible for free agent status until after performing for six years under contract and a renewal year at the club's option. This provision discouraged the rookies and newer players from signing short contracts, playing out their renewal year, and becoming free agents early in their careers. Further, the new agreement established a free-agent draft. This allowed teams to restrict some players who had become free agents from complete, free negotiation. In effect, the Messersmith-McNally case gave the players union power where it had little before and caused the League to address longstanding concerns of the players.

Selected Bibliography

Champion, W., Jr. *Fundamentals of Sports Law.* Deerfield: Clark, Boardman, Callaghan, 1990.

Kuhn, B. *Hardball: The Education of a Baseball Commissioner.* New York: Times Books, 1987.

Miller, M. *A Whole Different Ball Game: The Sport and Business of Baseball.* New York: Carol Publishing Group, 1991.

Baseball Owners Called "Out" for Collusion

Jan Stiglitz

Major League Baseball Arbitration Panel
Decision Nos. 86-2 (1987), 87-3 (1988), and 88-1 (1990)

Until 1975, baseball operated under a "reserve system" in which players were bound to a team and could not freely market their services. Clubs maintained a reserve list which gave them the exclusive right to negotiate with players they reserved. There was also a renewal clause in the individual contract between a player and his team which gave a club the unilateral right to renew a player's contract for one year, even if the player did not want to re-sign with the club. The clubs took the position that the new contract contained the renewal clause, so players would find themselves perpetually bound to their teams.

In 1975, however, with the Messersmith-McNally decision, baseball players won the right to become free agents. The neutral arbitrator, Peter Seitz, ruled that players Andy Messersmith and Dave McNally were not perpetually bound by the renewal clause. Instead, the renewal clause only operated to bind a player for one year. He also ruled that the reserve clause only gave teams the right to reserve players with whom they had a contractual relationship. Since Messersmith and McNally had played under their renewed contracts without signing a new agreement, they were declared free to negotiate with any team in baseball.

The Messersmith-McNally decision led the players to negotiate a league-wide system of free agency which was incorporated into the 1976 Collective Bargaining Agreement between the clubs and the players. This system gave players the right to free agency after six years of service. It also gave clubs that were losing players some compensation, such as high draft picks, for the clubs that signed the free agents.

The dawn of free agency had a dramatic effect on player salaries. In the five-year period preceding free agency (1970 to 1975), the average salary in baseball rose from $29,303 to $44,676, an increase of about 50 percent. In the five-year period after free agency (1976 to 1981), the average salary in baseball jumped from $51,501 to $185,651, an increase of approximately 350 percent. By 1985, the average salary had risen to $371,571.

There were other significant changes in the contracts that free agents were able to negotiate. For the first time, players had the leverage to negotiate guaranteed, multiyear contracts. Such contracts were virtually unheard of prior to 1976. The benefits of free agency were not limited to those who actually achieved that status. As players approached free agency, clubs were often willing to negotiate longterm, guaranteed contracts in order to prevent the players from entering the free-agent market.

The first collusion case against owners dealt with the free-agent market that existed after the 1985 season. Following the 1984 season, all twenty-six major league clubs had signed free agents from other clubs. Suddenly, however, after the 1985 season, the free agent market changed dramatically. Players such as Carlton Fisk and Kirk Gibson found that no one was bidding against their current teams for their services. As a result, twenty-nine free agents re-signed with their own clubs.

Suspecting that this was not a random occurrence or the result of twenty-six independent business decisions, the Major League Baseball Players' Association ("the Association") filed a grievance. The Association claimed that this frozen market was the product of "collusion," an agreement by the teams not to bid on free agents until the team that had previously contracted with the player had decided not to re-sign the player.

The Association claimed that such collusive behavior violated the "Individual Nature of Rights" provision in the Collective Bargaining Agreement. That provision stated:

The utilization or non-utilization of rights under this Article . . . is an individual matter to be determined solely by each Player and each Club for his or its own benefit. Players shall not act in concert with other Players and Clubs shall not act in concert with other Clubs.

The use of this provision by the Association was rather ironic. In the absence of such a provision, collusive behavior by the owners would not be illegal. The courts have repeatedly held that baseball is exempt from attack under the antitrust laws, for instance in *Flood* v. *Kuhn*. The individual nature of rights provision had been included in the 1976 collective bargaining agreement at the insistence of the clubs. The clubs had remembered how successful the joint holdout by Sandy Koufax and Don Drysdale had been in pressuring the Dodgers into agreeing to higher salary demands. After the Messersmith-McNally decision, the clubs feared that the newly freed ball players would again resort to such tactics.

The clubs did not contest the enforceability of the individual nature of rights provision. Instead, they denied that there had been any collusion. They maintained that the "depressed level" of the 1985 market was "simply the culmination of a ten-year trend" and other factors. For example, the clubs argued that the economics of baseball required fiscal restraint. Thomas Roberts, the neutral arbitrator, however, did not find that the individual rights provision had an exception for fiscal problems, nor was such an exception warranted. A club could simply decide to bid or refrain from bidding on a free agent to accommodate its own fiscal constraints.

The clubs also cited a number of other factors that might have contributed to the frozen market. These included a dissatisfaction with the performance decline that allegedly accompanied longterm contracts, a newly revised system of free agent deadlines, and the recent productivity of teams' farm systems. But the arbitrator found that "only a common understanding that no club [would] bid" on a former player could have resulted in the "universal effect" on the market.

The arbitrator noted that in the 1984–85 off-season, twenty-six of the forty-six free agents changed clubs. In the 1985–86 off-season, all but four of the thirty-two free agents were forced to sign with their former clubs. Why? Because only one of the twenty-nine had even received a bona fide offer from anyone other than his former club. As the arbitrator ultimately found: "The clubs showed no interest in the available free agents *at any price* until such time as their former club declared that the player no longer fit into their plans."

For example, Kirk Gibson, who was eligible to leave the Detroit

Tigers, had initially been approached by both the Kansas City Royals and the Atlanta Braves. But immediately after meetings of the owners in October and of the general managers in November, the Royals announced they would not make any efforts to sign any free agents and the Braves terminated discussions with Gibson's agent.

Numerous witnesses testified for the clubs. Each explained why his club had not bid on another team's free agents, and all denied the existence of any agreement. Even though the Association was not able to prove directly any such agreement, the circumstantial evidence of collusion was compelling. The arbitrator concluded there simply could be no explanation for the lack of offers except for an agreement by the teams.

The free-agent market that existed after the 1986 season was similar to the one that existed after the 1985 season. As in 1985, a number of star players were available, including Andre Dawson, Tim Raines, Jack Morris, and Reggie Jackson. In the previous year, the Association noted that clubs did not show any attention to a free agent until the player's old club decided it was no longer interested. With one exception, no player ever received competing offers. The clubs once again asserted that there was no agreement. Instead, they claimed, the flat market was simply the result of "unilateral, non-consensual responses to similar competitive conditions." The clubs also attempted to show that there was more activity in 1986. Regardless of what had happened in 1985, in 1986 there was a different market.

A new neutral arbitrator, George Nicolau, was selected to hear Collusion II. But he, too, ruled in favor of the players. Because of the decision in Collusion I, the arbitrator in Collusion II assumed the existence of collusion in 1985 and focused on whether this collusion continued in 1986. As in Collusion I, the arbitrator in Collusion II noted that collusion need not be expressed in writing. Instead, the signs of the illegal agreement will be found in the actions of the parties. In Collusion II, the arbitrator found that the few meager deviations from the prior year's experience did not negate the existence of a common (and prohibited) understanding and goal. Instead, he found that the collusion had continued unabated.

The first part of the decision focused on the period prior to January 8, the deadline for a team re-signing its own player. The clubs maintained that, in contrast to 1985, there were attempts by clubs to bid for players that were still negotiating with their old teams. Specifically, the clubs argued that Jack Morris had received an offer from the Minnesota Twins while he was still in active negotiations with the Tigers and while the Tigers' offer of salary arbitration was still outstanding.

At the time, Morris was coming off of a 21–8 won and lost season. In his previous eight years, Morris won more games than any other pitcher in baseball. The arbitrator detailed the attempts that agent Dick Moss had made with a number of clubs on behalf of Morris. The arbitrator first noted that Moss had received virtually identical letters from the Angels, the Expos, and the Cubs, all of whom declined to engage in competitive bidding. The arbitrator then concluded that the purported negotiations with Minnesota were a sham. He found that the Twins had pretended to engage in serious negotiations in order to appease fans, but that the team never made a serious offer. After talks with Minnesota broke down, Moss made specific proposals to the Yankees, the Phillies, and the Angels, but all rejected these proposals without making any counteroffers.

The arbitrator also cited the experience of Darrell Evans, who had accumulated forty home runs and ninety-four runs batted in during the 1985 season and twenty-nine home runs and eighty-five RBIs in 1986. Bob Teaff and Jerry Kapstein, Evans's representatives, called every club in the major leagues to determine if there was any interest in a one-year deal. No club responded, and Evans was forced to re-sign with the Tigers.

The lack of interest in Morris and Evans sharply contrasted to the market that existed for any player whose team showed no interest in re-signing him. Players such as Reggie Jackson, Rick Dempsey, and Ray Knight had no problem obtaining contracts, once their clubs announced a lack of interest. The second part of the decision focused on the players who did not re-sign with their clubs by January 8. Unlike the prior year, some players in Collusion II were able to change teams. The clubs argued that this demonstrated there was a free, albeit reserved, market in 1986. But the arbitrator found that the facts did not support this conclusion. The clubs cited Andre Dawson as an example of a player who was able to change clubs. But Dawson was only signed after he handed the Cubs a blank contract and told them to pay him whatever salary they deemed appropriate.

Tim Raines presented another clear illustration of the absence of a truly free market. Since Raines failed to sign with Montreal by January 7, the Expos were precluded from negotiating with him again until May. Raines was a twenty-seven-year-old perennial All-Star who was coming off a season in which he hit .334 and stole seventy bases. As evidence of the free market, the clubs claimed that Raines received offers from the Mariners, the Padres, and the Astros. But the arbitrator found that the Mariners never put any figure on the table. He found that the Padres had made an offer, but it was $400,000 less than Raines had earned with Montreal. Houston, too, had made a belated offer, but its offer was even lower than San Diego's.

The arbitrator noted other evidence that suggested continued collusion by the clubs. There was questionable communication between clubs, which they had characterized as a matter of "courtesy." For example, when Oakland decided that it did not want to bid for Bob Boone, Sandy Alderson, the general manager, made a courtesy call to the Angels to tell that club that the As would not extend an offer. Similarly, when the owner of the White Sox sent a letter to Dick Moss saying that he would not make an offer to Jack Morris, he sent a blind copy of the letter to the Tigers as a "courtesy."

Perhaps the most compelling evidence was cumulative. The 1987 free agents took an average pay cut of 16 percent. Similarly, the average salary for all players in 1987 (after the second year of collusion) decreased from the prior year. The arbitrator also noted that approximately three-fourths of the free agents received one-year contracts.

The arbitrator's decision in Collusion I came down in September 1987. This ruling forced the clubs to change their approach to bargaining in the 1987–88 off-season. Their new plan included the creation of a data bank that let each club know the up-to-the-minute status of all negotiations with free agents.

Once again, the Association filed a grievance, and neutral arbitrator George Nicolau ruled in favor of the players. The arbitrator found that the information bank "converted the free-agency process into a secret buyers' auction, to which the sellers of services—the players—had not agreed." He found that the clubs used the bank to track "just how far they would have to go with particular players."

Damages from the collusion were initially fixed in stages. Arbitrator Roberts found a salary shortfall of $10.5 million as a result of the collusion in 1986. Arbitrator Nicolau found salary shortfalls of $38 million and $64.5 million for 1987 and 1988. These numbers, however, do not fully reflect all of the damages caused by the collusion. Other damages were caused by the shorter length of contracts signed, fewer guaranteed contracts, fewer option buy-out agreements, fewer and smaller bonuses (performance and signing), and fewer no-trade provisions.

In December 1990, the clubs and the Association executed a comprehensive settlement agreement of Collusion I, II, and III. The clubs agreed to pay damages in the amount of $280 million. The settlement also provided for additional service credit to certain players and granted others the right to walk away from their contracts and become "new look" free agents. Finally, the settlement included a stipulation, for purposes of future salary arbitration, as to how much salaries had been depressed as a result of collusion.

Technically, the players won, and the pool of money that they divided was substantial. It is not clear, however, that it was enough. So far, more than eight hundred players have filed claims totalling in excess of $1.3 billion. Many observers also claim that the owners still saved an enormous amount of money by virtue of their actions. After a decade of rapidly rising salaries, the salary picture for the late 1980s was relatively stagnant. The average salary increased from $412,520 in 1986 to $497,254 in 1989. While this 20 percent increase might seem healthy in other industries, it pales by comparison to salary patterns prior to collusion. Since 1989, salaries have again risen dramatically. From 1989 to 1992, the average salary has more than doubled. No one knows, however, what the salaries would now be if the owners had not colluded.

Collusion damages, moreover, are only distributed to players who can prove that the collusion had an impact on their salaries. Many believe that free agency had a trickle-down effect on all salaries. If so, there were many victims who will never be compensated for the harm caused. Finally, there is a problem with how quickly the money is being distributed. As of the end of 1992, more than two years after the settlement, no money had been distributed to any player.

If the teams had been subject to federal antitrust laws, the damages would have been trebled. This pattern, presumably, reflects the belief that either some penalty is needed to prevent violations or the computation of damages from collusive behavior does not amount to the profit that is gained from the behavior. At the players' insistence, the Collective Bargaining Agreement now provides for treble damages for any future collusion by the clubs.

Selected Bibliography

Major League Baseball. *Basic Agreement*. New York: 1976, 1980, 1985, 1990.
Miller, M. *A Whole Different Ball Game: The Sport and Business of Baseball*. New York: Carol Publishing Group, 1991.
Zimbalist, A. *Baseball and Billions*. New York: Basic Books, 1992.

Joe Kapp's Fight for Free Agency

Michael W. Flamm

Kapp v. National Football League, 586 F. 2d 644 (9th Cir. 1978), cert denied, 441 U.S. 907 (1979).

"Football is a kids' game, invented to give a lot of people a lot of fun. The minute a player loses sight of that fact, he's in trouble." So said Minnesota Vikings quarterback Joe Kapp in 1970 shortly after he and his overly serious teammates had dropped Super Bowl IV to the Kansas City Chiefs. But as he soon discovered, football is also a business, and the player who loses sight of that fact has little chance of success or survival in the National Football League (NFL).

After leading the University of California to the Rose Bowl in 1958, Kapp was drafted by the Washington Redskins but refused to sign with the team. For the next eight years he played in the Canadian Football League until he joined the Minnesota Vikings in 1967 as a twenty-nine-year-old, third-string rookie. In his third season, he guided the Vikings to their first-ever Super Bowl appearance and became a star.

Then the trouble began. As a rookie, Kapp had signed a two-year contract with the Vikings who, under the contract's option clause, in 1969 exercised their option for a third year (at 90 percent of his 1968 salary). But after the Super Bowl, Minnesota offered Kapp, now a free agent, another two-year contract on the same terms as his original one. He rejected the offer and sought to negotiate with other teams. Although the Philadelphia Eagles and the Houston Oilers expressed interest, neither team made a firm offer. The reason, according to Kapp, was that both teams feared the "Rozelle Rule," which would have obligated them to compensate the Vikings with players and/or draft choices.

Eventually, however, the New England Patriots traded a player and a first-round draft choice to the Vikings for the rights to Kapp, whom they signed to a memo of agreement in October 1970. Kapp then played the remainder of the season with the Patriots. But, in May 1971, Commissioner Pete Rozelle told New England that Kapp could not compete in the NFL unless he signed a Standard Player Contract (SPC). Kapp refused, objecting to various provisions in the SPC, including the "Rozelle Rule," the option clause, the college draft, and the tampering rule (which forbade teams from negotiating with players on another team's active or reserve rosters). In July the Patriots ordered Kapp to leave training camp, which he did. Thus ended his brief but colorful NFL career.

The legal game, however, had only begun. Kapp quickly filed suit in California District Court, charging the New England Patriots with breach of contract and alleging that the "Rozelle Rule," option clause, and the tampering provision constituted a *de facto* boycott of free agents and a *per se* violation of the Sherman and Clayton Acts. Even if the "rule of reason" was imposed allowing the NFL to justify these provisions, they would be found unreasonable, Kapp added. Nevertheless, the *per se* doctrine was crucial to Kapp's case because, if applicable, the NFL would then have no right to contend that these provisions were justified, and Kapp would have no need to produce elaborate statistical evidence that countered the NFL's assertions.

The NFL position rested on two major points. The first was that its rules were reasonable and were not a violation, *per se* or otherwise, of the federal antitrust laws. Here the NFL, which, unlike major league baseball has no antitrust exemption, argued that professional sports were a unique business where fan interest and economic success depended upon competition on the field and cooperation off the field. Unrestricted free agency, the NFL contended, would allow the wealthier franchises to corner the best players and destroy the competitive balance essential to the league's popularity. The second point was that the collective bargaining agreement between the league and the NFL Players Association (NFLPA), which had gone into effect in February 1970, immunized the NFL from the antitrust laws even if its rules violated them.

The trial's outcome was mixed. The judge accepted the NFL's contention that the issues merited examination by the "rule of reason," but upon examination he found that the NFL rules were "patently unreasonable" and in violation of antitrust laws as Kapp had argued. The judge also rejected the NFL's assertion regarding the collective bargaining agreement, noting that the agreement became retroactively effective in February 1970 but was not actually ratified until June 1971 (after Kapp's refusal to sign the SPC), but the jury ultimately decided not to award Kapp any damages because he could not prove that the NFL's rules had harmed him directly.

Predictably, both sides placed different spins on the decision. Ed Garvey, Executive Director of the NFLPA, called the judge's opinion "the most significant development in the history of professional sports from the point of view of the athlete." "It is just one district judge's opinion," responded NFL Commissioner Rozelle, who decided to appeal the decision. Kapp did likewise.

In 1978 the U.S. Court of Appeals upheld the lower court's judgment. It again found the NFL's rules unreasonable and in violation of federal antitrust laws, but it again found, as well, that Kapp deserved no damages because he could not prove injury.

Thus the court dismissed the NFL's cross-appeal. The court also accepted the argument of NFL attorney Paul Tagliabue, now the league's commissioner, who contended that Kapp had voluntarily left the NFL to pursue an acting career in Hollywood and had voluntarily rejected the opportunity to sign an SPC with the right reserved to challenge it in the future.

As expected, Kapp next appealed to the Supreme Court, but in 1979 it refused to hear his case. By then new cases and new controversies between the NFL and the NFLPA had emerged. The Kapp decision faded into legal history. But Kapp had struck the first major blow against the NFL's restrictions on free agency and had laid the groundwork for later precedent-setting lawsuits by players such as John Mackey and Freeman McNeil.

Selected Bibliography

Freedman, W. *Professional Sports and Antitrust.* Westport: Quorum Books, 1987.
Roberts, G. "Sports League Restraints on the Labor Market: The Failure of Stare Decisis." *The University of Pittsburgh Law Review* 47 (Winter 1986): 337–405.
Sobel, L. *Professional Sports and the Law.* New York: Law-Arts Publishers, Inc., 1977 and Supplement, 1981.

Tight End Mackey Blocks Commissioner Rozelle

Richard M. Terry

Mackey v. *National Football League*, 407 F. Supp. 1000 (D. Minn. 1975), *aff'd,* **543 F. 2d 606 (8th Cir. 1976),** *cert. dismissed,* **434 U.S. 801 (1976)**

John Mackey entered the National Football League (NFL) in 1963 with impressive credentials. Born on September 19, 1941, in Brooklyn, New York, Mackey excelled in several sports at Hempstead High School, Long Island. Following graduation in 1959, he attended Syracuse University where he starred on the football field and earned a bachelor's degree in history and political science. The Baltimore Colts drafted Mackey in the second round. Mackey flourished as a blocker and as a pass-catching tight end. He and quarterback Johnny Unitas teamed up so effectively that he earned Pro-Bowl selection five times. The NFL in 1970 named Mackey the top player at his position in the league's history. In that same year, Mackey, as president of the recently formed National Football League Players Association (NFLPA), organized a strike by the players. Then five years later, in *Mackey* v. *National Football League,* Mackey mounted a legal challenge to the "Rozelle Rule" which resulted in one of the most important cases in the field of labor and sports.

From its inception in the 1920s to the present, the NFL has been an association of member clubs that own and operate football teams. As a result these clubs constitute a monopoly over this sport, with regulation accomplished by a constitution and bylaws. In 1960 the NFL hired Alvin "Pete" Rozelle as commissioner with duties and powers defined by the constitution of the NFL.

Several issues ignited conflict between the players and the league. One had to do with the "reserve" or option clause of the standard player contract. The contract specifically stated that once a player signed, he had to play for the signing team for at least two years, with an option year at the discretion of the signing team, in which the player performed with a 10 percent reduction in salary. At the end of the option year, the player could become a free agent. The main issue, however, dealt with the compensation that a new club had to pay the player's former team in order to sign the free agent. Before 1963, when a player signed with a new team, his former team received no compensation. After 1963, however, the belief developed that teams in lucrative markets would attract the best players and thus tilt the balance of competition. To protect a club's investment in scouting and developing players, the "Rozelle Rule" was added to the NFL's constitution and bylaws. The provision dealt with situations in which players sought freedom to negotiate with other teams. If the original team and the acquiring team failed to agree on compensation to the former, Commissioner Rozelle would determine the appropriate compensation. Options for Rozelle included money, future draft picks, and other players. The NFLPA maintained that this rule violated the Sherman Antitrust Act, which states that every combination in the form of a conspiracy in restraint of commerce is illegal and that every person who monopolizes or combines to monopolize will be guilty of a felony. Because many leagues, especially the NFL, have been sanctioned as legitimate monopolies, they have been exempt from certain provisions of the Sherman Act and also from the nonstatutory exemptions of the Clayton Act and the Norris-LaGuardia Act.

In 1973, Edward R. Garvey, former executive director of the NFLPA, described the conditions that brought about Mackey's suit: "First of all, the National Football League is a monopoly, and I think that this is an important fact. It has exclusive control of the labor market. If a talented player decides that he is going to play football for pay in this country, he must do so under rules established by the owners and by their commissioner." The "Rozelle Rule" was not included in two successive collective bargaining agreements between the NFL and the NFLPA. *Mackey* v. *National Football League,* therefore, was not only a challenge to the NFL league in general, but also to the "Rozelle Rule" in particular, because of the apparent collusion that could exist between the club owners and the commissioner to the detriment of the players.

In U.S. District Court, Judge Larson ruled in favor of the players and stated that the "Rozelle Rule" was a *per se* violation of the Sherman Act. He also decided that the NFL no longer could claim antitrust immunity under certain nonstatutory exemptions, ruling that, since the union was rather new, the preceding collective bargaining agreements were negotiated from weak positions. This decision was a major blow to the power and pride of the NFL. The NFL sought relief from the Court of Appeals. Judge Lay, however, agreed with Judge Larson's determination that the NFL violated antitrust legislation. Through a new collective bargaining agreement in 1977, the "Rozelle Rule" was modified. The struggle started in earnest by Mackey in the 1970s continued into the early 1990s, when in the *McNeil* v. *National Football League* case the players achieved virtually total free agency.

Tight end John Mackey finally gained admission into the NFL Hall of Fame in 1992. Qualified observers of professional football believed that were it not for his legal challenge to the league, he would have been admitted much sooner. Al Davis, managing partner of the Oakland Raiders and one of the other inductees in 1992, had also long been an irritant to the league. Mackey observed that "they decided to let all the troublemakers in at once."

Selected Bibliography

Champion, W., Jr. *Fundamentals of Sports Law*. Deerfield: Clark, Boardman, Calleghan, 1990.

Freedman, W. *Professional Sports and Antitrust*. Westport: Greenwood Press, Inc., 1987.

Porter, D., ed. *Biographical Dictionary of American Sports: Football*. New York: Greenwood Press, Inc., 1990.

Scher, J. "Mackey Finally Catches a Break." *Sports Illustrated*. February 3, 1992: 66.

Sobel, L. *Professional Sports and the Law*. New York: Law-Arts Publishers, Inc., 1977 and 1981 Supplement.

"These People Just Plain Don't Like Each Other"

David M. Allyn

McNeil v. National Football League, 790 F.Supp. 871 (D. Minn. 1992)

In August 1992, the field at the Hubert H. Humphrey Metrodome in Minneapolis, Minnesota, was transformed from the baseball home of the Twins to the football home of the Vikings. The field was undergoing preparation for pre-season football. The hardest hitting, fastest blitzing football in Minneapolis, however, would not occur at the Metrodome. The real action would take place a few blocks away in the courtroom of United States District Court Judge David S. Doty, before a jury of nine women and three men. Here, twenty years after John Mackey of the Baltimore Colts first challenged the National Football League (NFL) for the right of free agency and five years after the failed players' strike of 1987, the clock ending the litigation game between the National Football League Players Association (NFLPA) and the league owners might run out. As one trial observer remarked, "These people just plain don't like each other; they see the courtroom as a place to pound lumps on the other side."

The judge and jury in Minneapolis heard the legal challenge of eight former and current NFL players to the league's Plan B free-agency system: Freeman McNeil (New York Jets), Tim McDonald (Phoenix Cardinals), Mark Collins and Lee Rouson (New York Giants), Don Majkowski (Green Bay Packers), Niko Noga (Detroit Lions), Dave Richards (San Diego Chargers), and Frank Minnifield (Cleveland Browns). Under Plan B, each team could protect thirty-seven players on its roster. The rest of a team's players became unrestricted free agents who could then negotiate with any NFL team.

Why did the NFLPA and the NFL find themselves in this position while other professional sports, such as baseball, had long before settled the free agency question? In 1975, the same year that an arbitrator struck down baseball's "reserve clause," another federal court judge in Minneapolis found that the "Rozelle Rule," which provided compensation to a free agent's former team, violated U.S. antitrust laws. But the new free agency system negotiated by the NFLPA under the less-than-brilliant leadership of Ed Garvey was a disaster for players. It still allowed NFL teams to match offers to their free agent players or to receive stiff draft choice compensation for lost players. Very few players moved, and the fact that NFL players have careers that average three to five years less than those of baseball players further weakened the individual football player's position. In the early 1990s the average baseball salary was about $1.1 million; the average salary of an NFL player was around $440,000.

The agreements between the NFL and the NFLPA lasted until 1987. That year, the players went out on strike over the free agency issue. The strike was a total failure. The owners brought in "scab" players, fans continued to attend games, and, more devastatingly, the television networks continued to televise games. The players returned to work after twenty-four days. When the strike was over, the NFLPA decertified itself as the bargaining unit for the players but agreed to finance the suits of Freeman McNeil and seven other players whose contracts expired after the 1988 season. These players contended that they should be free to negotiate with any team in the NFL.

The case finally came to trial in the summer of 1992. The NFL's lawyers argued against free agency, contending: first, that the NFL was a joint venture of twenty-eight teams; second, that competitive balance in the NFL existed only because of restricted movement; and third, that these and other factors placed the NFL in a different world from normal business.

The players' lawyers agreed that unlimited free agency might cause chaos and the possible destruction of some franchises. But they also pointed to the unfairness of a system that allows untested rookies to earn more than all-star veterans because they can hold out before signing their initial contract. Plan B was also attacked by noting that more-talented, but protected, players earned less in 1990 than less-talented, unprotected players who signed free-agent contracts with other teams. Protected New York Giants defensive back Mark Collins and running back Lee Rouson earned $551,000 and $165,000 respectively for the 1990 season. Defensive back Terry Kinard earned $640,000 from the Houston Oilers and running back George Adams earned $470,000 from the New England Patriots after being left unprotected and becoming Plan B free agents. At the same time, economists for the players testified that owners, such as Norman Braman of the Eagles who paid himself $7.5 million annually, lowered team profits through large salaries for themselves.

The trial lasted from June through September, 1992. Twice during the summer, Judge Doty declared recesses to give the parties a chance to reach an out-of-court settlement, but no agreements were reached. Then, on September 10, 1992, the players' arguments paid off as the jury reached a verdict in the case. It ruled that the NFL's Plan B system was a violation of United States antitrust laws and awarded four of the eight plaintiffs a total of $543,000. Under antitrust laws, these damages were trebled to a total of $1.63 million. The largest award ($240,000) went to David Richards, while ironically, the player whose name marqueed the case, Freeman McNeil, received nothing.

The owners' reaction to the verdict seemed to indicate that they were living in a dream world. Though having lost fourteen court actions brought by their players since March 1991, owners promised to appeal the ruling and replace Plan B with a proposed "Plan C." The NFLPA, meanwhile, followed up with motions to block any Plan C, to challenge the legality of the NFL draft, and to declare immediately four unsigned hold-outs to be unrestricted free agents. Judge Doty accepted the players' arguments in declaring Garin Varis, Webster Slaughter, Keith Jackson, and D.J. Dozier free agents and was quoted by King in *Sports Illustrated* as observing that "economic injuries claimed by the players, such as their inability to play for teams that best utilize their skills . . . or to play on natural grass may be impossible to quantify in monetary terms."

The NFL owners immediately and hypocritically took advantage of the ruling by bidding for free agents Varis, Slaughter, and Jackson. Jackson received $1.45 million per season from the Miami Dolphins, more than either of Miami's two all-star receivers, Mark Clayton and Mark Duper. In typical, surrealistic style, NFL management then blamed the players for disrupting team salary structures. Don Shula, Dolphins coach, who opposed free agency, predicted a backlash and warned the players of the ramifications of the pursuit of free agency.

If Shula were worried about the players not understanding the "ramifications" of their actions in October, 1992, then his concern for the players must have been greatly magnified in January, 1993. Though some owners continued to posture, such as Lamar Hunt of the Kansas City Chiefs who boasted, "We have never backed away from a fight," the majority of owners, under pressure from Judge Doty and under the leadership of Commissioner Paul Taglibue, finally reached a settlement with the NFLPA. The agreement called for five-year veterans whose contracts had expired to become free agents on March 1, 1993. The NFL draft would be reduced to seven rounds, and a $2 million annual salary cap for rookies would be instituted. Teams, however, would be able to designate one player as a franchise player. As long as that player's pay ranked among the top five at his position, he would not be able to become a free agent. Furthermore, in 1993, teams will have the right of first refusal on two other players and the same right on one player in 1994. Finally, as a concession to the owners' concern for balance, the four playoff finalists would be unable to sign free agents in 1993 unless they lost one of their own.

What does the future hold for the NFL, the NFLPA, and the players themselves? Remembering that "these people just plain don't like each other," and that the waters ahead are uncharted, there probably will neither be smooth sailing nor an end to all litigation. With their legal fees now over $10 million, the NFL owners hope to concentrate on other issues, the most immediate being expansion, which could take place as early as 1995. Norman Braman and the Philadelphia Eagles filed tampering charges against the Houston Oilers and their then defensive coordinator Buddy Ryan. As for the players, some are also grumbling. Most players, however, probably agreed with Pittsburgh Steeler linebacker Hardy Nickerson's feelings: "I couldn't ask for anything more than my basic freedom. In baseball, basketball, and society in general, you can at some point of your life shop yourself around. Now I have that right, too." Yes, you do, Hardy, but beware—there are some people who are still not very happy about it.

Selected Bibliography

Bartok, R. "NFL Free Agency Restrictions under Antitrust Attack." *Duke Law Journal*
    (1991): 503–559.
George, T. "In the Run to Daylight Players Are Winning." *The New York Times*. August
    9, 1992: 13.
King, P. "Inside the NFL: Let Freedom Ring." *Sports Illustrated*. October 5, 1992: 60.
Kirshenbaum, J. "To Market We Go." *Sports Illustrated*. January 18, 1993: 12.
Schneider, J. "Unsportsmanlike Conduct: The Lack of Free Agency in the NFL." *Southern California Law Review* 64 (1991): 797–857.

Oscar Robertson
The Player and the Case

Daniel J. Murphy

**Robertson v. National Basketball Association, 389 F.
Supp. 867 (S.D. N.Y. 1975).**

Oscar Robertson is one of several players whose name is enshrined
in sports record books and in legal treatises. A member of the all-
time National Basketball Association (NBA) team, Robertson also
gave his name to a lawsuit that challenged some of the fundamental
labor-relations issues in professional basketball.

At every level of the game, the talented player nicknamed "Big
O" dominated the competition. At Crispus Attucks High School in
Indianapolis, Robertson led his squad to forty-five consecutive victories. In the classroom he also excelled, graduating in the upper 10
percent of his class and earning National Honor Society recognition.
Robertson then chose to attend the University of Cincinnati. He proceeded to pace the Bearcats to three twenty-plus victory seasons.
Robertson led the nation in scoring for three successive seasons and
received All-American recognition.

Graduating in 1960, Robertson quickly established himself as a
dominating performer in the NBA. Robertson easily made the switch
from forward to guard with the Cincinnati Royals and was known
as a skilled ball handler. "Big O" showed equal proficiency at scoring and handing out assists. For his first several years in the NBA,
Robertson showed amazing consistency by averaging nearly thirty
points and about eight to twelve assists a game.

The Royals, while vastly improved thanks to Robertson and
other talented players such as Jack Twyman, never won a league
championship. Robertson was traded to the Milwaukee Bucks in
the early 1970s, and, along with Lew Alcindor (later known as
Kareem Abdul Jabbar), led the squad to a 66–16 regular season

record in 1970–71 and to the NBA championship.

Robertson directed the players off the court as well. As president of the NBA Players Association, Robertson joined in a class-action law suit against the league in 1970. Robertson and other team player representatives charged the NBA with conspiring to restrain competition through such measures as the "reserve clause" and the compensation plan that accompanied it. The Players Association also took aim at the college draft as well as a rumored merger of the two leagues, the NBA with its newer rival, the American Basketball Association (ABA).

The players initially obtained an injunction prohibiting the merger. The owners sought to dissolve the injunction and moved for a summary judgment on all of the issues brought by the players. The owners contended that the draft and other challenged practices were subjects of collective bargaining with the Players Association. This "labor exemption" issue raised by the owners was ill-received by the court, which found that the draft, reserve clause, and Uniform Player Contract were never the subject of serious collective bargaining. Judge Robert Carter also ruled that there was no labor exemption which protected the two leagues from suits avoiding antitrust violations. The court relied upon a 1965 United States Supreme Court decision in *United Mine Workers* v. *Pennington* which held that an agreement reached in collective bargaining does not automatically exempt the parties from scrutiny for antitrust violations.

In an unusual step the court ruled that though the players were only defending against the owners' attempt at summary judgment before trial, the facts were nearly so strong as to permit the court to enter a judgment for the players that the two leagues had violated the Sherman Antitrust Act by both attempting to merge leagues and by instituting the draft and reserve clause outside of collective bargaining. The court specifically required that any attempted merger between the leagues would require Congressional approval. The court's ruling shook the foundation of professional basketball.

Seeing the writing on the wall, the NBA relented and offered to reach agreement with the players. In what became known as the "Robertson settlement," the league negotiated a new collective bargaining agreement and obtained the permission needed to eventually merge with the ABA. For its part, the NBA accepted the jurisdiction of the court in the *Robertson* case and did not appeal the ruling.

During the next several years the NBA functioned under a free-agent compensation plan. In this process, the NBA commissioner decided the compensation that the player's new club had to pay the former one. The Players Association successfully argued in cases involving players Marvin Webster and Bill Walton that the compensation awards to clubs were so excessive that they restrained clubs from signing free agents. The *Robertson* v. *National Basketball Association* decision, therefore, represented an important step in the ongoing field of labor-management relations in professional basketball.

Selected Bibliography

Berry, R. and G. Wong. *Law and Business of the Sports Industries: Volume I: Professional Sports Leagues.* Dover: Auburn House Publishing Company.

Foraker, S. "The National Basketball Association Salary Cap: An Antitrust Violation?" *Southern California Law Review* 59 (1985–1986): 157–181.

Yasser, R. *Sports Law: Cases and Materials.* Lanham: University Press of America, 1985.

The Letter of Intent and Collegiate Athletes

Joseph J. Craciun

Lesser v. *Neosho County Community College*, 741 F. Supp. 854 (D. Kan. 1990)

In early 1989, Darren Krein was an All-American linebacker from Aurora, Colorado. The University of Miami, a collegiate powerhouse then coached by Jimmy Johnson, was one of many schools that recruited him. Krein claimed that he signed his "letter of intent" to attend Miami only after receiving the assurance that Johnson planned to stay on as coach. Two weeks later, Johnson left Miami to coach the Dallas Cowboys. Krein, feeling misled, wanted out of his letter of intent. Krein initially appealed but later abandoned that strategy.

National Collegiate Athletic Association (NCAA) recruiting rule 13.02.7 states, "The National Letter of Intent referred to in this bylaw is the official document administered by the Collegiate Commissioners Association and utilized by the subscribing member institution to establish the commitment of a prospect to attend a particular institution." NCAA recruiting rules 14.6.5.1 and 14.6.5.3.7 hold, with some various exceptions, that a valid transfer authorized by the former institution costs one year of eligibility while an unauthorized transfer, that is, without release from a letter of intent, costs an athlete two years of eligibility. Institutions, therefore, seem to wield great power over new signees, making them pay a high cost for future movement, but placing no similar limitations or penalties on coaches and others involved on the other side of the recruiting table.

Given an absence of coverage in the NCAA rules regarding the obligations of coaches and administrators for letters of intent, one must look elsewhere in order to predict the outcome of future cases like the Krein situation and, in turn, the possible ramifications those cases would have on NCAA rules and policies.

In one such case, *Lesser v. Neosho County Community College*, a former student-athlete, who was cut from the baseball team after four practices, brought suit against the college for failure to let him out of his letter of intent for various reasons, including breach of contract and fraudulent misrepresentation theories. Let us compare and contrast this case and Krein's situation.

The court held that Lesser's elimination from the team and the college's subsequent refusal to release him from his letter of intent did not constitute a breach of contract. Because most contracts are read at face value, the NCAA only guaranteed Lesser a scholarship through his letter of intent, not an assurance that he would not be cut. Krein could argue that his letter of intent contained an ambiguity that arose when the terms were applied and thus warranted the use of outside (extrinsic) evidence to establish the agreement. He could then introduce statements regarding the decision-making process that went into picking the right coach, including research of the coach's objective resume as well as personal observations made during his informal contacts with Johnson. Where a letter of intent may not guarantee a player's not getting cut, at least it should assure the presence of the key individual who played the vital role in obtaining the player's confidence to sign.

In *Lesser*, the letter of intent stated that it was voidable only for failure to meet admission requirements, not failure to make the team. In Krein's case, the opposite was true. Neither Johnson, nor any school official, made any prior or contemporaneous, oral or written statement, regarding Johnson's departure.

The court in *Lesser* also stated that NCAA's failure to disclose a fine system for team rules was harmless error because it was not a material fact that went into the decision of Lesser to sign. In contrast, according to Krein and others, the coach is often the most important element, and often the only discernable factor, separating a choice between relatively similar educational opportunities. Certainly the person with whom the recruit has had the most contact prior to signing and with whom he plans to spend the next four years might well be considered a material factor affecting his signing.

The court in *Lesser*, however, denied the school's motion for summary judgment under the fraudulent misrepresentation claim, stating that questions of fact remained for the jury regarding Coach Steve Murray's making statements with "reckless disregard of truth or falsity." Krein, in turn, would be able to show directly that Johnson left only two weeks after assuring Krein that he would not leave. Johnson would have difficulty showing that he did not make those statements with "reckless disregard for truth or falsity," assuming that a deal of such magnitude as the replacement of the legend in Dallas, Tom Landry, could arise and be completed within such a short span of time.

University of Miami athletic director Sam Jancovich stated he would not release Krein from his letter of intent because he wanted him to fulfill his "commitment." The one-way street of commitment is patently unfair to the Darren Kreins of the world who remain trapped by an archaic system that fears change even though change is already taking place around it. Perhaps through the use of litigation or as a result of the outcry of public opinion, the NCAA will institute necessary amendments to a rigid system of often unworkable and overly technical rules. Krein symbolizes a young person who wants to play football, possibly cash in on a draft-day bonanza, and take advantage of a free education, for the days when the knees ache and the stopwatch cannot click off under 5.0 seconds for the 40-yard dash.

Selected Bibliography

Moran, M. "At Miami, As Player Ponders Re-entering a Race to Fight the System." *The New York Times*. October 7, 1992: Section B, 13.

National College Athletic Association. *1992–93 NCAA Manual*. Overland Park: NCAA Legislative Services Department, 1992.

Reilley, R. "Here Today; Gone Today: A Coach May Swear He's Staying but Who Can Believe Him?" *Sports Illustrated*. March 27, 1989: 102.

Agents, Athletes, and Academics

Chris Kanzius and Charles E. Quirk

United States v. Walters, 704 F. Supp. 844 (N.D. Ill. 1989)

United States v. Walters, 913 F. 2d 388 (7th Cir. 1990)

From 1985 to 1989, Ronnie Harmon's name frequently appeared in Iowa's leading newspaper, *The Des Moines Register*. For the first two years, Harmon made news on the sports pages because of his performance as a highly talented running back for the University of Iowa's football team. Later on he became the subject of hard news stories and editorials because of revelations made in legal actions involving two sports agents, Norby Walters and Lloyd Bloom.

Fans of the University of Iowa's football squad celebrated regularly during the 1985 season as the Hawkeyes compiled a seven wins, one loss Big Ten Conference season on the way to a league championship and a Rose Bowl invitation. Coach Hayden Fry's offense featured the accurate passing of consensus All-American quarterback Chuck Long and the hard running of Harmon. For the 1985 season Harmon finished sixth on the list of all-purpose runners, tucked in between Bo Jackson of Auburn and Oklahoma State's Thurman Thomas. With rushing, pass receptions, and kick-off returns, Harmon averaged around 168 yards a game.

The 1986 Rose Bowl game, however, turned into a disaster for the Hawks and their intensely loyal fans. Harmon, who had fumbled only once during the season, dropped the ball on Iowa's first offensive play. He went on to fumble three more times in the first half. In the second half Harmon dropped a sure touchdown pass. Despite a strong performance by Long, the Hawks could not overcome the fumbles, and the team lost to UCLA 45–28.

In the worlds of professional basketball and football, colleges, arguably, function as unofficial "farm clubs." Harmon is one of many student-athletes who receive athletic scholarships. The universities expect these athletes to perform to the best of their abilities both in the classroom and in their sports. Their athletic talents produce substantial revenue and recognition for the universities in the forms of ticket sales, alumni support, and radio and television contracts.

The National Collegiate Athletic Association (NCAA) regulates the relationship between athletes and the institutions of higher education. It protects both the athletes and their schools through established recruitment procedures and scholarship practices. The NCAA requires that athletes retain amateur status in order to preserve eligibility to play at the college level, and therefore prohibits payments to student-athletes. The NCAA also forbids student-athletes from signing with an agent or from receiving funds or anything of value before the end of their collegiate athletic eligibility. Schools that belong to the NCAA require their players to sign forms stating that they have not signed a contract with an agent or received money or gifts that would affect their eligibility.

Harmon's story illustrates the breakdown of the system. Clever agents such as Norby Walters and Lloyd Bloom have given money to premier football players before their eligibility expired and signed them to postdated contracts. Walters claimed to have spent $800,000 on about thirty athletes, including at least five of the first-round 1987 draft choices. A notorious fast-talker, Walters specialized in signing African-American athletes. Some of his clients, however, switched to other agents, leading Walters to bring suit against them and to speak out publicly.

During the period 1987–1993, followers of football witnessed a federal grand jury investigation of Walters and Bloom, two court decisions and reversals, disclosures of academic irregularities, and calls for reform of college athletics. In 1987, a federal grand jury investigated the two agents for alleged involvement in fraud and racketeering. The following year the University of Alabama successfully prosecuted a civil action against Walters for the recovery of revenues lost due to the resultant ineligibility of student-athletes to whom Walters had given money for signing agency contracts. The agent settled the suit by agreeing to pay the university $50,000 and to sign a $150,000 promissory note.

In 1988, the United States government brought criminal charges against Walters and Bloom in a seven-count indictment of mail fraud, violations of the Racketeer Influenced and Corrupt Organizations Act (RICO), and conspiracy. The RICO charges included extortion, attempted extortion, mail fraud, wire fraud, and the use of interstate facilities in the furtherance of unlawful activity.

Bloom was found guilty of five of the seven counts but appealed the decisions. The 7th U.S. Circuit Court of Appeals reversed the convictions in 1989. Walters and Bloom entered conditional guilty pleas to two counts of mail fraud but retained their right to appeal. Early in July 1993, writing for a three-judge panel of the federal appeals court, Judge Frank Easterbrook ruled that the prosecution had not provided sufficient evidence to justify a mail-fraud conviction.

The seven-year controversy proved costly. Legal battles led Walters to lose his clients, business, and residence. Several weeks after the favorable decision by the appeals court, Bloom was mysteriously shot to death in his home in Malibu, California. During the investigations, Iowans learned that athlete Ronnie Harmon received around $54,000 from Walters while enrolled at the Iowa City institution. More significantly, they found out about academic transcripts showing that in three years in college Harmon took only one course in his computer-science major while finding time to take courses such as billiards and watercolor painting and that defensive back Devon Mitchell responded to the intellectual rigors of billiards, advanced slow-pitch softball, and recreational leisure.

Embarrassed University of Iowa President Hunter Rawlings ordered more stringent academic requirements. In addition to fulfilling the NCAA rule that student-athletes make steady progress toward a degree, he decreed that players could no longer receive credit for athletic participation and must carry at least a fourteen-hour course load each semester. Rawlings then escalated the demand for reform by calling upon the NCAA to ban freshmen from participating in athletics. This proposal infuriated coach Fry and sparked a debate that extended well beyond the boundaries of the Hawkeye State. Understandably, relations between Rawlings and Fry remained strained, at best. More significantly, however, the proper interrelationship between agents, athletes, and academics appears no more settled in the mid-1990s than it was a decade earlier.

Selected Bibliography

Champion, W., Jr. *Fundamentals of Sports Law*. Deerfield: Clark, Boardman, Callaghan,
      1990.
McKenna, K. and J. DiGiuseppe. "Policing Sports Agents: The First Four Years." *Uni-
      versity of Miami Entertainment & Sports Law Review* 8 (Spring 1991): 1–69.
Sloan, P. *The Athlete and the Law*. New York: Oceana Publications, Inc., 1983.
Woods, R. and M. Mills. "Tortious Interference With an Athletic Scholarship: A
      University's Remedy for the Unscrupulous Sports Agent." *Alabama Law Review*
      40 (Fall 1988): 141–186.

Minnesota Gopher Basketball
Problems on the Court and in the Courts

John W. Johnson

**Behagen v. Intercollegiate Conference of Faculty Repre-
sentatives, 346 F. Supp. 602 (D. Minn. 1972) [U.S. District Court, Minnesota].**
**Regents of the University of Minnesota v. National Col-
legiate Athletic Association, 560 F. 2d 352 (8th Cir.
1977) [U.S. Court of Appeals, 8th Circuit],** *cert. dismissed,* **434 U.S. 978 (1977).**

The men's intercollegiate basketball program at the University of
Minnesota has endured more than its share of legal problems. Two
federal court cases from the 1970s document some of these difficulties and, in a larger sense, highlight the issue of how effectively the
organizations that regulate collegiate athletic competitions afford due
process of law to member universities and their student-athletes.

The first case, *Behagen v. Intercollegiate Conference of Faculty
Representatives,* grew out of an attempt by the University of Minnesota to temper the conference-mandated punishment of two of its
athletes for their participation in a fight in the closing seconds of a
big game; the second, *Regents of the University of Minnesota v. NCAA,*
resulted from the university's challenge to NCAA sanctions against
three of its players who were found to have received "extra benefits
not made available to members of the student body in general."

The altercation that led to the contested punishments in *Behagen
v. Intercollegiate Conference* occurred on the evening of January 25,
1972. The Gophers were playing at home against perennial Big Ten
basketball power Ohio State. On the eve of the game both teams
were undefeated in conference play; the Associated Press rated Ohio
State sixth nationally and Minnesota sixteenth. Minnesota Coach
Bill Musselman, hired in 1971 following several winning years at a

small midwestern college, had brought to Gopher basketball a tight man-to-man defense and a flamboyant pregame routine inspired by the Harlem Globetrotters. To such tunes as "Sweet Georgia Brown" and "Your Love Is Taking Me Higher," the Gopher players entertained the crowd with exhibitions of dribbling and ball-handling. By the time of the Ohio State game, word had circulated that the Gophers' warmup was the best show in town, and Minnesota's cavernous old basketball/hockey facility, Williams Arena, began to sell out regularly.

The crowd on January 25 was announced at the maximum capacity figure of 17,775, although the Twin City newspapers later reported that well over 19,000 had packed into the arena that night. After the pregame routine stirred the crowd to a high level of intensity, the game itself developed into a rough, low-scoring defensive battle. As the clock wound into its final minute, Ohio State looked like it was finally pulling away. With the visitors ahead 50–44, Luke Witte, Ohio State's star center drove for a basket but was hauled down roughly from behind by a Minnesota player. A flagrant foul was called. A Minnesota reserve, Marvin ("Corky") Taylor reached a hand down to help the Buckeye player to his feet. As he was pulling up the groggy player, Taylor kneed him in the groin. Taylor later stated that he had been provoked by Witte spitting at him and by the rough play and racial taunting throughout the game. Almost spontaneously both benches emptied onto the floor and a massive fight ensued. The situation was exacerbated by hundreds of fans who jumped onto the raised arena floor and began attacking members of the Ohio State team. It took almost half an hour to restore order. Recently appointed Big Ten commissioner Wayne Duke happened to be in attendance. He consulted with both coaches and declared the game terminated even though thirty-six seconds still remained on the clock.

Six Ohio State players were injured, three of whom—Witte, Mark Minor, and Mark Wagar—were hospitalized in order to receive stitches for cuts and X-rays for suspected concussions. Witte sustained severe head injuries and never played effectively again. Filmed footage of the game, which aired on news and sports broadcasts for days, clearly revealed several Minnesota players and scores of fans slugging and kicking Ohio State players. In a February 1972 issue, *Sports Illustrated* ran a story on the game, complete with lurid pictures, titled "An Ugly Affair in Minnesota."

On January 26, the day following the game, Commissioner Duke launched an investigation into the incident. He viewed films of the game, talked to the referees, and interviewed participants, coaches, and athletic officials. As stipulated by the Handbook of the Inter-collegiate Conference of Faculty Representatives (the "official" name for the Big Ten), Duke also consulted with the Committee on Inter-collegiate Athletics of the Twin Cities Campus Assembly, the appro-priate University of Minnesota body dealing with athletic issues [here-after termed the "Minnesota Committee"]. The Big Ten Handbook dictated that the commissioner and the appropriate university com-mittee come to an agreement on action in such cases but that "the primary responsibility for remedial action falls on the member schools themselves."

It appeared initially that Commissioner Duke and the Minne-sota Committee were of the same mind because on January 28, 1972, the committee ordered the suspension of star forward Ronald Behagen and reserve Corky Taylor for the remainder of the basket-ball season. Behagen was caught in many camera shots stomping on the neck of Witte, and Taylor was the player whose kneeing of Luke Witte set off the brawl. It soon became clear that the Minnesota Committee intended that the suspension would cover games only while allowing Behagen and Taylor to participate in team practices. Commissioner Duke, on the other hand, believed that the suspen-sion included practices. On January 31, 1972, the commissioner presented a report outlining his position to a meeting of Big Ten athletic directors; they agreed with Duke's position that the suspen-sion should include practices as well as games. On February 1, the University of Minnesota appealed the athletic directors' decision to the Big Ten Faculty representatives who subsequently affirmed the decision of the athletic directors.

The Minnesota Committee then reopened its investigation of the brawl and the Big Ten's imposed penalties. It held five days of hearings and ultimately concluded that Behagen and Taylor should have their suspensions lifted because of "significant omissions re-garding 'due process.'" These omissions included the Big Ten's fail-ure to have advised the players in writing of the charges against them and the conference's failure to have afforded them the opportunity to speak in their own defense. Notwithstanding the points raised by the Minnesota Committee, Commissioner Duke, on February 11, 1972, acting pursuant to his power to "promote the general welfare of the Conference," once again suspended Behagen and Taylor. At an apparent impasse, attorneys for Behagen and Taylor sued in federal district court for an injunction to lift the suspensions pending a full hearing of the charges against the athletes.

Federal District Judge Earl Larson moved quickly. After listening to the arguments of attorneys for the players and the conference, Judge Larson issued his opinion on February 22, 1972. Since both parties agreed that the Big Ten was clothed with the power of "state action" under the Fourteenth Amendment to the U.S. Constitution, the paramount question was whether the conference had afforded the plaintiffs satisfactory due process in the face of the charges against them. Judge Larson found that it had not. He determined that the Big Ten's ban of Behagen and Taylor from practicing was levied without affording the players due process of law. He cited the Big Ten's own handbook to the effect that the conferences directors, in the aftermath of an alleged infraction, "shall afford the institution, its employees or students, concerned an opportunity to appear at the meeting in which the Commissioner's report is made and to be heard in defense against charges."

Judge Larson reasoned that "the opportunity to participate in intercollegiate athletics is of substantial economic value." Just as the right to an education cannot be arbitrarily interrupted or terminated without attention to minimum standards of due process, the judge argued that courts recognize the need to provide similar protection under the due process clause of the Fourteenth Amendment for "the property interests" of superior college athletes.

Larson ordered that, no later than February 25, 1972, the Big Ten hold a hearing in which Behagen and Taylor be allowed to answer the charges against them and have an opportunity to present their own version of what happened on January 25. This proceeding was also intended to afford Behagen and Taylor with other due process protections, such as receiving notification in writing of all of the witnesses who would be called by the Big Ten's attorneys. If this hearing did not take place by February 25, the judge's ruling stipulated that he would lift the suspensions.

Judge Larson's opinion appeared to portend good news for the Minnesota basketball players. The hearing was held on February 25, and the players were afforded the protections specified by Judge Larson. But the outcome of the hearing was the same as before: the players were deemed culpable of deplorable behavior, and the suspensions from games and practices for the entire season were continued.

Surprisingly, in the aftermath of the brawl and the various administrative setbacks, the Minnesota basketball team continued to play well. On more than one occasion, the undermanned Gophers played their starting five for an entire game. The Gophers ultimately won the Big Ten conference title and, without Behagen and Taylor, represented the Big Ten in the national basketball tournament. The following year the Gopher basketball team was again ranked high nationally, but it faded at the end of the season. Two Minnesota players, Jim Brewer and the embattled Ron Behagen, went on to modest success in the National Basketball Association. Another Gopher cager, Dave Winfield, who had been plucked from an intramural team in early 1972, went on to a stellar career in major league baseball. Still playing in his forties, Winfield is a cinch Hall of Fame selection. After the 1972–73 season Coach Musselman abandoned Minnesota for the pros, leaving behind memories of two years of hard fought victories, one conference title, and a vicious brawl.

A scant four years later, in a case known as *Regents of the University of Minnesota* v. *National Collegiate Athletic Association,* the University of Minnesota was back in federal court to contest punishments for alleged irregularities of its men's basketball program. This time the adversary was the National Collegiate Athletic Association (NCAA). The Gopher men's basketball program had been cited in an NCAA "letter of inquiry" (essentially an indictment) for 98 violations of NCAA rules. Although agreeing to the factual nature of most of the NCAA's charges, Minnesota felt that several of the players involved had not been afforded due process of law; specifically, the university refused to rule ineligible three members of the basketball team who were cited by the NCAA as receiving "extra benefits not made available to members of the student body in general."

The players were Philip Saunders, Michael Thompson, and

David Winey. Saunders admitted to placing long-distance telephone calls on a university WATS line, using the automobile of an assistant coach's mother-in-law to provide transportation to prospective athletes to a Minnesota summer basketball camp, and accepting a cost-free room for one night at the summer basketball camp. Thompson confessed that he had sold two complimentary basketball season tickets for about twice their face value. And Winey acknowledged that he had received transportation, food, lodging, and entertainment from a university athletic booster. In comparison to the seriousness of some of the NCAA's charges against other universities' athletic programs (e.g., cars given to players, crimes concealed, and grades changed), the alleged violations against the three Minnesota athletes appeared trifling.

Shortly after receiving the accusations, Minnesota granted the three players hearings before two campus committees dealing with student behavior and athletics. These committees found that, however questionably the three players had behaved, they had not violated NCAA rules and should not be declared ineligible. When Minnesota, thus, refused to rule the players ineligible, the NCAA, which takes the position that it has exclusive authority to determine eligibility of athletes, placed *all* Minnesota men's intercollegiate athletic teams on probation. A flurry of correspondence ensued between Minnesota President Peter Magrath and the NCAA. Eventually the NCAA Committee on Infractions granted Minnesota a hearing to consider "new evidence." The hearing only seemed to harden the position of the NCAA: it now insisted that Minnesota must declare the three players ineligible and that the university must face the sanction of probation for not declaring the athletes ineligible earlier. Minnesota President Magrath was left with the Hobson's choice of following the recommendation of his campus committees and thus submit to NCAA sanctions or bow to the NCAA position and ignore the legal duty to its athletes as emphasized by the university's internal university committees.

To attempt to resolve this dilemma, attorneys for the University of Minnesota made the short trip to the U.S. District Court Building in Minneapolis. There the university maintained that the NCAA-mandated probation caused "irreparable injury" to its athletic programs and sought a temporary injunction, both to restrain the NCAA from suspending the three players and to declare void the NCAA enforcement decree against Minnesota.

As in *Behagen* v. *Intercollegiate Conference*, the district court in *Minnesota* v. *NCAA* determined that the regulatory body, in this case the NCAA, is clothed with the power of state government and thus must adhere to recognized standards of due process under the Fourteenth Amendment to the federal constitution concerning the accused athletes. The court determined that internal Minnesota committees had held appropriate due process hearings and found that the conduct of the players had not violated NCAA eligibility rules. For the NCAA to act counter to the findings of the Minnesota student conduct committees imperiled the rights of the students and placed the university in an awkward position.

On December 2, 1976, Chief Judge Edward J. Devitt of the U.S. District Court in Minnesota found for the university. He granted the preliminary injunction and directed the NCAA to lift its probation against the University of Minnesota because he foresaw a strong possibility that the university would win its case on the merits. In a terse opinion Judge Devitt cited with approval the reasoning of Judge Larson in *Behagen* v. *Intercollegiate Conference* four years earlier, that is, that the athletes involved have a substantial property interest which should be afforded appropriate due process protection. Devitt submitted that "the opportunity to play intercollegiate basketball for the University of Minnesota is a property right entitled to due process guarantees because it may, albeit only in exceptional circumstances, lead to a very remunerative career in professional basketball . . ." He further stated: "It apparently has not been fully appreciated by the NCAA that its member institutions have a dual obligation to the NCAA *and* to the students" [Devitt's emphasis].

Once again Minnesota won a due process claim in federal district court. On appeal to the Eighth Circuit Court of Appeals in St. Louis, however, Judge Devitt was reversed. In a lengthy opinion, the Court of Appeals on August 2, 1977, concluded that the university had little chance of winning on the merits, so it dissolved the preliminary injunction.

The appeals court first declared that there were no serious factual disputes at issue. The three Gopher cagers acknowledged that they had committed the infractions of which they were accused, and

the factual findings of the two internal Minnesota review committees were corroborated by the NCAA. The appeals court, unlike the
two Minnesota review committees and the district court, refused to
enter into a discussion of whether the punishment of ineligibility fit
the "crimes." While acknowledging that the infractions were petty,
the appeals court adhered to the letter of the law, at least as it was
promulgated by the NCAA constitution.

Two of the three judges on the appeals panel accepted the contention that the NCAA was a state actor and, thus, under the Fourteenth Amendment could be held to normal standards of due process. Even Judge Bright, who in his concurrence claimed to "have
some doubt that the activities of the NCAA constitute 'state action,'" acknowledged that four appellate circuits were on record as
holding to the contrary.

The reasoning of the two appellate judges in the main opinion,
Judges Van Oosterhout and Webster, was essentially syllogistic: that
Saunders, Thompson, and Winey did in fact receive "extra benefits
not made available to members of the student body in general," that
the penalty specified by the NCAA constitution for such violations
(i.e., a declaration of ineligibility) was in effect when the infractions
occurred and, therefore, the commission of these infractions required
that the athletes be declared ineligible by the member institution,
the University of Minnesota. In the alternative, given this fact situation, the failure of Minnesota to declare the players ineligible exposed the university to NCAA sanctions.

Having reached this conclusion, the two-person majority of the
appeals court submitted that it did not need to reach the issue of
"whether Saunders, Thompson, and Winey had a property interest
in Intercollegiate basketball participation or a liberty interest in their
good names . . . sufficient to invoke the guarantees of due process."
Following its review of the district court record, the appellate court
concluded that the NCAA had not violated the due process rights of
the three players. In fact, the appeals court stated that the Minnesota review committee hearings themselves had afforded an adequate
measure of due process to the three athletes and that, given the infractions of NCAA rules disclosed by these committee hearings, the
players should have received the mandatory penalty of ineligibility.

The majority opinion concluded with a reminder that the NCAA was on record during the proceedings of this case that, since the infractions were slight, it would consider mitigating circumstances in reducing the penalties of ineligibility. But, before it would consider doing so, the University of Minnesota would have to comply with NCAA rules and declare Saunders, Thompson, and Winey ineligible.

What the NCAA apparently objected to was the attitude of the University of Minnesota. Because the university sought to contest the right of the NCAA to demand that Minnesota declare the three players ineligible, the NCAA would not waver in its position that the sanctions against Minnesota athletics should stand. If, and only if, Minnesota declared the three players ineligible, the NCAA appeared to say, would it then consider reducing the penalties. In essence, the NCAA was declaring that it could be charitable to the three athletes, but that its compassion would only be manifested *after* the University of Minnesota demonstrated that it would bow to strict NCAA rules. In his concurrence, Judge Bright made an apt observation. He stated that the NCAA rulings against Minnesota which led to this litigation "seem to reflect some degree of vindictiveness . . . against the University of Minnesota, to punish it for the previous improprieties of the basketball coaching staff." Possibly Bright was referring to the controversy between the University of Minnesota and the Big Ten over the suspensions of Behagen and Taylor in 1972.

The University of Minnesota petitioned the U.S. Supreme Court to hear its appeal of the 8th Circuit Court's decision in *Minnesota* v. *NCAA*. On November 29, 1977, the nation's highest court, however, dismissed the petition without explanation, thus making the appeals court decision final. Pending Supreme Court review, Minnesota had refused to declare the three basketball players ineligible. Nevertheless, a month before the Supreme Court dismissed the case, the University of Minnesota went ahead and declared ineligible Thompson and Winey (Saunders had by this time completed his eligibility). Minnesota officials were, by their own statements, acquiescing to the pressure from other Minnesota men's sports teams which were laboring under NCAA-imposed probation.

The Minnesota federal cases of *Behagen* v. *Intercollegiate Conference* and *Minnesota* v. *NCAA* are representative of two propositions in the field of sports law: first, that American courts generally recognize the activities of athletic regulatory associations such as the Big Ten and the National Collegiate Athletic Association as exercising "state action" under the terms of the Fourteenth Amendment to the U.S. Constitution; second, that as clothed with the raiment of state action, these associations must generally afford student-athletes due process of law so as not to deny their rights, including the "property right" of an athletic scholarship.

Although the legal principles enunciated in both cases appeared to bolster the rights of the college athletes vis-à-vis regulatory bodies, the athletic conferences and the NCAA were the ultimate winners. In *Behagen* v. *Intercollegiate Conference* the suspension of Behagen and Taylor by the Big Ten was upheld after additional administrative proceedings, and in *Minnesota* v. *NCAA* the sanctions against the University of Minnesota were lifted only after the university declared ineligible the offending players.

Essayists in recently published law reviews have argued that due process protection for college athletes may not be as far-reaching as a quick reading of the relevant court cases would indicate. In addition, they maintain that the rights to due process won in one court may be lost in later administrative or judicial proceedings. One way or another, the legal experts submit, athletic conferences and the NCAA eventually get their way in disputes with players, coaches, and universities. This was certainly borne out in the aftermath of *Behagen* v. *Intercollegiate Conference* and *Minnesota* v. *NCAA*.

Selected Bibliography

Green, R. "Does the NCAA Play Fair: A Due Process Analysis of NCAA Enforcement Regulations." *Duke Law Journal* 42 (October 1992): 99–144.

Miller, T. "Home Court Advantage: Florida Joins States Mandating Due Process in NCAA Proceedings." *Florida State University Law Review* 20 (Spring 1993): 871–905.

Porto, B. "Balancing Due Process and Academic Integrity in Intercollegiate Athletics: The Scholarship Athlete's Limited Property Interest in Eligibility." *Indiana Law Journal* 62 (1987): 1151–80.

Reed, W. "An Ugly Affair in Minnesota." *Sports Illustrated* February 7, 1972: 18–21.

Riguera, J. "Case Note: *NCAA* v. *Tarkanian*: The State Action Doctrine Faces a Half-Court Press." *University of Miami Law Review* 44 (1989): 197–232.

Sports Broadcasting
Who Owns the Property Rights?

Michele Murphy

Pittsburgh Athletic Company v. KQV Broadcasting Company 24 F. Supp. 490 (W.D. Fa. 1938)
Zacchini v. Scripps-Howard Broadcasting Co. 433 U.S. 562 (1977)
WCVB-TV v. Boston Athletic Association 926 F. 2nd 42 (MA 1991)

Sports broadcasting law did not exist until the 1930s when disputes began to arise over who had the right to broadcast sports events. Club owners began to challenge broadcasters who produced play-by-play descriptions of games without receiving any type of consent or authorization from the owners. Sports club owners first began to bring their complaints about these unauthorized broadcasts to the Federal Communications Commission (FCC) in 1934. The form of the challenge was to request the FCC to deny renewal licenses for those who broadcast detailed descriptions during games without club consent. Although the FCC found that unauthorized broadcasting violated concepts of fairness, they rarely found that this unfairness amounted to actual violations of the Communications Act of 1934 and therefore rarely denied renewal licenses.

Because club owners were not very successful in these endeavors and because unauthorized broadcasters continued to have their licenses renewed, owners began to bring their disputes into the courtroom. The landmark decision of *Pittsburgh Athletic Company v. KQV Broadcasting Company* in 1938 vested concepts of property rights in sports broadcasts in favor of club owners.

In 1938, KQV Broadcasting Company broadcast play-by-play reports of Pittsburgh Pirates baseball games at Forbes Field by placing employees at strategic locations outside the ballpark where their view enabled them to report the happenings in the games. Admittance to a game by the ball club was conditional on the requirement that those purchasing the tickets refrain from disseminating news of the game while it was in progress. KQV, therefore, saw no problem with their broadcasting practice since they were not members of the ticket-purchasing public, nor were they trespassing. Indeed, in response to the suit by Pittsburgh Athletic Company, KQV asserted their intention to continue doing what they thought was their legal right.

The Pittsburgh Athletic Company, owner of the Pirates, having granted General Mills, Incorporated, exclusive rights to broadcast Pirates games, had a strong monetary interest in stopping KQV's activity. General Mills had, in turn, contracted with the National Broadcasting Company, granting them radio broadcast rights of Pirates games. Socony-Vacuum also had a monetary interest in General Mills's contract with Pittsburgh Athletic, as it had purchased half of the interest in that contract.

KQV's broadcasting cost each of these four companies money because advertising pays considerably less to broadcasters, and pays off considerably less for advertisers, when the broadcasts are not the only source from which the public can obtain news of the games while they are being played. This loss to General Mills, National Broadcasting, and Socony-Vacuum in turn lowered the value of Pittsburgh Athletic's contract power regarding the broadcasting of its club's games. But without KQV committing trespass, and, in fact, doing nothing but reporting a newsworthy event, what redress existed for Pittsburgh Athletic and these broadcasting companies?

Pittsburgh Athletic requested the district court of Pennsylvania to grant a preliminary injunction requiring KQV to cease broadcasting Pirates games. The district court granted Pittsburgh Athletic's request. In this, the court relied on the fact that Pittsburgh Athletic had put forth great expenditure in the ballpark and players' salaries and concluded that the company had the right to capitalize on the value of its investment. The court also held that Pittsburgh Athletic had the sole property rights in the news of its games and, therefore, had the right to control the use of such news and contract with whomever it wished to broadcast such news and receive profit therefrom, basing its findings on the fact that Pittsburgh Athletic created the game, controlled Forbes Field, and restricted the dissemination of news from Forbes Field while the games were in progress.

In addition to investing the property right of broadcasts of games in the owners of sports clubs, the court also concluded that, as a matter of law, KQV was interfering with Pittsburgh Athletic's business in several ways: it wrongfully interfered with Pittsburgh Athletic's ability to contract with broadcasters and advertisers; it had deprived Pittsburgh Athletic of revenue it could secure in selling its broadcast rights; and, although KQV argued that it had not directly made money from its broadcasts, it had acquired the goodwill of the public by winning some of the public ear away from Pittsburgh Athletic. In this way, KQV indirectly misappropriated funds that would have been incorporated into the value of Pittsburgh Athletic's broadcasts. This misappropriation was not only unjust enrichment of KQV from what was actually a product of Pittsburgh Athletic's labor but also constituted fraud against the public. The court found that KQV engaged in unfair competition and granted the exclusive rights of broadcast to the sports club owners.

This is a landmark case because it permanently changed the nature of sports broadcasting rights. Prior to this case, anyone who could get information about the game, provided they were acting in a lawful manner (meaning not trespassing or stealing, for example), could broadcast the game while it was being played. Now, the right to broadcast was placed solely within the hands of the sports club owners, which automatically increased the monetary value of owning a sports team. Although this case was decided over fifty years ago, it still defines the property right of broadcasts today.

The Supreme Court decision in *Zacchini* v. *Scripps-Howard Broadcasting Co.* further solidified the property right one retains in a broadcast of one's performance. In that case, the Court held that the First Amendment right of freedom of speech did not prevail over the right of persons to capitalize on the broadcast of their own performances. A television news station which had broadcast the entire fifteen seconds of a famous "human cannonball" act had misappropriated the performer's monetary interest by publicizing the event without the performer's consent. This case is the landmark decision of the Court in protecting one's professional performance from being shown to the public without one's consent.

The fact that the Supreme Court had held that property rights belong to owners did not mean that players did not challenge those rights. Players on the teams challenged the interpretation that the sole property right in broadcast of sports events rested with the owners of the sports clubs. Players have brought complaints into court claiming that, since it is their performance that is being broadcast, the broadcast of such events without their consent (in other words, without their being paid) is similar to publishing a book without the consent of, or payment to, its author. An example of one such case is *Baltimore Orioles Inc. v. MLB Players Association* (1986). Deciding in favor of the club owners, the court looked at the federal Copyright Act of 1976, which gave federal protection to the owners of sports clubs in the live broadcasts of their teams' performances and their right to publicize and contract with whom they wish regarding the dissemination of the broadcasts of their clubs' games to the public.

The Copyright Act also protects the actual broadcast medium (the form in which it is recorded); the statute simply requires that a broadcast be "fixed" (recorded) and have "modest creativity" in order to become the club owners' copyrighted property. The courts have found that sports events satisfy the modest creativity requirement because of the broadcast producer's choice of angles, lights and the like, while the fact that all modern sports broadcasts are recorded and saved satisfies the "fixed" requirement.

With this federal protection on their side, the owners have little to fear from lawsuits brought by the players. The only protection players have is that given to them by state laws that protect the property interest that one retains in broadcasts of one's performances. When, however, both the federal and state government have valid laws that conflict as to whom they protect, the federal law prevails. Since the federal Copyright Act vests copyright protection in the owner of the "fixed" copy of the performance, which is the owner of the ball club, owners' rights are protected over those of the player. This is the conclusion that the court came to in *Baltimore Orioles*. It seems highly unlikely, therefore, that players will profit from broadcasts unless part of their contract with the club gives them a portion of the money generated thereby. This, however, is a matter to be negotiated privately between the player and the club rather than in the courtroom.

From all of the prevailing case law up to this point, it seems clear that the owners of sports clubs retain all rights to the dissemination of broadcasts of the games in which their clubs participate. A 1990 case decided by a Massachusetts circuit court, however, suggests that those rights might not be as solidly protected as they appear. *WCVB-TV* v. *Boston Athletic Association* held that property rights are not absolute simply because one owns the sponsorship of an event. The Boston Athletic Association (BAA) owns the registered trademark, "Boston Marathon," and has incurred great expense in their promotion of the annual event. The BAA contracted with Channel 4, WBZ-TV, of Boston to give WBZ the exclusive broadcast rights to the event. Notwithstanding, Channel 5, WCVB-TV broadcast the live event in 1990 and, like KQV in *Pittsburgh Athletic,* asserted its intention to do so in 1991. Although this scenario seems the same as *Pittsburgh Athletic,* the district court denied the motion brought by the BAA for a preliminary injunction to prevent WCVB from broadcasting the marathon again.

This decision, however, is not necessarily inconsistent with *Pittsburgh Athletic.* In the *WCVB-TV* case, the district court found it problematic to prevent broadcasting newsworthy events that occur on the public streets. Pittsburgh Athletic, of course, controlled its game performances by holding them in a privately owned stadium. The BAA has taken no simlar steps to bring the Boston Marathon within its exclusive control. Given the nature of a marathon race, conducting it on private property is not possible. Unable to restrict access to the general public, the BAA cannot forbid others from disseminating the news of the event. Thus, the event cannot be considered a protected performance; rather, it is a public newsworthy event about which anyone can report to the public.

The Massachusetts court of appeals, in reviewing *Boston Athletic,* affirmed the district court's decision for different reasons. It focused entirely on trademark law in its decision. Trademark law protects monetary investment in the distinctive quality of a symbol that the public recognizes as belonging to a particular company or product. The BAA had argued that the public, when seeing its "Boston Marathon" trademark on Channel 5, would mistakenly believe that Channel 5 was authorized by the BAA to broadcast the event. The court pointed out that trademark protection is to prevent the consumer from being misled as to which company is the producer of a product or event. No purpose is served, therefore, by enforcing the trademark law where danger of confusion to the public is minimal or absent. The court said that whatever confusion did exist here was unlike the type of confusion that trademark law was meant to protect against. But the court pointed out that trademark protection would apply to situations in which someone with no affiliation with the BAA sold T-shirts bearing the "Boston Marathon" trademark without the BAA's consent. Whereas the public would have a legitimate interest in the authenticity of the T-shirt they paid for, when people watch the marathon on TV, they could not care less who is affiliated with whom. They want to see the race, and they want to see the result. The public is not getting any less for its money nor is it being deceived or confused by watching the event on Channel 5 instead of Channel 4.

As the law stands now, the owners of sports clubs have the sole right to contract with others regarding the broadcast of games in which their team participates when they maintain control over public access to the games. This property right can withstand challenges by the players on such teams by virtue of the domination of federal law over state law. One who controls the production and sponsorship of a sporting event may not have such property rights when the event occurs on the public streets, with unrestricted access to the public, because it then becomes a newsworthy event unprotected by property law.

Selected Bibliography

Federal Communications Commission. *Federal Communications Commission Reports,* 1935.

Garrett, T. and P. Hochberg. "Sports Broadcasting and the Law." *Labor Law Journal* 59 (Spring 1983): 155–193.

Sagle, R. "The Nature and Effect of Major Sports Restrictions on Radio and Television Broadcasting Rights under the Sherman Act." *The George Washington Law Review* 21 (March 1953): 466–482.

Sobel, L. *Professional Sports and the Law.* New York: Law-Arts Publishers, Inc., 1977.

The Land of the Free Disputes Homes for the Braves

Patrick Allitt

**Wisconsin v. Milwaukee Braves, Inc., 1966 CCH Trade
Cases 71,738 (Wisc. Cir. Ct. 1966)**
**Wisconsin v. Milwaukee Braves, Inc., 144 N.W. 2d 1
(Wisc. Sup. Ct. 1966)**

The baseball Braves were a venerable institution, older than the century, when the team announced in 1953 that it was leaving Boston and moving to Milwaukee. A few fans grumbled at the news but consoled themselves with the thought that the more popular Red Sox were still in town. The threadbare Braves, said owner Lou Perini, desperately needed the revenue that Milwaukee offered. For a while the shift was a big success: star players such as Warren Spahn, Eddie Matthews, and Hank Aaron led the Braves to victory in the 1957 World Series and to three other pennants.

Lean years followed, however, and attendance fell off in the early 1960s. In 1962 Perini sold the franchise to a group of young Chicago businessmen, chaired by William Bartholomay, who planned to recoup their costs and boost income. The city of Atlanta, under image-conscious Mayor Ivan Allen, Jr., approached the Braves consortium and offered them a new home in the rapidly growing "city too busy to hate." They accepted the offer, and the National League endorsed the Braves' projected move. Under a secret agreement which soon became public knowledge, Atlanta began to build Fulton County Stadium as the new home field for the Braves. At that time there were no major league franchises in the deep South, so an Atlanta-based team stood to gain much larger annual fees from the sale of broadcasting rights over a larger area than a Milwaukee team which had to compete with nearby Chicago. This was not the first time a franchise had tried to move (as the Braves' own earlier history showed), but it was the first time a team from a one-team city had planned to exit, leaving its local fans bereft of major league baseball.

The shift out of Milwaukee caused more anguish than had the 1953 move. African-American star Aaron, for example, said publicly that he did not relish going to the racist South and that he would first investigate conditions in Atlanta before going with the club. The franchise owners, hoping to play the 1965 season in Atlanta, were compelled by a court order to stay in Milwaukee for that season to fulfill a stadium contract that they had signed with the county. The mayor's office claimed that Milwaukee would lose two million dollars and two thousand jobs if the Braves left, and these grim estimates formed part of the background to an antitrust lawsuit the state of Wisconsin filed in late 1965.

Wisconsin Attorney General Bronson C. La Follette, grandson of the famous Progressive Era politician Robert La Follette, sued the National League and the Braves, claiming that they were in effect unlawfully boycotting Milwaukee and violating the state's "Little Sherman Antitrust Act" by conducting an illegal monopoly. He hoped that the National League, then undergoing expansion, would be ordered to grant a replacement franchise to Milwaukee in compensation for its loss if the Braves left.

The drama reached its height in March 1966 in a packed Milwaukee courtroom with each side bringing batteries of lawyers before the judge (there was no jury). The National League and the Braves took the case very seriously because of the millions of dollars at stake and because the decision might set a precedent for their operations elsewhere. Among the heavy hitters the NL brought to court was attorney Bowie Kuhn, who was to become the commissioner of baseball three years later. When lawyer Willard Stanford, for the state, declared that he was going to bring back the Braves "screaming or otherwise," Earl Jinkinson, for the Braves, answered with equal melodrama, "This could be the death-knell of baseball."

At the end of twenty-eight days of court arguments, the plaintiffs were pleasantly surprised to find that Circuit Court Judge Elmer Roller of Milwaukee agreed with them. Roller, a sixty-four-year-old baseball fan with a good reputation for scholarly decisions, ruled that the National League had indeed violated the Wisconsin antitrust law. Despite working on the ruling for thirty-seven hours straight, however, Roller was unable to deliver his verdict until the day after the Braves played their 1966 home opener in Atlanta before a crowd of fifty thousand. He ordered the Braves back to Milwaukee, even though the season had begun, unless the National League guaranteed the city an expansion team in return. In addition, he fined the Braves and the National League a total of $55,000 plus court costs.

The Braves and the National League appealed at once. They had not waited passively for this blow to fall. Instead they had persuaded a Georgia judge to issue an injunction ordering the Braves to fulfill the terms of the twenty-five-year contract by playing all their home games at Atlanta and nowhere else. A Texas federal court upheld the injunction. On July 27, 1966, two weeks after the All-Star break, the Wisconsin Supreme Court, acting quickly in view of the possible chaos a mid-season move might create, overturned Judge Roller's decision. It agreed with him that baseball was a monopoly, but added that a continuous body of precedent existed that exempted baseball from the antitrust laws.

On Monday, December 12, 1966, well after the end of the season, the United States Supreme Court, Milwaukee's last hope, voted 4–3 against hearing the case, thus allowing the Wisconsin Supreme Court's verdict to stand. Only three of the justices who considered the issue, Hugo L. Black, William O. Douglas, and William J. Brennan, favored reviewing the case; a minimum of four is necessary if the case was to be added to the Supreme Court's docket. La Follette and the other Milwaukee malcontents said they would try to reopen the case, but they had no luck. The major leagues' longstanding exemption from antitrust laws, therefore, enjoyed further confirmation. The Braves stayed in their Atlanta home, and within a few years, the arrival of the Brewers mollified Milwaukee's wounded civic pride.

Selected Bibliography

Campbell, D. "Antitrust Analysis in Professional Sports Management Cases: The Public Cries 'Foul.'" *Arizona Law Review* 25 (1983–1984): 995–1021.

Eckhouse, M. "More Woes Than Wahooes for Baseball Wanderers." In P. Bjarkman, ed., *Encyclopedia of Major League Baseball Team Histories: National League*. Westport: Meckler, 1991, 20–71.

Sobel, L. *Professional Sports and the Law*. New York: Law-Arts Publishers, Inc., 1977.

Fear, Attack, and Pressure

The Relocation of the Raiders

Wayne S. Quirk

NFL et al v. Oakland Raiders, 726 F. 2nd 1381 (9th Cir. 1984), *cert denied*, 105 S. Ct. 397, 83 L. Ed. 2d 331, 53 U.S.L.W. 3342 (1984)

City of Oakland v. Oakland Raiders, 32 Cal. 3d 60, 646 p. 2d 835, 183 Cal. Rptr. 673 (1982); 150 Cal. App. 3d 267, 197 Cal. Rptr. 729 (1983)

On August 27, 1988, the National Football League (NFL) solemnly paid last respects to former Pittsburgh Steelers owner Art Rooney. At one point during the funeral service, the presiding cleric asked the mourners to offer each other the sign of peace. NFL Commissioner Pete Rozelle and Los Angeles Raiders managing partner Al Davis shook hands, sharing one of the very few moments of harmony between the two longtime adversaries. The conflicts between these powerful figures have spanned almost thirty years. Davis's controversial decision to relocate the Raiders contributed to critical judicial pronouncements on the issue of franchise movement in sports. The rulings stimulated consideration of significant sports industry antitrust issues and led to the introduction of protective legislation.

These important and far-reaching issues originated with the seemingly innocent 1978 relocation of the Los Angeles Rams from the Los Angeles Coliseum to the "Big A" stadium in Anaheim. Many franchises in the NFL, as well as in other sports leagues, previously changed locations with little resistance from administrative bodies. In fact, legal scholars contend that only unusual circumstances inhibit franchise movement. During Rozelle's tenure, considerations of franchise movement usually met objective assessment of the costs and benefits for both the club and the league. The unusual situation in the Raiders case derived from the deep-seated personal feud between Davis and Rozelle. Davis decided against following established channels, choosing to do things his own way, that is, the "Raider way."

The Raider way is distinguished by many of Davis's favorite terms and phrases, such as "domination," "pressure," "attack," "fear," "intimidation," "commitment to excellence," and "getting it done." One of the most telling anecdotes regarding Davis's approach to football and business involves a brief conversation with Raider Mark van Eeghen. During a media session, the Raider fullback went into a tirade about the ethics of relocating the team. Later, van Eeghen confronted Davis and inquired if he were disturbed about the comments. Davis simply replied, "Just win."

The approved relocation of the Rams to Anaheim left the Coliseum without a tenant, so the Coliseum Commission quickly filed suit against the NFL for antitrust violations. The suit remained essentially dormant until the Raiders became a potential tenant for the stadium. Unable to reach a resolution with the Oakland-Alameda County Coliseum Commission, Davis signed a memorandum of agreement with the LA Coliseum.

The existing mechanism for franchise relocation involved a 75 percent approval vote from team owners. This approval mechanism is part of the NFL Constitution and is referred to as Rule 4.3. The annual NFL meeting in the spring of 1980 provided team owners with an opportunity to vote on the potential relocation of the Raiders. The final tally revealed an overwhelming twenty-two opposed, zero in favor, five abstentions and one, the Raiders, not voting. Ironically, league votes over the previous years on an assortment of issues often tabulated twenty-seven to one, with the individualist Davis representing the minority vote.

Talk of lawsuits dominated the meetings in Rancho Mirage, California, and the *Los Angeles Times* dispatched a reporter with a law degree to cover the proceedings. The colorful field slang of the NFL rapidly added legal terms to the established language. Instead of discussions of defensive strategies using red dogs or line stunts, the talks focused on temporary restraining orders, stays, injunctions, and the British-born concept of "eminent domain."

The vote to deny the franchise move prompted the Los Angeles Coliseum Commission to renew its action against the NFL. Unusual court proceedings, punctuated by a hung jury and mistrial, eventually led to judicial consideration of the "single business entity" status of the NFL. Ultimately, in the *NFL* v. *Oakland Raiders* decision, single entity status was ruled inappropriate. The court reasoned that NFL clubs are separate business entities whose products have independent value. Furthermore, while cooperation is necessary to produce a football game, it is the independent attributes of each of the teams that distinguishes the clubs within the NFL.

After rejecting the single entity defense of the NFL, the appeals court applied the (to some) infamous "rule of reason" for determination of the potential trade restraint of Rule 4.3 under the Sherman Antitrust Act. Section 1 of the act prohibits every contract, combination, or conspiracy in restraint of trade. Most possible trade restraints, such as the Coliseum's suit, are subjected to the rule of reason, which weighs the positive and negative effects of an agreement on competition to determine whether the agreement imposes an unreasonable restraint on trade. The factors evaluated by the court for this case included the characteristics of the market, the history and intent of Rule 4.3, and the reasonableness of the rule. Following four years of injunctions, temporary restraining orders, permanent injunctions, and litigation, in *NFL* v. *Oakland Raiders* the Ninth Circuit Court of Appeals found that Rule 4.3 violated Section 1 of the Sherman Antitrust Act.

The conclusion of the court provided the NFL with a formula to protect Rule 4.3 from antitrust scrutiny. The court advised the NFL to use objective factors such as population, economic projections, facilities, and regional balance instead of a simple vote of the owners. Almost as an afterthought, the court suggested fan loyalty as a consideration. The use of these specified criteria served to objectify the process. Alternatively, an arbitrary vote was viewed as a potential conspiracy by the owners against single franchise relocation.

Legal scholars speculated that the narrow scope of the decision reflected the appeals court's reluctance to establish a precedent that could make the NFL incapable of violating Section 1. It is also probable that the prevailing antiregulatory climate of the Reagan years influenced the direction of the decision.

As this case slowly advanced through the California courtrooms, the Raiders dominated action on the football field. Super Bowl victories in 1981 and 1983 highlighted their twenty-one-year NFL supremacy in winning percentage. In fact, the Raider's .715 winning percentage during this period far exceeded the success of the best clubs in other major sports. One of the elements of the Raiders' success was the approach used by Davis to build the team. The most apparent strategy involved acquiring renegades or castoffs from other clubs and turning them into championship-caliber players. Over the years the roster brimmed with players finding prosperity with the Raiders after floundering with other teams.

The scouting strategy employed by Davis, however, probably contributed more to the success of the team than the rejuvenation of misfit players. Davis operatives populated the coaching ranks at every level of organized football. Topflight players such as Howie Long, Fred Biletnikoff, and Mark van Eeghen were selected in low draft positions, much to the bewilderment of other teams. The subtle yet effective skills of these players didn't score high on the timed and measured formulas used by other scouts, but caught the attention of the Raiders' grass-roots scouts.

These types of players meshed well with the aggressive Raiders style. The legacy of the Raiders' on-field tactics is an offense that attacks the opposition with length. Pass patterns are run deeper, quarterbacks hold the ball longer, and linemen sustain their blocks until the whistle sounds. The defense strikes with an aggressive territorial claim to their side of the line of scrimmage. The strategy most annoying to Davis is ball control designed to keep defenses off the field. In stark contrast, Davis admonishes, "Attack, fear, pressure. Don't take what they give you. You're going deep and they're not going to stop you by design or location. They have to do it on the field. Screw it. You say you can stop us. Prove it."

Unquestionably, this football strategy was consistent with Davis's approach to negotiations and administration. Despite his success and unusual style, Davis's fellow owners seemed quite charmed with him until he began dragging them into court. The treble damages awarded to Davis in the antitrust violation decision further distanced the Raiders owner from his colleagues.

The Davis style of not taking what is given but rather going deep regardless of the opponent's design stood almost in direct contrast to Commissioner Rozelle's preference for negotiation and conciliation.

The growth of the NFL during the Rozelle years was marked by competitive parity on the field and financial prosperity off the field. It was popularly believed that Rozelle established himself as the best commissioner in the history of sports during his twenty-nine-year reign.

Among the many court cases entangled in the Raiders' move from Oakland to Los Angeles was the highly publicized eminent domain suit, *City of Oakland* v. *Oakland Raiders*. This action found the City of Oakland petitioning to exercise eminent domain powers that are normally used for seizing land to build parks, streets, or bridges in order to stop the Raiders' move to Los Angeles.

The history of these eminent domain powers began with the seventeenth-century English Parliament. In principle, the doctrine provides that, upon seizure of personal property, the Crown must return a fair price to the owner. America's founders wrote the idea into the Fifth Amendment with the codicil that condemnation was permissible only for public use. In California, the definition of public use became especially expansive and the state court upheld the City of Oakland's eminent domain action to acquire all of the Raiders' franchise rights related to the NFL Franchise Certificate of Membership. This action included the right to operate the team as well as to administer the player contracts associated with the franchise. The justices curiously reasoned that there was no difference between seizing land to build an arena and seizing the team to play inside.

The decision allowing condemnation for public use forced the Raiders to rely upon other arguments to allow the proposed move. The grounds which proved successful for the Raiders supply a valuable lesson: that even an apparently meritless argument should not be underestimated. In a surprising decision, the court found that the condemnation violated a curious principle termed the "dormant commerce clause."

The commerce clause (U. S. Constitution, Article 1, Section 8) grants Congress the power to regulate commerce among the states. Since there is no expressed limit to the extent of state regulation, the Supreme Court determines the extent to which states may regulate interstate commerce when Congress remains silent. The ensuing body of law is known as the dormant commerce clause.

The City of Oakland argued for exemption from the clause, relying on case doctrine, the market participation doctrine, and a lack of precedent. Ultimately, each argument failed and the court found that the city sought not to advance the health or safety of its citizens, but rather to promote public recreation, social relations, and economic benefits. In the view of the court, the burden placed on interstate commerce by the condemnation outweighed any benefit to Oakland. The court thus disallowed the attempted condemnation of the Raiders' franchise based only on dormant commerce-clause grounds.

During the bizarre unraveling of the court cases and a 1982 strike, the NFL somehow continued to prosper. Commissioner Rozelle successfully lobbied Congress for an innovative revenue-sharing plan that both made the owners rich and stabilized the league. He deftly negotiated a network television contract that secured the league's future into the next decade. Franchise values escalated from an average of around $1 million in the early 1960s to well over $140 million in recent transactions. In a stroke of irony, the increase in franchise value was now clearly linked with the effects of the Raiders' court decisions.

Reviews of Rozelle's career following his 1989 retirement speculate that the turmoil of handling Davis ranked among the most challenging of his tasks. It is most probable that the animosity between Rozelle and Davis began with the commissioner's decision to remove the Raiders owner from the competition committee in 1977. Steelers coach Chuck Noll accused Raiders defensive back George Atkinson of being part of the criminal element in the game. Davis, of course, sided with his aggressive defensive player, and Rozelle removed him from the prestigious competition committee. Davis also found himself excluded from other committees' activities. Davis further alienated himself as he collected antitrust treble damages and decided to testify for the United States Football League in an unrelated antitrust suit.

As Rozelle approached retirement in the late 1980s, the two adversaries seemed close to a reconciliation. They shared that rare moment of peace at the Rooney funeral. Davis also raced to become the first to shake Rozelle's hand at the announcement of the commissioner's retirement. In an act of incredible compromise and vision, Rozelle appointed Davis to the committee to select his successor. His reasoning for such a move probably rested both in capitalizing upon Davis's previous experience as commissioner of the American Football League, as well as attempting to solidify the ranks of the owners. Rozelle retired peacefully and the owners accepted Davis back into their inner circle. Unfortunately, within a few months Davis fell back into the fray, separating himself from the owners as well as football fans and city officials.

The reluctance of the courts to set precedent with a decision in either of these two major cases left only the uncertain power of the free market and regulatory legislation to control franchise movement. There was simply nothing to stop greedy owners from using the leverage of the threat of movement to negotiate with both existing locations and potential sports cities.

Anecdotes illustrating this legal blackmail littered the sports world during the past several years. In Chicago, only brilliant last-minute maneuvers by then Governor James Thompson stopped the baseball White Sox from relocating to the Sundome in St. Petersburg, Florida. In Detroit, previous Tigers owner Tom Monahan and Bo Schembechler, the team president, joined forces in an attempt to steamroll an economically depressed community into financing a new stadium. The football Cardinals left St. Louis for Phoenix, and Minnesota hockey fans watched the North Stars relocate to Dallas.

The most brazen examples, of course, came from Davis and the Raiders. Davis was clearly not satisfied with the situation in Los Angeles. The Coliseum houses relatively few seats in between the goal posts and dwindling attendance in the 90,000 seat stadium made the crowds seem small and removed. Many fans speculated that the Raiders no longer had a home field advantage. Over the past several years, Davis entertained offers from Oakland, Sacramento, Los Angeles, and Irwindale, a southern California municipality boasting one gravel pit for every fifty-five citizens. Irwindale experienced the misfortune of watching Davis pocket a $10-million-dollar nonrefundable deposit when the town's proposal failed due to lack of financing and a suitable site. In recent negotiations, it now seems clear that the Raiders franchise is moving back north to Oakland. Pending only a review by the Oakland City Council and the Alameda County Board of Supervisors, an agreement was reached approving the Raiders' relocation to Oakland. Terms of the agreement include $85 million for stadium modernization and a $31.9

million loan for timely relocation to Oakland for the 1995 season. After thirteen years of playing in front of dwindling Los Angeles crowds and a bizarre series of negotiations, the Raiders are returning to Oakland. In a move reflecting the current climate, the NFL issued what is termed a "terse" statement which offered no opinion concerning the move.

In contrast, there is at least one example of a lesson well learned from this decade of movement and expansion. In 1994, the National Basketball Association forestalled the relocation of the Minnesota Timberwolves to New Orleans. Learning perhaps from the earlier court prescription for antitrust exemption, Commissioner David Stern employed an objective analysis of conditions almost identical to the factors delineated by the court in the antitrust decision.

The pressures of the free market and increasing sophistication of some sports league administrators do not appear sufficient for control of sports franchise owners. Several members of Congress initially responded to the courts' silence on the matter by submitting legislation designed to protect the professional sports community. To date, however, no protection has been enacted and avaricious owners continue to prosper while loyal fans and municipalities are either pressured into financially challenging agreements or into waving goodbye to local sports teams.

Selected Bibliography:

Amoroso, R. "Controlling Professional Sports Team Relocations: The Oakland Raiders' Antitrust Case and Beyond." *Rutgers Law Journal,* 17 (Winter 1986): 283–319.

Berry, R. and G. Wong. *Law and Business of the Sports Industries.* Volumes I and II. Dover: Auburn House Publishing Company, 1986.

Hofer, R. "Lord of the Rings." *Sports Illustrated.* December 11, 1989: 104–113.

Lazaroff, D. "The Antitrust Implications of Franchise Relocation Restrictions in Professional Sports." *Fordham Law Review,* 53 (November 1984): 157–220.

Mead, L. "Raiders: 7.2 million, City of Oakland: 0. Was That the Final Gun? A Story of Intrigue, Suspense and Questionable Reasoning." *Loyola Entertainment Law Journal,* 9 (Spring 1989): 401–424.

Nack, W. "A Commitment to Cynicism." *Sports Illustrated.* September 17, 1990: 102.

Press, A. and R. Sandza. "Oakland Blitzes the Raiders." *Newsweek,* July 26, 1982: 68.

Weistart, J. "League Control of Market Opportunities: A Perspective on Competition and Cooperation in the Sports Industry." *Duke Law Journal,* 1984 (December 1984): 1013–1070.

Wiley, R. "Less Than Colossal in the LA Coliseum." *Sports Illustrated.* September 2, 1982: 22–29.

York, D. "The Professional Sports Community Protection Act: Congress' Best Response to Raiders." *The Hastings Law Journal,* 38 (January 1987): 345–375.

Zimmerman, P. "Whither the Raiders?" *Sports Illustrated*. May 24, 1980: 56–60.
Zimmerman, P. "Al to World: Get Out of Our Way." *Sports Illustrated*. July 5, 1984: 86–101.

Colts Gallop to Indianapolis

Lester S. Brooks

Indianapolis Colts v. Mayor and City Council of Baltimore—741 F. 2d. (1984), 733 F. 2d. (1984)

"Unitas to Berry—Touchdown!" This was a familiar phrase heard by thousands of Baltimore Colts fans on many Sunday afternoons and represents part of the glorious tradition of football in Baltimore. But that tradition came to a jarring end in March 1984, when the Baltimore football franchise moved to Indianapolis, Indiana.

The Colts had a rich history in Baltimore filled with sensational victories, painful losses, and Hall of Fame performers. The National Football League (NFL) came to Baltimore for good in 1953. The Colts defeated the New York Giants in a 1958 sudden-death overtime NFL Championship game at Yankee Stadium, 23–17. "The game" is supposed to have changed the face of sports in America by propelling football to the top of the sports world. The Colts went on to establish a notable football tradition highlighted by a dramatic last-second victory in Super Bowl VII over the Dallas Cowboys in 1973. An integral element to Colts football tradition was the players themselves, such as Johnny Unitas, Raymond Berry, Alan Ameche, Gino Marchetti, "Big Daddy" Lipscomb, Art Donovan, and Lenny Moore. These Colts were just some of the stars who brought excitement, character, and personality to Baltimore. Indeed, a symbiotic relationship seemed to have developed between the team and the city.

When the Colts moved in 1984, they were owned by Robert Irsay, who had obtained the club in an unusual trade of franchises. Irsay received the Colts in July 1972 in an exchange with Carroll Rosenbloom, who received the Los Angeles Rams franchise. But late in the evening of March 28, 1984, the nightmare for the city of Baltimore became a reality. Mayflower Company moving vans arrived at the Baltimore Colts' Owings Mills training facility and under the direction of the general counsel to the team, Michael Chernoff, packed up team equipment and office supplies and departed for Indianapolis. The long relationship between team and city came to a midnight halt and precipitated the ire of Baltimore Colts fans everywhere. From the governor and mayor to the average citizen, a feeling of betrayal gripped all.

Talk of an impending move by the Colts had appeared in the Baltimore newspapers since early in 1984. Irsay entered into negotiations with officials from Phoenix and Indianapolis. Although Phoenix eventually withdrew its bid, Indianapolis successfully enticed the Colts to Indiana, despite frenzied attempts to keep the Colts in Maryland. The *Baltimore Sun* newspaper reported on March 30, 1984, that included in the attempt to keep the Colts was a plan, unveiled by Governor Harry Hughes, consisting of a low-interest (8 percent) loan of $15 million, a guaranteed attendance of 43,000 at home games, and the purchase of the Owings Mills training facility that would alleviate a multimillion-dollar debt for Irsay. Baltimore mayor William Donald Schaefer was particularly bitter at the move because Irsay never responded to him regarding the package that was offered to persuade him to keep the franchise in Baltimore.

Not only did Baltimore officials attempt to entice Irsay to remain, but coercive measures were used to prevent him from abandoning the city. On Tuesday, March 27, 1984, the Maryland legislature introduced an emergency bill allowing for the condemnation of the Colts under eminent domain. This legislation seems pivotal in Irsay's decision to move, for when news reached him about the city's intention, he immediately set into motion the removal of the Colts to Indianapolis. The law of eminent domain would have allowed the City of Baltimore to buy the franchise at market value (the city solicitor's office set market value at $40 million) or condemn the football franchise in order to keep the team from being transferred. Interestingly enough, not only did the Maryland legislature pass a bill allowing the city to utilize the law of eminent domain, but Baltimore Circuit Judge Robert L. Karwacki also signed an injunction blocking the Colts' departure, and the mayor and City Council of Baltimore enacted Emergency Ordinance No. 32 authorizing condemnation of the team and forbidding the further movement of the ment of the franchise. Finally, Joseph DiBlasi introduced a resolution in the Baltimore City Council pleading with the NFL to allow Baltimore to retain the name, logo, and colors of the Colts for only a Baltimore franchise.

Eminent domain proved to be a troubling issue. The principle held that private property could be taken by the government for public use only. But it was not clear what "public use" meant and if the government had the liberty to take anything it wanted. Additionally, in the case of the Colts, did eminent domain allow for condemnation of property beyond the state boundaries? That is, the Colts franchise was no longer operating within the territorial jurisdiction of Maryland and therefore eminent domain could not be applied. In answer to this quandary Maryland officials countered with a "minimum-contacts argument," claiming that since some of the property of the Colts still remained in Maryland, the entire franchise could be classified under eminent domain. The U.S. District Court did not allow the city's argument since a team appearing in another state for a game established minimum contacts with that state which could claim the entire franchise.

Meanwhile, the Colts filed suit in the U.S. District Court of Indiana on April 5, 1984. The resolution of this case would determine who should be awarded the Colts, Baltimore or Indianapolis. The Colts, now of Indianapolis, argued against Baltimore condemnation of the franchise while claiming that the team had contracted with the Capital Improvement Board of Indianapolis to play its games in the Hoosier Dome for twenty years. Although the court decided that there were no adverse claims in the case and therefore did not award the team to either defendant, filing of the case shows that the Colts attempted to bolster their right of franchise relocation.

Circumstances surrounding the Colts' relocation were complex. The owner, Irsay, had headquarters in Chicago, Illinois; the Baltimore Football Club was incorporated in Delaware; the Colts played their games in Baltimore, Maryland; and the team had been transferred to Indianapolis, Indiana. When the city of Baltimore initiated condemnation against the Colts, the U.S. District Court held that, under Maryland law, Baltimore had no right to prevent the owner of the football franchise from moving outside of the state without payment of compensation and that the mere filing of a condemnation petition was insufficient to establish rights over the franchise. The court stated that the general rule is for a condemning authority to pay compensation prior to obtaining possession. Since the Colts were beyond the jurisdiction of Baltimore and had left the city prior to the filing of condemnation proceedings, the owner was free to remove the franchise.

Also, at an NFL meeting on March 2, 1984, Article 4.3 of the NFL Constitution and Bylaws came under consideration. The bylaw stated that franchises have no right to transfer to a different city without prior approval by three-fourths of the members in the NFL. The NFL, however, according to Commissioner Pete Rozelle, decided to waive the provisions of this bylaw, claiming that this was a "Colt decision." The NFL thus refused to express approval or disapproval on Irsay's impending move to Indianapolis. But for the city of Baltimore, the worst defeat in its sports history had occurred, the loss of the beloved Baltimore Colts football franchise.

The transfer of sports franchises has a long and involved history dating back to the nineteenth century. The Baltimore Colts' move to Indianapolis is just one recent case of franchise transfer. By no means have we seen the last of sport franchise relocations nor the emotional turmoil that follows.

Selected Bibliography

Mayor and City Council of Baltimore vs. Baltimore Football Club, Inc. 624 Federal Supplement. United States District Court, D. Maryland. December 9, 1985: 278–290.

Mufson, E. "Jurisdictional Limitations on Intangible Property in Eminent Domain: Focus on the Indianapolis Colts." Indiana Law Journal 60 (1984–1985): 389–410.

Staudoher, P. "Team Relocation in Professional Sports." Labor Law Journal 9 (September 1985): 728–733.

"Though the Colts Bolted for Indy, the Band Marches on in Baltimore." Sports Illustrated. September 19, 1986: 10–12.

The NFL-AFL Merger
Law, Politics, and the Power of Money

H. Daniel Holm Jr.

American Football League v. National Football League,
205 F. Supp. 60 (D. Md. 1962)

In September 1970, the twenty-six teams of the newly merged National Football League (NFL) took to the field of play and ended one of the longest and costliest wars in the history of professional sports. The teams, now organized into the National Football Conference and the American Football Conference, had originally belonged to the established NFL and its upstart rival, the American Football League (AFL). The merger concluded over ten years of legal maneuvering, political intrigue, and a financially draining struggle for television rights and player talent.

Professional football dates from 1895. The game as played at its inception bears little resemblance to the multimillion-dollar industry of today. In its early years, professional football was not much more than a hobby, as most of its players simultaneously played for college teams. Little organization existed until 1920, when the American Professional Football Association was formed. In its first year, the association included eleven teams, five located in the state of Ohio alone. The association changed its name in 1921, and the "National Football League" was born. Initially much less popular than college football, the NFL attracted increasing numbers of fans as it attracted "name" players. For example, in 1925 the Chicago Bears signed University of Illinois star Red Grange, and fan interest soared. By 1933 the NFL teams were organized into a Western Division and an Eastern Division. In 1936, the NFL held its first player draft. Prior to the middle of the 1940s, the NFL was unchallenged as the major professional football organization. In 1946, the eight-team All-America Football Conference began play, but it lasted only four years. However, three of its teams, Baltimore, Cleveland, and San Francisco, became part of a thirteen-team NFL in 1950.

The AFL arose out of the frustration its founders experienced in trying to purchase NFL teams or to obtain expansion franchises. Two of the prime movers behind the AFL were businessmen Lamar Hunt and Bud Adams, Jr. In 1957 and 1958, both had unsuccessfully attempted to purchase the Chicago Cardinals. When that failed, they approached then NFL commissioner Bert Bell, requesting expansion franchises. Bell rejected the requests, responding that no expansion franchises would be granted until the early 1960s. Thus rebuffed, Hunt and Adams immediately made plans to create the AFL.

Organization of the AFL began in earnest in early 1959. By midyear, Hunt approached Commissioner Bell and disclosed his intent to form the new league. Initially, Hunt proposed an immediate merger of the two leagues. Bell flatly rejected the proposition. Undeterred, the AFL was officially formed in 1959 by Hunt and Adams, along with businessmen Barron Hilton, Harry Wismer, Bob Howsam, Max Winter, and H.P. Skoglund.

Joe Foss, World War II hero and former South Dakota governor, received the nod as the AFL's first commissioner. He later commented that for the first six weeks of his job he worked without pay because the AFL had no money. He deemed it a "miracle" that the AFL ever survived its early days.

The AFL began a full schedule of games in 1960. Affiliated with it were eight teams located in eight cities: Boston, Buffalo, Houston, New York, Dallas, Denver, Los Angeles, and Oakland. After the 1960 season, the Los Angeles team moved to San Diego. At the same time, the NFL operated with twelve teams located in eleven cities: two teams in Chicago, and one each in Cleveland, New York, Philadelphia, Pittsburgh, Washington, Baltimore, Detroit, Los Angeles, San Francisco, and Green Bay. In 1960, the NFL gave franchises to Dallas and to Minneapolis–St. Paul. The Dallas franchise began play in 1960, and the Twin Cities started the following year (the delay occurred because of an NFL-imposed requirement that the franchise construct an adequately sized stadium).

The NFL and the AFL immediately engaged in vigorous confrontation on several fronts. While the two leagues did not initially recruit each other's veteran players, they did compete for college athletes. The predictable effect of this battle was to drive up player salaries. The NFL and the AFL also fought for television contracts. For many years, NFL games had been broadcast by CBS, through arrangements made by the teams or their sponsors. The AFL did not have the financial resources to wrestle this contract away from the NFL but was able to negotiate a modest pact with ABC. Hunt, recognizing that the AFL could not compete as an equal with the NFL, tried to blunt the effect of unbridled competition when he met with Bell in 1959. Hunt proposed a common player draft and a prohibition on broadcasting any game of either league into a city where either an NFL or AFL game was being played. Bell, with the vigorous backing of NFL owners, rejected both proposals. The ensuing cost of competition between the NFL and the AFL threatened the financial solvency of franchises in both leagues and eventually resulted in merger.

On October 14, 1960, the AFL filed an antitrust lawsuit against the NFL in the Federal District Court of the state of Maryland. The resulting decision in *American Football League* v. *National Football League* provides a fascinating look at the economics and power politics of professional football in the early 1960s. The court established the framework for its decision when it identified three factors as requisites for the successful operation of a major league professional football team: first, membership in a league in which the several clubs are reasonably well matched in playing strength and are located in areas which can and will support the teams by attendance, and throughout the season show sufficient interest to provide adequate revenues for both the home and visiting clubs; second, the acquisition of a group of capable players; and third, the sale of television rights.

The essence of the AFL suit was that the NFL had monopolized, attempted to monopolize, and conspired to monopolize the market for professional football, thereby blocking the AFL from obtaining the three requisites noted above. Therefore, the court was required to decide whether the NFL had monopolized the metropolitan areas in which franchises could successfully locate, whether the NFL had monopolized player recruitment, and whether the NFL had monopolized the sale of television rights. The court began its decision by observing that to prove monopolization, the AFL had to first demonstrate that the NFL possessed monopoly power, and second, show that the NFL undertook a course of action the consequence of which was to exclude competition or prevent competition in professional football or engage in any activity which was undertaken with the purpose or intent of accomplishing that end.

According to the court, monopoly power "is the power to control prices or exclude competition." To determine whether the NFL had such power, the court had to identify the "relevant market" involved. It held that the market for professional football was essentially nationwide. For example, professional football teams competed for players and coaches from across the nation. In addition, competition for television and radio contracts and commercial sponsors was national. The only area of competition not nationwide in scope was the competition for attendance at games and the competition between the telecast of a game from one city and the actual playing of the game in another city. The court found that this aspect of competition was generally confined to the area in which the game was played. The court characterized the competition between the AFL and the NFL for metropolitan areas in which to locate franchises as "the most important aspect of the competition in this case."

After reviewing the evidence, the court concluded that the NFL had no monopoly power and had not monopolized professional football. With respect to the metropolitan areas in which franchises could be located, the court found that there were many cities in the United States capable of supporting competently managed professional football teams. Even Lamar Hunt testified that a metropolitan area of 500,000 or more could support a professional football team. In 1962, there were fifty-two metropolitan areas in the United States with a population over 500,000, of which thirty-one had more than 700,000, and twenty-four more than 1,000,000. The court pointed out that the NFL was not financially able to expand into all cities in which the AFL might place teams and that "even during 1959, after the AFL was organized, the NFL owners were unwilling to weaken their own league by expanding into any area which they did not believe would prove a suitable addition to the NFL." The court concluded, therefore, that the NFL had no monopoly with respect to metropolitan areas suitable for franchising. The court reached the same conclusion with respect to players, citing evidence that AFL teams signed six of the first twelve choices of NFL teams in the 1959 draft. The court found that the NFL had "no power to prevent the AFL from signing an adequate number of qualified players." Finally, the court concluded that the NFL did not have the power to exclude the AFL from adequate television outlets and, consequently, there was no monopoly power exercised in this arena.

After determining that the NFL did not have monopoly power, the court went on to consider the AFL's claim that the NFL attempted or conspired to monopolize. The AFL relied primarily on the NFL's grant of franchises to Dallas and Minneapolis–St. Paul. The AFL argued that these franchises were established in an effort to restrict competition from the AFL in the same areas. The court determined, however, that the evidence did not support the AFL's contention that the granting of these franchises was done with an intent to injure the AFL. Having decided that the NFL did not monopolize and had not conspired to monopolize professional football, the district court ruled against the AFL on its claims. The district court's ruling in favor of the NFL was affirmed on appeal in *American Football League* v. *National Football League* (1963).

Losing its antitrust suit in the federal courts did not put an end to the fledgling AFL or to its competition with the NFL. Rather, the next four years produced heated struggles between the two leagues, fueled by unprecedented sums of money. CBS and NBC both coveted broadcast rights for the NFL. In 1964, then NFL Commissioner Pete Rozelle signed a $14 million broadcast contract with CBS. The contract provided the NFL nearly three times as much money as the 1962 television contract and gave each team approximately one million dollars per year. After losing out to CBS, NBC took a major gamble on the AFL. NBC signed a five-year contract to broadcast AFL games. The pact brought approximately $850,000 per year to each AFL team. The importance of the agreement was that it provided the AFL with sufficient capital to engage in an all-out bidding war with the NFL for top college football talent. As the conflict between the AFL and NFL escalated, rumors of questionable college-player recruiting tactics were rampant. Large bonuses were paid to college players to sign, thereby angering veterans. In 1965, the AFL scored a major coup by signing Joe Namath out of the University of Alabama for the then astronomical sum of $420,000 for three years. His signing turned out to be a bargain for the New York Jets, who saw their ticket sales double in his first year.

By 1965, owners of teams in both leagues were concerned that the recruiting war for college players could financially devastate a number of franchises. Unsuccessful merger discussions had taken place throughout the early 1960s between the NFL and the AFL. Even as concern about player salaries mounted, the NFL continued to publicly maintain that it did not want a merger and/or a common player draft. In an effort to stop the financial blood flow, the AFL went so far as to persuade Senator Gordon Allott of Colorado to propose an amendment to a sports bill pending in Congress which would have allowed only one player draft in each professional sport. Senator Allott's amendment, however, was never debated.

The beginning of the end of the NFL's resistance to merger with the AFL occurred in the spring of 1966. Prior to that time, the NFL and the AFL had an "understanding" that they would not recruit the other league's veterans. But in 1966, the agreement disintegrated. Pete Gogolac of the AFL Buffalo Bills was signed by the NFL New York Giants. Two established quarterbacks in the NFL, Roman Gabriel of the Los Angeles Rams and John Brody of the San Francisco Forty-Niners, indicated that at the expiration of their contracts, they would join AFL teams. While the NFL owners had been willing to compete with the AFL for college players, they did not relish the prospect of getting into a bidding war with the AFL over veteran players. Consequently, the AFL and the NFL announced their intention to merge in June 1966. The merger agreement included several provisions: first, Pete Rozelle would become the sole commissioner; second, establishment of a common player draft to end the talent-bidding war; and third, a championship game (Super Bowl) between the winners of the two leagues beginning in 1966, which would become a championship game between the winners of the National Football Conference and American Football Conference after the merger was completed.

After the AFL and NFL entered into their merger agreement, the only remaining hurdles were the antitrust laws. The merger of the NFL and the AFL was clearly designed to eliminate interleague competition and to monopolize professional football. The owners, fearing antitrust lawsuits, turned to Congress for help. In September of 1966, senators Russell Long of Louisiana and Everett Dirksen of Illinois introduced the Football Merger Bill in the Senate. The bill exempted professional football from the antitrust laws. Within two weeks of its introduction, the bill was reported out of the Senate Judiciary Committee with a recommendation in favor of passage. The Judiciary Committee cited several reasons for urging passage of the bill, including the following: the merger insured that all of the twenty-four AFL and NFL teams would be able to continue operating in their present locations; the merger would improve player strength and financial resources of weaker teams in both leagues; and, the retention of existing teams and addition of new franchises would increase the overall employment opportunities for professional football players and coaches. Within days of introduction, the bill passed the Senate on a voice vote.

Passage of the bill in the House of Representatives proved much more difficult. The chairman of the House Judiciary Committee, Representative Emanuel Celler of New York, opposed passage of the bill. Chairman Celler told Commissioner Rozelle, however, that the merger should go ahead since he saw no antitrust problems with it. He, therefore, believed the legislation was unnecessary. In direct response to Celler's assurances to Rozelle, a group of disgruntled potential investors filed an antitrust lawsuit against both the AFL and NFL designed to block the merger. Nevertheless, Celler maintained his opinion that the proposed legislation was not needed. While members of the House pressured Celler into scheduling hearings on the bill, it became obvious to them that he intended to block the bill altogether. Because of Celler's intransigence on the issue, it became necessary for merger proponents to bypass the House Judiciary Committee.

A strategy was devised to make the bill an amendment to an unrelated piece of legislation. The Senate and House were both considering a bill relating to the investment tax credit provisions of the Internal Revenue Code. In the upper chamber, Senator Dirksen offered an amendment to the investment tax credit bill exempting the merger of the American and National Football Leagues from the antitrust laws. The Senate approved the amendment and passed the investment tax credit bill. The House of Representatives had already passed an investment tax credit bill which did not contain the football merger amendment. Consequently, the House version and the Senate version were referred to a Conference Committee. The House conferees agreed to accept the Senate version containing the merger amendment. The Senate passed the conference committee report and after extensive debate, so did the House. As a result, the exemption of the NFL-AFL merger from the antitrust laws became law in late 1966. The tactic of bypassing Celler's committee by appending the merger proposal to the Investment Tax Credit Bill had been devised by Senator Long and Representative Hale Boggs of Louisiana. The payback for their legislative acumen came swiftly. Nine days after the Football Merger Act became law, the NFL awarded New Orleans an expansion franchise.

The passage of the Football Merger Act effectively brought to an end the financial war between the NFL and the AFL. While practical problems with the merger developed, all were effectively handled. In May 1969, a major crisis was averted when the Cleveland Browns, Baltimore Colts, and Pittsburgh Steelers agreed to leave the proposed National Football Conference (containing the former NFL teams) and joined the American Football Conference (containing former AFL teams). Finally, any thought that the AFL teams were inferior to the NFL teams ended with the victory of Namath and the New York Jets over the Baltimore Colts in the 1969 Super Bowl. In the intervening years, no one has questioned the wisdom of the merger, since it began an unprecedented period of financial success and popularity for professional football.

Selected Bibliography

Berry, R. and G. Wong. *Law and Business of the Sports Industries, Volume I: Professional Sports Leagues.* Dover: Auburn House Publishing Company, 1986.

Rader, B. *American Sports.* 2nd Edition. Englewood Cliffs: Prentice-Hall, 1990.

Sobel, L. *Professional Sports and the Law.* New York: Law-Arts Publishers, Inc., 1977.

Weistart, J. "Article: League Control of Market Opportunities: A Perspective on Competition and Cooperation in the Sports Industry." *Duke Law Journal* 1984 (December 1984): 1013–70.

Yasser, R. *Sports Law: Cases and Materials.* Lanham: University Press of America, 1985.

Part Four

Sports Law: Racial and Gender Discrimination

Sports, like all games, are played by human beings. Regrettably, bias over race and gender continues to afflict the world of sports just as it does virtually all spheres of human behavior.

The essays in Part IV analyze cases and issues involving discrimination against racial minorities and women in the field of sports. The effort of organized athletics to come to terms with the meaning of "equal protection of the laws" in the Fourteenth Amendment and various federal legislation is, therefore, part of the much larger subject of how American society in the second half of the twentieth century has attempted to address racial and gender inequities.

"Wyoming's 'Black Fourteen'" begins the essays on racial discrimination by examining the dynamics of race in a Rocky Mountain state in the years surrounding 1970. In "White Ball/Black Ball," discrimination against African Americans in private country clubs receives scrutiny. "The Stone Left Unturned: Marge Schott's 'Suspension'" treats the controversies swirling around the owner of the Cincinnati Reds in particular and the problem of minority hiring in professional baseball in general.

Five essays examine gender discrimination. The opening essay, "The Quest for Gender Equality: Setbacks and Strides," concentrates upon legal cases involving high school athletes. "Let's Play, Too: Sex Discrimination in Intercollegiate Athletics" offers a thorough treatment of developments for college athletes since the early 1970s. The next essay, "Little League Baseball: Where Are the Girls?" focuses on the quest for equality in one important sphere. "Barely

There: Female Reporters in Male Locker Rooms," examines the *Ludtke* v. *Kuhn* (1978) decision and well-publicized incidents in professional football in the early 1990s. The concluding article, "Major League Baseball Called for Balk!" discusses Pam Postema's efforts to umpire in the big leagues.

Wyoming's "Black Fourteen"

Steven Schulte

Williams v. Eaton 443 F. 2d. 422 (1971)

The civil rights movement of the 1960s and 1970s touched nearly every aspect of American life. Martin Luther King, Jr., Malcolm X, the Black Panthers, and other activist individuals and organizations combated America's racist heritage using a diversity of tactics in a variety of forums. By the late 1960s, racism in organized athletics had also become a target for promoters of civil rights.

Laramie, Wyoming, home of the University of Wyoming, the rural state's only four-year institution of higher learning, seemed an unlikely place for a major civil rights confrontation. As late as the mid-1960s, when many of the nation's college campuses smoldered under the fires of antiwar and racial protests, Laramie remained a placid, idyllic college town, an academic refuge in a sorely divided country. While the nation experienced shock at the assassinations of Martin Luther King, Jr. and Robert F. Kennedy, and at the excesses of Mayor Richard Daley's Chicago Police, people in Wyoming congratulated themselves that their state, and indeed, their university, had remained aloof from these reminders of a nation gone mad. In September 1968 a Wyoming newspaper crowed with obvious pride that the University of Wyoming, at an elevation of 7,200 feet, "full of the spirit of the West's last frontier—stands serene, proud, and aloof from the turmoil which has rocked other campuses."

Yet, at the same moment, throughout the United States and the West, African American student-athletes had begun to recognize that their visible public profiles allowed them to influence debate over the nation's racial status quo. It started with the highly publicized proposed boycott of the 1968 Mexico City Olympics by African American athletes. Although the boycott failed to transpire, the vivid raised-fist salute of African American track and field winners on the medal stand signified that a new era in American sports had dawned.

African American athletes targeted signs of discrimination nationally. In the American West, racial policies of the Mormon Church—Church of Jesus Christ of Latter Day Saints (LDS)—became the focus of strident protests in 1968 and 1969. In the aftermath of the Olympic protests, African American track athletes at San Jose State University and the University of Texas at El Paso proposed boycotting meets with the flagship LDS institution of higher learning, Brigham Young University (BYU). A series of protests and other expressions of racial discontent blazed across campuses in the West. In early October 1969, African American students at Arizona State University demonstrated outside the football stadium when BYU visited the hometown Sun Devils.

African Americans objected to the LDS policy of denying the priesthood to black church members. While African Americans could join the church, priesthood membership enabled its all-white, male members to enjoy full church rights, including the authority to act in God's name. African Americans had been barred from the LDS priesthood since an antebellum revelation by Church leader Brigham Young declaring that "a man having one drop of the seed of [Cain] . . . in him cannot hold the priesthood."

The 1969 University of Wyoming football team seemed intent on surpassing the high laurels of its three previous seasons when the Cowboys had won twenty-seven of thirty-two games, playing in both the Sugar and Sun bowls. Cowboy coach Lloyd Eaton had garnered numerous Coach of the Year honors and had been rewarded with a handsome bonus and a new contract. The 1969 Cowboys looked awesome as they began the season with a 4–0 start and ranked twelfth in the nation. Nothing seemed to threaten Eaton's goal of another major bowl appearance.

A stern disciplinarian, Eaton took a Vince Lombardi–like approach to the job: more than a game, football offered vivid lessons for life. Most Wyomingites applauded Eaton's philosophy, including his rule that team personnel never participate in any form of demonstration or protest. Eaton justified his rule on the grounds that most football players were only average students and neither their football nor their academic careers could afford such "outside" distractions.

On October 16, 1969, Eaton's iron resolve was tested. Two days before Wyoming's game with BYU, letters from the University of Wyoming's Black Student Association were delivered to Eaton, the university president, and the athletic director, demanding that Western Athletic Conference schools cancel and refuse to schedule further games with the Mormon university. It also suggested that right-thinking blacks and whites should protest the "racist" LDS doctrines by wearing black armbands in any scheduled athletic contests with BYU. Upon receiving his letter and, perhaps, anticipating trouble, Eaton reminded Joe Williams, an African American athlete who was one of three team captains, of his no-protest rule.

The following day, fourteen African American players wearing armbands marched into Eaton's office to discuss the rule. Seeing his discipline breached, an angered Eaton ruled the players in open defiance and dismissed them from the team.

The episode had serious ramifications for the coach, the players, and Western race relations. The fourteen players never again played football as Wyoming Cowboys, and several players had their chances for college transfers or pro careers undermined. The incident so divided the Laramie campus that the football team crumbled at Eaton's feet. Although the team defeated BYU, it lost its remaining games. In 1970, Eaton's team could only muster one victory in ten games, leading Eaton to accept reassignment in athletic administration, a position he left a year later.

The players fared no better. With legal assistance provided by the National Association for the Advancement of Colored People (NAACP), the case of *Williams* v. *Eaton* was filed in Federal District Court in Cheyenne, Wyoming, October 29, 1969. The former Wyoming football players sought to recoup damages caused by the abrupt termination of their college football careers and to offset harm to future professional football earnings. The decision, announced in March 1970, went against the plaintiffs, citing the team's established rule against player demonstration or protest. After three of the fourteen withdrew their names from the case, an appeal before the 10th Circuit Court of Appeals, *Williams* v. *Eaton* (1971) affirmed the original decision. In a final legal maneuver, the athletes argued that their constitutional right to protest had been abridged by Eaton and the University of Wyoming. The Circuit Court of Appeals in *Will-*

iams v. *Eaton* (1972) again denied the athletes' motion. The court held that the Board of Trustees of the university acted reasonably in refusing to allow black football players to wear armbands during a game against BYU, and that such a policy was not a violation of the right of expression provided in the First Amendment.

The "Black Fourteen" affair may be viewed from many levels. From a national perspective, it demonstrated how by the late 1960s civil rights issues impacted not only the college campuses but the athletic arena as well. Regionally, the incident highlighted the cultural clash between Western conservatives and minority groups. The university's antiprotest policy and the law-and-order philosophy underlying it elicited an overwhelmingly positive response throughout the Rocky Mountain states and anticipated the rise of the New Right as a potent political force by the late 1970s. The issue also exposed the difficulties facing a predominantly white university in a rural state operating within a rapidly changing national social milieu. The university and the State of Wyoming itself remain divided over this incident, which devastated not only Cowboy football for many years, but also the campus environment for minority students.

Selected Bibliography

Bullock, C. "Racism, Mormonism, and Black Protest: Wyoming and the Western Athletic Conference, 1968–1970." M.A. Thesis, University of Wyoming, 1992.

Hansen, K. *Mormonism and the American Experience.* Chicago: University of Chicago Press, 1981.

Hardy, D. *Wyoming University: The First Hundred Years, 1886–1986.* Laramie: University of Wyoming, 1986.

White Ball/Black Ball

L. John Gable and John W. Johnson

While little white balls were dropping on putting greens at private country clubs all across the country, little black balls were dropping into membership ballot boxes inside their exclusive clubhouses. Like a deep, dark family secret that everyone knew existed but no one dared admit, little had been said, and still less done, about the longstanding, widespread practice of racial and ethnic discrimination at America's private country clubs. Everyone knew that one day it would become a public issue, but no one could have imagined that the catalyst for disclosure and change would be a man of the stature and standing of Hall Thompson.

On July 20, 1990, Thompson, founder and chairman of Birmingham, Alabama's exclusive Shoal Creek Country Club, was interviewed by Joan Mazzolini, a general-assignment reporter for the *Birmingham Post-Herald*. Shoal Creek had once again been selected as the site for that year's Professional Golf Association's (PGA) Championship tournament. In an extended interview regarding discriminatory practices at various private clubs, Mazzolini asked Thompson for his reaction to a black city councilman's demand that city monies set aside for an advertisement in the PGA Championship program be withdrawn because of Shoal Creek's exclusionary policy concerning membership for African Americans.

Thompson said, "Bringing up this issue will just polarize the community . . . but it can't pressure us." When asked if the club was receptive to admitting black members, he responded, "That's just not done in Birmingham. . . . We have the right to associate or not to associate with whomever we choose. The country club is our home and we pick and choose who we want. . . . I think we've said that we don't discriminate in every other area, except the blacks." While the openly discriminatory comment was hardly considered newsworthy in Birmingham, it touched off a ripple of revolt, a wave of panic, and a sea of change at similarly exclusive clubs across the country.

The issue of memberships at private clubs is a difficult one. Do the rights that protect an individual's freedom of association take precedence over court-mandated civil rights legislation? Should private clubs that set their own membership qualifications be exempt from laws that prohibit racial-ethnic discrimination? There are moral and ethical questions involved. By nature, private country clubs are discriminatory and exclusive because they vote into membership only certain hand-picked individuals. There may exist no written rules prohibiting members of racial or ethnic groups; such policies would be flagrant violations of civil rights laws. There may exist, however, unwritten but clearly understood policies among the membership as to "who is" and "who is not" welcome to belong. In essence, it may be that many clubs privately believe what only Thompson was bold enough to admit publicly.

It is interesting that it took an incident, such as the one at Shoal Creek, to bring to light the longstanding discriminatory policies that exist in many private clubs. Why is it that previously there had been no action from the courts, no demonstrations by civil rights groups, no boycott of events by tour players, no public outcry against the clubhouse color bar? "Looking back, it was inevitable that racism in golf would become an issue, but we were not preparing for it," said Deane Beman, then the commissioner of the PGA Tour. Even at Shoal Creek it was none of the above that finally forced the issue of racial discrimination into the open. Ironically, it was corporate America that finally blew the whistle. Immediately after publication of Thompson's statements, and his subsequent refusal to retract them, saying only they were "taken out of context," corporate sponsors began pulling financial support away from the PGA tournament, fearing damage from the fallout. This is ironic considering the number of memberships these same corporations sponsor at similarly exclusive clubs across the nation.

It has taken years to bring this well-known country club secret out in the open. Now what will it take to put an end to these discriminatory practices? In an unrelated incident in 1991, an African American high school golfer, Dondre Green, was denied permission to play in a school-sanctioned tournament at the Caldwell Parish Country Club, a private club in Columbia, Louisiana. The club manager told the school's coach that the young man would not be allowed to play because he was African American. "It's a club rule. This is a private club, and it has the discretion to bar anybody it wants." When informed that "blacks can't play at this club," the team unanimously decided to forfeit the match.

Since the Shoal Creek incident, several significant changes have occurred. Previously, course selection for major golf tournaments had been made on the basis of course quality alone. Within weeks of the debacle in Birmingham, however, the PGA of America instituted a new site selection policy requiring prospective host courses to have "demonstrably open membership policies and practices prohibiting discrimination on the basis of race, creed, color, national origin, or gender." The PGA Tour (including the Senior PGA Tour and the Ben Hogan Tour), the United States Golf Association, and the Ladies Professional Golf Association have all reevaluated their selection policies.

Nationwide, since 1990, Shoal Creek and many private clubs have changed longstanding exclusionary practices and have accepted as members blacks and other racial and ethnic minorities. Such changes have not come easily. At Shoal Creek, for example, only the PGA's threat of removing its 1990 national championship to another site caused the Birmingham club to admit a black golfing member. Just five months after the Shoal Creek incident, golf legend Tom Watson resigned his membership at his home course, the Kansas City Country Club, as an act of conscience over its refusal to admit a prospective member who was Jewish. Within a week the club's board met in closed session and invited the prospective member to join.

In 1994 Shoal Creek was again in the news. An Associated Press story in August reported that Louis J. Willie, the black Birmingham insurance man who was admitted to Shoal Creek in the aftermath of the 1990 controversy, was still the only African-American member of the club. The president of the Southern Christian Leadership Conference characterized the admission of Willie as tokenism: "It was just as I thought," the SCLC president stated. "They had a gun to their head. Once you remove the gun, they do nothing." Shoal

Creek refused to offer a rejoinder, saying that it would not discuss its membership policies in the press.

According to his own statements, Louis Willie appears to be quite happy as a Shoal Creek member. He says that he "doesn't mind that he is the [club's] only black." He reports that his golf outings have taken place without racial incident, regardless of whether he has joined white threesomes or brought black guests to the club to play with him.

Shoal Creek also made the national sports news in October 1994 when eighteen-year-old Tiger Woods, the reigning U.S. amateur champion and the best African American golfer to come along in twenty years, was scheduled to play in a collegiate tournament at the Birmingham club. In anticipation of this event, reporters besieged Woods with questions about the significance of his playing at a fa-cility so identified with racism on the links. Woods played his rounds at the club without incident, but he declined to talk specifically about the discrimination he had faced growing up as a African American man playing a game involving a dimpled white ball.

What will it take to finally put an end to the black ball in the white-ball world? Certainly new policies such as those adopted by the governing boards of golf on course selection are necessary, but the issue of racial-ethnic discrimination must ultimately be addressed at the local level, on a club-by-club basis all across the country. What began at Shoal Creek certainly will not end there. History may one day show that what Rosa Parks did to legalized segregation in Mont-gomery in 1955, Hall Thompson unintentionally did to the private black ball thirty-five years later in Birmingham.

Selected Bibliography

"A First Step." *Sports Illustrated*. December 17, 1990: 30.

Garrity, J. "An Act of Conscience." *Sports Illustrated*. December 10, 1990: 110.

Johnson, W. "The Gate's Open." *Sports Illustrated*. August 13, 1990: 54–57.

"Off Course." *Sports Illustrated*. April 29, 1991: 15.

"Picking and Choosing." *Sports Illustrated*. July 9, 1990: 13.

"Shoal Creek." *Sports Illustrated*. August 13, 1990: 14.

"Shoal Creek Club Agrees to Begin Admitting Blacks." *The New York Times*. August 1, 1990: 13.

The Stone Left Unturned
Marge Schott's "Suspension"

David Rodgers

"Baseball Bans Cincinnati Owner for a Year Over Racial Remarks," read the headline on the front page of the *New York Times* for February 4, 1993. Thus culminated an impressively cunning and successful two-month effort by the baseball establishment to do absolutely nothing about the Marge Schott racial controversy and to pay no price for its lack of focus on racial issues.

Like all raging thunderstorms, the Marge Schott controversy started with quiet rumbles in the distance. Tim Sabo (no relation to the then Cincinnati Reds third baseman Chris Sabo), having been fired from his position as controller of the club in 1992, brought a $2.5 million lawsuit against Schott, the majority owner of the Cincinnati Reds. He claimed that he was fired without sufficient cause. Late in 1994 the Ohio Supreme Court allowed Sabo's suit against Schott to proceed.

In depositions, Sabo and two other employees claimed that Schott had made racist remarks. She was overheard calling ex–Red player Dave Parker "that dumb nigger," and on another occasion she referred to "sneaky goddamn Jews." Schott herself admitted in a deposition that she had used the word "nigger," and that she may have referred to Martin Luther King, Jr., Day as "Nigger Day." She also confessed to keeping a Nazi swastika armband in her home, as a memento from an employee, and said that she could not understand why a former Jewish employee was offended by it. When this information became public, a former employee of the Oakland As recalled that she had overheard Schott saying, "I'd rather have a trained monkey working for me than a nigger." In an interview in the *New York Times* concerning the racial comment controversy, Schott added the statement, "Hitler was good in the beginning, but he went too far."

Minority leaders from across the country called for action against Schott, threatening boycotts and warning that they would pressure the government for reform of the sport. Clearly, the team owners had to take measures to assuage the public outrage. On December 1, 1992, the owners appointed a four-member committee to investigate the allegations against Schott. All of the members were from major league baseball's Executive Council that was acting in lieu of the vacant post of commissioner of baseball. The committee consisted of league presidents Bill White (National League) and Dr. Bobby Brown (American League), and owners Jackie Autry (California Angels) and Doug Danforth (Pittsburgh Pirates).

The committee confronted a complex problem. Schott's crime, in the eyes of the public, was that of bigotry. Bigotry in thought or speech is not a crime in the United States. Expressing bigotry in actions, such as hiring practices, however, is illegal. Although Schott had a very poor minority hiring record, so did most of the other owners. Clearly they would not want the censure to be on those grounds, but to base the censure solely on bigotry in speech would offend Americans' longstanding respect for and protection of freedom of speech. The fact that Schott was widely considered to be unpopular with the other owners was another complication. In its weekly "Scorecard" section, *Sports Illustrated* announced, "For years other owners have wanted Schott to go away and the revelation of her racism and anti-Semitism may be just the excuse they need to take action."

By late in January 1992 Schott undertook an effort to repair her standing. She started making conciliatory statements. Schott established and defended her position as a member of a minority herself, that is, as a female owner of a professional baseball team. In her shrewdest move, she hired Washington, D.C., attorney Robert Bennett to represent her interests in regard to any action that baseball might wish to take against her.

Bennett's skills as a powerful litigator and his aggressive defense of Schott's rights effectively stayed the owners' hands from inflicting serious penalties. The hiring of Bennett signaled that any action unacceptable to Schott would result in a very lengthy legal procedure that would surely cause the other owners more public-relations harm than they were prepared to handle. The suit would most certainly have called into question baseball's stricture forbidding an owner from bringing suit against the commissioner or Executive Council.

By late January 1993, the Executive Council moved toward its judgment. In an example of both public relations acumen and gutlessness, almost the entire extent of its intended punishments for Schott was leaked to the press. Whether this was intentional or not, it tested whether the decision would be palatable to the public. On February 3, 1993, the official punishment was announced. This punishment, despite being worded in strongly condemnatory terms, was very light. Not one single aspect of the censure would be a serious irritation to the power or the pocketbook of any owner of a major league franchise.

The major negatives for Schott were that she could not make day-to-day decisions for the 1993 season and that she would have to pay a $25,000 fine. The suspension also stated that she must attend a multicultural awareness program. She was banned from the owners' box seats for the season and from the front office and playing field. The suspension left intact Schott's position as the team's managing general partner. She could still earn revenue from the club, make major policy and financial decisions, and vote at owners' meetings. It also allowed her to designate who would be able to make the day-to-day decisions that she had been barred from making. The agreement represented a deal in which Schott was allowed to remain as general partner, and baseball was able to avoid a potentially long court case that might have ended in limiting its power. Both sides were able to dampen public outrage.

Schott put her attack lawyer back in her pocket. Public furor was satisfied, but nothing tangible had been done to alleviate the real problem of baseball ownership's inadequate minority hiring practices. The leadership of baseball reaffirmed its promise to promote minority awareness and minority hiring in upper-level positions. Throughout the winter months Schott made many high-level minority hirings, the most important of which was the hiring of Cuban-born baseball legend Tony Perez as team manager.

During her suspension Schott did a fair job of avoiding negative publicity. Some damage was caused by the perfunctory firing of Perez less than two months into the 1993 season. Many agreed that the move was uncalled for and far too early in Perez's tenure. While Schott claimed that the decision was out of her hands due to the suspension, the idea that general manager Bobby Bowden would have made the decision against her wishes is far-fetched. Interestingly, Perez's nonminority replacement compiled a worse won-loss record over the remainder of the season.

After the Perez incident Schott sailed through her suspension. She attended a multicultural training program and even had her suspension reduced to eight months, followed by a four-month probation. It soon became clear, however, that Schott's talent for negative publicity was only in a short period of dormancy. Early in the 1994 season she openly defied a city ordinance banning smoking in the seats in Riverfront stadium. Only the threat of forcible removal caused Schott to refrain. Soon thereafter she started a move to purchase the stadium. This caused some to make the comical observation that she was mainly interested in owning the facility so that she could lift the ban and resume smoking in her owner's box.

The most recent and more serious stir was caused by a comment that Schott made two months into the 1994 baseball season. Speaking before the Ohio County Treasurers' Association, Schott referred to the appearance of some modern ballplayers by saying, "Only fruits wear earrings." In reference to the comment, Todd Kamm, spokesman for a Cincinnati gay/lesbian group stated, "It's come to the point that the city has become used to being embarrassed by Marge Schott's mouth." In general, the fans of the Reds have been quite tolerant of Schott's more questionable observations. A commonly shared feeling is that the most important issue is keeping the team in Cincinnati and that Schott, as a longtime Reds fan and Cincinnati local, is very likely to do so. It is to be expected that the wider public and the baseball ruling council, which has announced that it will be looking into the "earrings" comment, will be less sympathetic.

Marge Schott seems likely to continue to make inflammatory comments. If these comments were of a less bigoted nature, Schott would rapidly become a beloved eccentric. As they tend, however, to reflect intense prejudice, it is possible that sooner or later matters will come to a head with either a more serious censure from the baseball ruling council or with Schott's voluntary exit from the public spotlight through the sale of the team.

The positive result of the light that has been thrown on Marge Schott's comments is that we have been given insight into the kind of thinking that can lead to poor minority hiring practices. Major league baseball has a dismal record in the area of minority employment. Each time that the spotlight is placed on the issue by comments such as Schott's, the baseball establishment finds itself in a dilemma: work to solve the problem, or work to hide the problem? Ira Berkow, columnist for the *New York Times*, noted that after the original announcement of Schott's suspension, baseball had no business punishing Schott for comments made in private, and that the real reason for punishment should have been Schott's abysmal minority hiring record. As all the other teams had hiring records that ranged from abysmal to slightly better than abysmal, the other owners left *that* stone unturned.

Selected Bibliography

Berkow, I. "Marge Schott: Baseball's Big Red Headache." *The New York Times*. February 4, 1993: 1.

Chass, M. "No Commissioner, and Perhaps No Penalty for Schott." *The New York Times*. November 22, 1992: Section 8, 11.

O'Brien, R. "Block That Schott." *Sports Illustrated*. November 30, 1992: 13.

"Schott Accused of Bias." *The New York Times*. November 16, 1992: Section C, 9.

Smith, C. "Baseball Bans Owner for a Year Over Racial Remarks." *The New York Times*. February 4, 1993: 1.

Whiteside, K. "Block That Schott (cont.)." *Sports Illustrated*. December 7, 1992: 15.

The Quest for Gender Equality
Setbacks and Strides

Brenda Holliday

Williams v. *The School District of Bethlehem, Pa.* Civil No. 90-06448 (E.D. Pa. July 14, 1992)

High school athletics is an arena generally regarded to be male dominated. Throughout history, women have been encouraged to maintain their femininity which stereotypically entails furthering an image of frailty and dependence upon male strength. Sports have always been a means for men to display their power and competitiveness, positive masculine attributes. Talented male athletes are rewarded with recognition, approval, and financial benefits in scholarships and professional opportunities. Athletic opportunities for females, however, have only become available within the past two decades. In the early 1990s there were about 1.9 million high school female sports participants compared to around 300,000 in 1970. Ironically, male high school athletes have decreased in number from 3,666,917 in 1971 to 3,406,355 in 1991. Although the number of males who play sports in high school continues to be almost double the figure for girls, public intervention and government legislation have given women's athletics a significant boost. Today, athletes seeking redress for discrimination in their high school athletic program have several federal avenues available to them. They include the Fourteenth Amendment of the United States Constitution and Title IX of the Education Amendments of 1972.

Many cases involving sex discrimination in high school athletics based their claims on violations of the Fourteenth Amendment to the United States Constitution. The equal protection clause prohibits states from enacting any laws that deny equal protection to all people within the state's jurisdiction. Because most sports discrimination cases involve a regulation enacted by a school, a school board, or an athletic association, a claimant of sex discrimination must first show that there is a close nexus between state participation and the challenged regulation. Upon a finding of state action, the court then uses a two-pronged test to determine the validity of that regulation under the Fourteenth Amendment. To stay in force, the regulation in question must: first, serve an important government objective; and second, be substantially related to achieving that objective.

State action may occur in a nongovernment institution that conducts activities which are so intertwined with the state that the entity can reasonably be perceived as performing those functions in a state capacity. When determining state action in a high school athletics sex discrimination case, the courts will consider whether or not a sufficient nexus exists between an athletic association or school board and the state. Factors to consider include: first, whether the decision makers are public officials or private individuals; second, whether or not public facilities are needed for the activity; third, whether the members are public or private groups; fourth, if it is a private institution, whether it has the ability to sanction public entities or not; and fifth, whether or not the state provides funding to the athletes covered by the challenged rules. Public schools are generally considered government entities for purposes of a constitutional challenge. Courts have frequently determined that the actions of both school boards and high school athletic associations constitute state action.

Claims of sexual discrimination in high school athletics often challenge regulations that require total separation of the sexes in athletic competition. Proponents of such regulations argue that important government objectives are served by them. Common justifications are that they prevent male domination of a team, redress past discrimination, and prevent injuries to female athletes.

Courts have varied in their acceptance of such justifications for separation of the sexes in athletics. The Supreme Court of the United States upheld a regulation prohibiting a girl from trying out for a boys' basketball team. The court said that if girls are allowed to try out for boys' teams, then boys will be able to try out for girls' teams, and under these circumstances boys would soon dominate the sport and eliminate the girls' opportunity to compete altogether. In a more recent Supreme Court decision, however, a regulation prohibiting males from trying out for female teams was deemed unconstitutional. Here the court reasoned that there is little male interest in joining a female volleyball team and, therefore, speculated that males would not dominate the team.

In other court decisions—for example *Morris* v. *Michigan Board of Education* (1973)—rules purporting to prevent sports injuries have been reviewed based on the nature of the sport. Contact sports more readily counter the arguments against banning female participation because of possible injury, and on this basis some courts have allowed such prohibitions. Some recent decisions—for example, *Brendan* v. *Indiana School District* (1973)—however, avoid upholding sex discrimination that is based on fear of physical harm to females. Courts have analyzed the physiological differences between males and females and found that while differences do exist, they do not constitute a justification for generalized discrimination, because the rationale is based on outdated forms of stereotypical paternalism. The stereotype reveals itself in the fact that males of smaller size or inferior ability, who might thereby be prone to injury, are nevertheless permitted to compete.

In addition to proving that discriminatory regulations serve an important government objective, a defendant in a suit has the burden of showing that the challenged rule is substantially related to promoting that state's interest. Courts have traditionally denied that there is a substantial relationship between promoting the state's interest in fostering female athletics and alleged discrimination in situations where no team for the sport in question exists for women. But while school officials today are quick to boast that equality between the sexes exists in their sports programs, much controversy concerns whether the existence of separate male and female sports teams does in fact constitute equality. Federal courts have held that prohibiting female access to male teams is not a violation of the Fourteenth Amendment where a comparable team exists for girls. One district court concluded that the separate-but-equal doctrine applied to the school's overall athletic program in general, even if no separate team was offered for a particular sport, and upheld prohibiting girls from boys' teams as long as the girls had an adequate athletic program. Conversely, other courts—in for example, *Brendan* v. *Independent School District 742* (1973)—have ruled that by denying women access to the only team available for a particular sport, their rights to participate in that sport are entirely obliterated.

Advocates of separate teams argue that females will be intimidated by the prospect of competing against stronger, more physically dominant males, and therefore sports participation in general will be bolstered if women and men compete only against members of their own sex. But the idea that athletes, especially of high school age, are more comfortable competing against those of their own gender stems from the stereotypical notion that boys are more athletically inclined than girls and, perhaps, also from the belief that boys fear losing to girls. Skeptics of the separate-but-equal rationale admit that there are physical differences between the sexes and agree that some form of regulation is necessary to prevent a regression to the time of male-dominated sports. However, those who reject the separate-but-equal doctrine do so primarily on the rationale that separate teams for boys and girls have not in reality been equal.

Much of the tremendous increase in female athletic participation in the past two decades is credited to the passage of Title IX of the Education Amendment of 1972. The amendment mandates equal educational treatment based on sex to all institutions receiving federal funds. Although equally applicable to males and females, the purpose of Title IX is primarily to rectify past educational disparities most often detrimental to females. Under Title IX, a school that receives federal funds must allow athletes to try out for noncontact sports teams if their gender has historically been athletically oppressed and if there are not equal teams currently in existence for that gender.

Since President Richard Nixon signed Title IX in 1972, it has met with vigorous opposition. Several attempts have been made to exclude specific types of sports from Title IX regulation. The Tower Amendment proposed to exclude revenue-producing sports from compliance, while another Senate measure attempted to exclude all nonrequired curriculum programs. Both of these proposals were unsuccessful and today Title IX applies to all athletic programs, high school and intercollegiate, revenue and nonrevenue producing, that are part of an educational institution that receives federal assistance.

The regulations imposed by Title IX apply to institutions that are assisted financially by the federal government. Generally, federal assistance includes granting or loaning funds, providing federal personnel, authorizing the use or low-cost sale of federal property, or any other federal contract, agreement, or arrangement meant to assist an educational program. The United States Supreme Court in 1984 narrowed the application of the Federal assistance requirement. In *Grove City College* v. *Bell*, the court ruled that Title IX encompasses only the specific departments that directly receive federal funds within an educational institution. This ruling practically excludes athletics from Title IX coverage since few athletic programs receive direct aid from the government. The Civil Rights Restoration Act of 1988, however, outlawed discrimination based on sex within all departments of an institution receiving federal assistance, thereby overruling *Grove City*. This act widens the scope of Title IX coverage so that athletic programs are required to adhere.

Title IX explicitly excludes contact sports from coverage. The language of the Amendment states that contact sports include boxing, wrestling, rugby, ice hockey, football, basketball, and other sports the purpose or major activity of which involves bodily contact. Although several sports are specifically designated as "contact," courts have interpreted the contact clause in various ways. For example, a 1991 Rhode Island District Court in *Kleczek* v. *Rhode Island Interscholastic League, Inc.* found that field hockey is an "incidental" contact sport in that contact is inherent when properly played. Conversely, in *Williams* v. *The School District of Bethlehem, PA*, the court concluded that although contact does take place in field hockey, the rules expressly penalize it, making it impossible for contact to be a "purpose or major activity" as outlined in Title IX. This 1992 Pennsylvania District Court also pointed to the fact that Title IX lists ice hockey as a contact sport, and by excluding field hockey in that category, intended it to be considered noncontact. This issue has yet to be uniformly decided and will continue to be reviewed on a case-by-case basis until presented to the U.S. Supreme Court.

Although an attempt to clarify Title IX provisions, the 1979 policy interpretation issued by the Department of Health, Education, and Welfare does not expand or explain the scope of "contact" sports. It does, however, state that "women can be excluded from a men's team where a contact sport is involved." Yet a 1981 court in *Yellow Springs* v. *Ohio High School Athletic Association* found that Title IX is permissive and flexible and does not mandate that girls do not play on boys' contact teams. What's more, some women have won suits allowing them to try out for football, an enumerated contact sport.

In analyzing past discrimination, the courts have been in dispute regarding the scope of the historical limitation needed to satisfy Title IX requirements. That is, does the amendment refer to previously limited opportunities for a particular sex in athletics in general or in a particular sport? While the majority of courts have construed the words to mean that one sex's "overall" athletic opportunities must have been previously limited, there is case law to the contrary. *Gomes* v. *Rhode Island Interscholastic League* (1979) first held that to read the regulation to refer to overall limitations would be constitutionally unsound. Several state courts have followed this reasoning.

The term "past athletic oppression" may automatically trigger thoughts of women's historical exclusion from sports. With the growth of women's athletic programs under Title IX, however, courts have recently been called upon to address the issue of limitations for male athletes. In 1992, when a high school boy was prohibited from playing on the girl's field hockey team, the court in *Williams* v. *The School District of Bethlehem, PA* compared the school's male and female athletic programs. In finding that the school had vigorously taken affirmative action to equalize athletics, the court concluded that it had, in effect, created a situation of reverse discrimination in which the girls had the opportunity to try out for all twenty-two teams offered, while the boys were only allowed to try out for twelve. The District Court found the school in violation of Title IX, determining that its longstanding policy of offering more athletic opportunities for girls than boys constituted previous denial of opportunity for boys.

Like the Fourteenth Amendment to the Constitution, Title IX's prescription for equality has been frequently debated, and often belied in practice. But unlike the separate-but-equal doctrine, Title IX outlines specific factors for determining compliance with its equal opportunity requirement. Generally, these include three broad areas to consider: first, whether the selection of sports and levels of competition effectively accommodates the interests and abilities of members of both sexes; second, whether athletic scholarships and financial assistance are equally distributed; and third, whether teams for each gender have equal equipment, facilities, and coaching.

While female participation in high school athletics has multiplied in the last twenty years, the majority of that growth occurred between 1972 and 1978. Women's sports teams today have about the same number of participants as they did in the late 1970s. Though great strides have admittedly been made, the increase in concern for eliminating sexual inequality might be harming women's athletics on some levels. Because the subject has come to the forefront of law and debate, it has become taboo to admit that inequality does, in fact, still exist. Many administrators and enforcement agencies are slow to stigmatize an institution as a sex discriminator. In fact, very little Title IX enforcement has occurred; few Title IX complaints end in a corrective reprimand; and no institution has ever been denied funding because of a Title IX violation. The increased popularity and money involved in women's sports has also attracted more men to coaching and administrative positions, reducing the number of female coaches by half that of twenty years ago. Additionally, in slow economic times proposals for cutbacks in athletics usually target women's programs.

The future is not without prospects for continued progress, however. As girls in age groups affected by affirmative action progress through the ranks of competition and training, each year new athletes show up who can compete on a level fairly comparable to men. The access to coaching from an early age increasingly provides talented females with opportunities to excel at almost any sport. Though debate continues over the extent to which equality in high school athletics has evolved, it has undisputedly progressed. The past twenty years have been decades of change. The next twenty years should prove equally as interesting.

Selected Bibliography

Avery, J. "Validity, under Federal Law, of Sex Discrimination in Athletics." *American Law Reports Federal* 23 (1975): 664–683.

Croudace, V. and S. Desmaris. "Where the Boys Are." *Southern California Law Review* 58 (September 1985): 1425–1465.

Geadelmann, P. *Equality in Sport for Women.* Washington, D.C.: AAHPER Publications, 1977.

Morse, S. "Women and Sports." *CQ Researcher.* March 6, 1992: 193–216.

Nelson, M. *Are We Winning Yet? How Women Are Changing Sports and Sports Are*

Changing Women. New York: Random House, 1991.

Tokarz, K. *Women, Sports, and the Law: A Comprehensive Research Guide to Sex Discrimination in Sports.* Buffalo: William S. Hein Company, 1986.

Let's Play, Too

Sex Discrimination in Intercollegiate Athletics

Timothy J. Wiles

Grove City College **v.** *Bell* **104 S. Ct. 1211 (1984)**

Franklin **v.** *Gwinnett County Public Schools* **112 S. Ct. 1028 (1992)**

Haffer **v.** *Temple University* **524 F. Supp. 531 (E.D.Pa. 1981)**

University of Richmond **v.** *Bell* **543 F. Supp. 321 (E.D. Va.1982)**

Civil Rights Restoration Act of 1987 Pub. Law No. 100-259, 102 Stat 28 (1988)

The last thirty years have seen a meteoric rise in sports participation by women in the United States. From 1971 to 1991, the number of females playing high school sports rose from 294,000 to 1.84 million. Thirty-four percent of college athletes are female, compared to less than 10 percent in the early 1970s. U.S. women's Olympic athletes won nine medals at the 1992 Winter Olympics at Albertville, France, including all of the five gold medals won by the entire U.S. team, while the male athletes brought home just two medals. In the 1994 Winter Olympics, the ratio improved: nine medals for the women, and four for the men. According to a 1991 *Sports Illustrated* poll, 69 percent of American women participate in sports or fitness activities. Advocates of women's sports attribute many of these positive changes to the effects of Title IX of the Education Amendments of 1972.

Many women, however, still complain of lack of access to sports teams and facilities, as well as to media exposure and the resultant monetary rewards. An analysis of the amount of television coverage allotted to women's sports versus men's sports would show an enormous disparity. Women's athletic departments at universities receive one of every five dollars allocated to intercollegiate sports. Women athletes receive about one-third of scholarship dollars, despite making up approximately half of the student body. The common defense to such statistics is that it is the big money sports, namely football and men's basketball, which provide the revenue necessary to support all the other sports. Yet *Sports Illustrated* reports that only about 13 percent of collegiate football programs covered even their own expenses in 1989. Despite such obvious disparities, enforcement of Title IX has been lax, and much of this is due to its legislative and post-enactment history, which has been characterized by confusion and bickering over the intended effects of the law.

Title IX reads simply:

No person in the United States shall on the basis of sex be excluded from participation in, be denied the benefits of, or be subjected to discrimination under any educational program or activity receiving federal financial assistance . . .

The wording of the law was modeled after Title VII of the Civil Rights Act of 1964, which prohibits discrimination on the basis of sex, race, creed, or national origin. From the beginning there were questions as to whether Title IX was intended to apply to intercollegiate athletics. Such discussion has centered upon the definitions of "educational program or activity," and "federal financial assistance." The teeth behind Title IX allowed the federal government to withhold funding to any institution found guilty of sex discrimination.

Senator John Tower of Texas attempted unsuccessfully to amend Title IX so that it would not apply to revenue-producing sports. Tower's 1974 amendment was defeated in committee and replaced by the "Javits amendment." This amendment directed the Department of Health, Education, and Welfare (HEW) to publish proposed regulations for implementing Title IX, including "with respect to intercollegiate athletic activities reasonable provisions considering the nature of the particular sports." Senator Jesse Helms of North Carolina also twice introduced bills which attempted to remove athletics from the jurisdiction of Title IX. Neither bill passed. The failure of Tower's and Helms's attempts to limit the scope of Title IX later became important legislative history supporting the view that Congress did, in fact, intend the statute to apply to intercollegiate athletics.

In 1975 the HEW issued the regulations mandated by the Javits amendment. These rules permitted separate women's and men's teams when selection was based upon competitive skill or when the sport in question was a contact sport, and required schools to make affirmative efforts to provide women equality of athletic opportunity and support. Additionally, schools were required to conduct an annual survey to ascertain interest levels for both men and women for particular sports. The regulations also specified what areas were intended for scrutiny with respect to whether or not equality in funding existed. This so-called laundry list included the provision of equipment and supplies; scheduling of games and practice time; travel and per diem allowances; opportunity to receive coaching and academic tutoring; assignment and compensation of coaches and tutors; provision of locker rooms and practice and competitive facilities, medical facilities and services, housing, and dining; and publicity. The 1975 regulations seemed to please no one, and HEW went back to the drawing board to prepare a final policy interpretation.

Published in 1979, the definitive scheme called for equal per capita funding in the area of athletic scholarships for male and female athletes. It also dropped the requirement for equal per capita funding in the "laundry list" areas, because some sports were seen to be inherently more expensive than others. The document, instead, called for equivalency in kind, quality, and availability as to the facilities and services in question. The policy allowed nonequivalent funding for football and basketball if the differences were due to "nondiscriminatory factors," such as equipment cost, injury rate, and facilities required for the particular sport. Critics of the final policy interpretation argued that, in a society in which men and women were equal, it would not take a larger arena to house a men's basketball game than a women's basketball game. The contention is that society itself is inherently discriminatory about sports, which is of course the very condition which Title IX was intended to address.

Despite having been diluted in the revised policy interpretation, Title IX seemed at last poised to begin its task of making sexual discrimination in publicly funded education an issue of the past. The final interpretation had, with regard to sports, two purposes.

The first was to eliminate inequality within existing programs, while the second was to correct affirmatively the effects of past discrimination by requiring institutions to encourage females to participate in sports, to increase the number of sports offerings for women, and to publicize the availability of sports to potential female athletes. All of these efforts were designed to help raise the profile of women's athletics in society and, therefore, promote the overall acceptance of women into full equality within the society at large.

Title IX enforcement is currently handled by the Office of Civil Rights within the Department of Education, which has devised a three-part test for determining if an institution is in compliance. First, a school must effectively accommodate the interests and abilities of both female and male student-athletes. Second, there must be an ongoing program expansion in any cases where there has been an underrepresented sex. Third, there must be proportionality in participation and opportunity for male and female athletes, that is, athletic opportunity must divide up about the same way as the student body does in terms of gender.

The landmark Supreme Court case, *Grove City College* v. *Bell*, decided in 1984, showcased the central area of contention in the interpretation of Title IX. What constitutes an "educational program or activity?" Should the phrase be interpreted in a broad, institutional manner, as the HEW (which after 1980 became the Department of Education), contended? Or should it be interpreted in a narrower, "program-specific" context? The broad approach holds that if an educational institution receives any federal funding at all, then it cannot discriminate in any of its programs, regardless of whether or not a specific program receives direct federal financial assistance. The narrow approach is just the opposite. Unless a specific program, activity, or department of an institution receives directly earmarked federal aid, it is free to act in any manner it chooses, whether discriminatory or not. Prior to the Grove City College case, federal courts were split on the issue. The two major cases were *The University of Richmond* v. *Bell*, and *Haffer* v. *Temple University*.

Responding to a charge of sex discrimination from students at the University of Richmond, the Department of Education sought to investigate Richmond's athletic department. The Department of Education claimed that, since the university, a private institution, received federal funds in the form of federal student financial aid, it should therefore comply with all provisions of Title IX. This contention was in line with an institutional interpretation of Title IX. The University of Richmond then filed suit against the Department of Education. The court found in favor of Richmond, in the process endorsing a narrow definition of the phrase "program or activity." According to the court, for the Department of Education to have any jurisdiction over the University of Richmond athletic department, not the university in general but the athletic department in particular, would have been the recipient of federal funds.

The opposite conclusion was drawn by another federal court in the case of *Haffer* v. *Temple University*. The athletic department at Temple, also a private school, was charged with sex discrimination by a group of eight female students. The plaintiffs charged that Temple received about 10 percent of its operating budget from the federal government, and, as such, was compelled to follow the provisions of Title IX. After a lengthy review of congressional intent, the court agreed, thereby endorsing an institutional interpretation of Title IX.

In *Grove City College* v. *Bell,* no one was accused of sex discrimination; instead the matter of contention was the breadth of Title IX jurisdiction itself. The Department of Education had requested Grove City College, a private school, to sign an "Assurance of Compliance" form, which promised that the college would conform with Title IX. The college refused on principle to sign the form. It had a history of refusing financial assistance from the government and it zealously guarded its independence.

Four hundred and eighty two of Grove City's 2,200 students, however, were eligible for and/or had received federal financial assistance in the form of Basic Educational Opportunity Grants (BEOGs), or Guaranteed Student Loans (GSLs). The government interpreted this as aid to the institution, whereas the college saw it as aid to the individual students.

The Supreme Court agreed with the Department of Education that Grove City College was the recipient of federal financial assistance and, thus, was subject to Title IX jurisdiction. The Court went on to assert, however, that only the financial aid department of Grove City was in receipt of federal assistance and, thus, it held that only that department, rather than the entire college, was required to comply with Title IX antidiscrimination regulations. The upshot of this finding was that, since very few collegiate athletic departments receive direct federal funding, Title IX effectively no longer applied to intercollegiate sports.

The effects of the Grove City decision were both immediate and far-reaching. At least 674 complaints filed under Title IX, Title VII, the Age Discrimination Act of 1975, and section 504 of the Rehabilitation Act of 1973 were disregarded following the decision. All of these laws contain wording very similar to that of Title IX. Much more far reaching was the possibility that institutions would be free to discriminate in certain of their departments or programs, provided that the particular department received no federal aid. This restricted the scope of Title IX and the other legislation in a manner clearly opposite to the letter and the spirit of the original legislation.

In so finding, the Supreme Court seemed to ignore much evidence that Congress originally intended Title IX to apply broadly to entire institutions. Several amendments had been introduced in Congress to limit the breadth of Title IX applicability, and all had failed. Congress took no action during the "laying before" period after Title IX enforcement regulations had been proposed, thereby indicating that, after Congressional consideration of these regulations, no disapproval with their scope was expressed. The Court, moreover, seemed to ignore the fact that the wording of Title IX's antidiscrimination provisions was very closely modeled after those of Title VI of the Civil Rights Act of 1964, which prohibited discrimination on the basis of race, color, or national origin. It had been widely assumed and argued that Title IX was patterned after Title VI in order to provide for it the same broad sweep.

In a long and passionate dissent, Justice William Brennan concluded that "the Court today limits the reach of Title IX in a way that was wholly unintended by Congress." Brennan found that the majority decision had given Grove City College its sanction to discriminate in all programs which do not directly receive specifically earmarked federal financial aid, which he believed to contradict Congressional intent. Brennan's closing paragraph questioned how the executive branch of government had come to view Title IX in such a radically different light from the original intent: "The inter-

pretation of statutes as important as Title IX should not be subjected so easily to shifts in policy by the executive branch." This
policy shift had been prefigured in a 1981 announcement by Vice
President George Bush that the government would begin a system-
atic review of regulations which it deemed "burdensome, unnecessary or counterproductive." Included in those regulations was Title
IX.

The legislative branch of the government was not ready to con-
cede the gutting of Title IX and other civil rights legislation. In early
1988, Congress passed the Civil Rights Restoration Act of 1987,
over the veto of President Ronald Reagan. The Civil Rights Restoration Act changed the wording of Title IX (and of Title VI), to explicitly state that entire institutions are subject to Title IX regulation if
any part of the institution receives federal funding. The passage of
this act was in direct response to the Supreme Court's ruling in the
Grove City case and effectively reversed the decision.

In an important 1992 case, the Supreme Court decided in
Franklin v. *Gwinnett County Public Schools* that plaintiffs alleging
sexual discrimination under Title IX are entitled to sue for compensatory damages. The suit brought by Christine Franklin against North
Gwinnett High School in Georgia did not involve sexual discrimination in athletics in itself, but rather was an allegation of sexual
harassment and rape against Andrew Hill, a teacher and coach at her
school. Franklin claimed that school officials attempted to discour-
age her from bringing charges against Hill, and that the investigation was dropped after Hill's resignation. The Supreme Court decided unanimously that it presumed that all appropriate remedies
were available under Title IX, since there was no evidence that Congress intended otherwise. This Court thus seemed to recognize that,
after the Congressional reversal of *Grove City College* v. *Bell* brought
about by the Civil Rights Restoration Act, it needed to pay closer
attention to Congressional intent.

The implications of the *Franklin* decision for educational institutions and their sports programs are potentially significant. First,
schools are now aware that they can face situations of massive liability if they discriminate on the basis of gender. Most commentators
agree that this will help create an environment in which athletic
administrators closely examine their programs in detail, looking for

possible discrimination, in order to forestall potentially expensive, time-consuming, and embarrassing litigation. Thus the *Franklin* decision places force behind Title IX for the first time. Prior to this decision, institutions were, of course, liable to lose federal funding if they were proven to be in noncompliance with Title IX, but not one of the over one thousand Title IX complaints which have been filed has ever resulted in such a penalty.

In the wake of the Civil Rights Restoration Act and the *Franklin* decision, the National Collegiate Athletic Association (NCAA) has finally begun considering how to ensure gender equity in intercollegiate sports, which former NCAA Executive Director Richard Schultz has called "a moral issue." In a 1992 study, the NCAA determined that men's sports receive over two-thirds of the scholarship money, almost 80 percent of operating funds, and 83 percent of recruiting expenditures.

The NCAA's gender equity task force in 1993 released a report and recommendations to member schools. The report began by defining gender equity as

an environment in which fair and equitable distribution of overall athletics opportunities, benefits and resources are available to women and men and in which student-athletes, coaches, and athletics administrators are not subject to gender-based discrimination. An athletics program can be considered gender equitable when the participants in both the men's and women's sports programs would accept as fair and equitable the overall program of the other gender.

The report asserted that it is up to the individual schools to comply with federal and state laws concerning gender equity, and set forth the principle of proportionality in achieving gender equity. That is, if a school's undergraduate student body is 55 percent female, then its population of athletes must also be approximately 55 percent female, as must its spending on athletics. The report upheld the current status of football and men's basketball by asserting that "maintaining current revenue-producing programs as one aspect of long range planning is preferable to decreasing the currently provided participation opportunities for men."

The report anticipated major discussion of gender equity issues at the NCAA's annual convention in January 1994, which some were even billing as "the gender equity convention." Yet the discussion of gender equity in January was inconclusive at best. Delegates voted 804–1 to support the principle that men and women athletes be treated fairly in college sports, a move which many considered to be empty rhetoric. No specific guidelines came out of either the convention or the NCAA Gender Equity Task Force to show member schools how to reach equity. Advocates of women's sports had also sought NCAA sanctions against schools not in compliance with Title IX, an idea which apparently did not come to pass at the convention.

These are not the best of financial times, neither for intercollegiate sports programs nor for higher education budgets in general. Since little money is available to increase spending on women's sports, many administrators and coaches fear that the only way to ensure equity will be to cut spending by large, well-established men's sports such as football and basketball. Others criticize this viewpoint and claim that there is plenty of fat for trimming off the sacred cow of football. The issue of asking football and men's basketball to make due with less is so contentious that some high-profile football coaches have threatened to leave the NCAA if such a directive were handed down. Women's Sports Foundation Executive Director Donna Lopiano is unconcerned with such threats. "They will still have to conform to Title IX, whether they are NCAA members or not. The law is still the law," she has said.

Several universities have canceled low-profile men's sports in order to bring ratios and expenditures into line between men and women. Notre Dame cut its men's wrestling squad, Miami did away with men's golf, and Illinois axed its men's swimming, diving, and fencing squads. Critics of this approach note that these relatively small sports are inexpensive compared to football and basketball, where changes in methods of travel, recruiting, quality of accommodations, coaches' salaries, numbers of scholarships, and related expenses could save similar amounts of money while preserving entire sports programs.

Male athletes are attempting to fight back against such cuts. Wrestlers at Drake University sought to block the University's cancellation of their program through court action in the fall of 1993.

U.S. District Court Judge Harold Vietor denied their request for an injunction, noting that the cancellation of wrestling at Drake appeared to be for financial rather than gender equity reasons. There have been several cancellations of wrestling programs around the country related to the attempt to comply with Title IX. Vietor said he wished he could just "wave a magic wand," to make both sides in the gender equity debate happy.

Male swimmers at the University of Illinois, whose program was canceled due to budget considerations, took a novel approach when they sued the university in 1993 alleging that they were being discriminated against based on their gender. The case was recently settled, decided against them by U.S. District Court Judge Joe B. McDade, who found that the university was already more than meeting the interests of the proportion of males in the student body, while not proportionately meeting the interests of female students. The male swimmers filed an unsuccessful appeal in the Seventh Circuit Court of Appeals.

Big Ten Athletic Conference commissioner Jim Delaney has asked member schools to ensure that there is no more than a 60–40 male to female ratio among its athletes by the year 1997. Acting unilaterally within the Big Ten, the University of Iowa has committed to approximate proportionality by the same date. When Iowa's Board in Control of Athletics made this commitment recently, the undergraduate student enrollment was 51 percent female and 49 percent male.

Legislators may not be willing to wait for the courts and/or the NCAA to solve the gender equity situation. Representatives Cardiss Collins of Illinois and Pat Schroeder of Colorado sponsored House Resolution 1793, known as the Gender Equity in Education Act of 1993. One of the bill's general purposes is to authorize the government to "conduct activities incident to achieving compliance with Title IX of the Education Amendments of 1972." Specifically, the bill includes the Equity in Athletics Disclosure Act, which would mandate that college and university athletic departments publish annual reports about their athletic participation rates and financial support data.

Within this volatile environment, a flurry of lawsuits are changing the face of intercollegiate sports. In July 1991, the proposed cancellation of the women's tennis program at the University of New Hampshire was met with a threatened lawsuit by the players, after which the program was reinstated. In 1993, a federal judge in Denver ordered Colorado State University to reinstate women's softball, which had been canceled due to a budgetary crisis. Ruling that the cancellation was discriminatory and contradictory to the goals of Title IX, U.S. District Judge Zita Weinshienk noted that "a financial crisis cannot justify gender discrimination."

Women coaches have sued their employers in several recent cases, alleging sex discrimination because they were paid less than their male counterparts. Oklahoma State's women's golf coach Ann Pitts, whose salary is $35,712 compared to men's golf coach Mike Holder's $63,000, sued the university. In April 1994, a jury awarded her $30,000 in compensatory damages and $6,000 for mental and emotional distress. The University of Washington has announced that it will increase the pay of women's basketball coach Chris Gobrecht to equal that of men's coach Bob Bender. USC basketball coach Marianne Stanley has not fared so well. After filing a sex discrimination suit in which she asked to be paid similarly to men's coach George Raveling, her contract was not renewed, though her team was 22–8 the previous season. Howard University's Sandra Tyler won a $1.1 million suit in which the university was accused of several offenses, including paying her about half as much as men's coach Butch Beard.

A recent lawsuit filed against the California State University (CSU) system by the National Organization for Women has resulted in what may come to be seen as a fair settlement of the gender equity issue. The CSU System has agreed to provide proportionality in several areas: overall athletic participation must be proportionate to overall student enrollment within 5 percent, and funding, grants-in-aid, and scholarships to women athletes must also be proportionate within 5 percent.

Competitive sports have long been dominated by men, and that domination has continued relatively unchecked even throughout the twenty years since the enactment of Title IX. Much of that continued dominance can be attributed to lax enforcement and conflicting interpretation of Title IX. Three major factors have now come together to create an environment in which institutions may have no choice but to comply with the provisions of Title IX. The Civil Rights Restoration Act of 1987 has clarified Congressional intent regarding Title IX, the *Franklin* decision has opened the door to compensatory damage claims under Title IX, and the NCAA itself has recommended that its member schools achieve gender equity through compliance with Title IX. These developments may help to create a society within which it is as natural to think of women as of men when sports are mentioned. In that future scenario, women may enjoy the same kind of societal encouragement and enthusiasm for their athletic endeavors as men traditionally have received.

Selected Bibliography

Carey, P. *"Grove City College* v. *Bell:* The Weakening of Title IX." *New England Law Review* 20 (4) 1984–85: 805–830.

Griffin, J. *"Grove City College* v. *Bell:* Restricting the Scope of Title IX." *Harvard Women's Law Journal* 8 (Spring 1985): 179–194.

Jensen, J. "Title IX and Intercollegiate Athletics: HEW Gets Serious about Equality in Sports?" *New England Law Review* 15 (3) 1979–80: 573–596.

Kadzielski, M. "Postsecondary Athletics in an Era of Equality: An Appraisal of the Effect of Title IX." *Journal of College and University Law* 5 (2) 1978–79: 123–141.

Moran, M. "Title IX: A 20-Year Search for Equity; Title IX Is Now an Irresistible Force." *The New York Times.* Sunday, June 21, 1992.

Villalobos, P. M. "The Civil Rights Restoration Act of 1987: Revitalization of Title IX." *Marquette Sports Law Journal* 1 (1) Fall 1990: 148–169.

Wolff, A. "The Slow Track." *Sports Illustrated.* September 28, 1992: 52–66.

Little League Baseball
Where Are the Girls?

Jennifer Turner

National Organization for Women, Essex County Chapter v. Little League Baseball, Inc.*, 127 N.J. Super. 522; 318 A. 2d 33; 66 A.L.R. 3d 1247 (N.J. Super. Ct. App. Div. 1974)

Little League baseball has been available for American youth since 1939. Until relatively recently, however, that meant boys only. In the mid-1970s, Little League bent to intense outside pressures and expanded its organization to include girls. At the same time, it started a softball league for girls who did not want to play baseball with boys. This league created yet another controversy when boys wanted to play softball. In the mid-1980s, a California court ordered Little League to allow boys to play in the softball league with the girls. Currently, Little League is an equal opportunity organization.

Little League was founded by William Stoltz in 1939. It was an organization created originally for boys, ages nine to twelve years. It was patterned after professional baseball, including farm teams, player drafts, spring training, and a World Series. Stoltz's program started with only three teams located in Williamsport, Pa., the League's headquarters. By the 1970s, the League had greatly expanded, with two million active players on fifty-nine thousand teams in thirty countries.

Little League Baseball, Inc. is a nonprofit organization that holds a federal charter by a 1964 Act of Congress. Little League has taken pride in its long history of relative absence of racial discrimination. The same, however, cannot be claimed for its history of sexual discrimination. According to its federal charter, the goals of Little League include the development of the qualities of citizenship and sportsmanship. The original charter specifically mentioned the development of the trait of "manhood." President Gerald Ford signed new legislation in 1974, expanding the organizations's goals to include the healthy development of young women as well as young men.

In 1974 suits against Little League were filed in fifteen states asking that girls be allowed to try out for the teams. Girls wanted the same chance as their brothers to play baseball. While the legal battle raged in all fifteen states, it was the New Jersey case that set the standard. The National Organization for Women (NOW) sought the admittance of girls to the all-boys Little League program in that state.

The New Jersey court found in favor of NOW and mandated that all Little League programs within New Jersey be open to girls as well as boys. The court based its decision on a finding that Little League conducted its tryouts and games at places of public accommodation, such as government-operated playing fields. A New Jersey statute prohibits discrimination at a place of public accommodation.

Little League weakly attempted to justify the discrimination by claiming that girls are more likely than boys to get hurt in a game played with a hardball. After extensive expert testimony from both sides, the court struck down the Little League's argument. It held that girls, ages nine to twelve years, are not so physiologically inferior to boys in the same age bracket that they should be precluded, as a class, from competing safely and successfully. The court found that a substantial number of girls wanted to play baseball and were qualified to compete with boys of the same age. These reasons were compelling enough for the court to allow New Jersey girls the liberty to play.

The New Jersey court handed down its decision on March 29, 1974. In June of that year, Little League officially abandoned its boys-only policy on the national level. Another factor in this decision was the renewal of its federal charter. A committee of the House of Representatives examined Little League's request for renewal. Congress made it clear that Little League's chances for renewal would be directly affected by its decision on whether to open the league to girls or not. Once Little League made its policy change, the federal charter was renewed and President Ford signed the new legislation which allowed girls to play baseball.

Some observers believe that Little League managed to thwart the will of Congress, while seemingly standing in compliance. They claim that the institutionalization of a softball league for girls was designed to draw girls away from the baseball teams. This softball league was also restrictive in that boys were not allowed to compete. The gender-specific restriction once again proved a stumbling block for Little League.

In 1985, the American Civil Liberties Union filed suit in California to enjoin a local Little League organization from banning boys from the softball league. The effect of this injunction was to allow boys, who then were limited to playing baseball, to compete in softball with girls. Softball and baseball are two different games, and just as there are some girls who prefer baseball, there are also some boys who prefer softball. The California court determined that the state's anti-sex-discrimination law, the Unruh Act, prohibits Little League from limiting the softball league to girls. Little League resorted to the shameless argument that boys would dominate the softball league by intimidating girls. The findings of the New Jersey Court, however, still applied. Girls nine to twelve years old are physically qualified to play competitively with boys in the same age group.

Selected Bibliography

Fairly, M. "Play Ball! Boys Win Right to Play on Little League Softball Teams." *Los Angeles Times*. March 15, 1985, Metro, Part 2, 1.

Fine, G. *With the Boys: Little League Baseball and Preadolescent Culture*. Chicago: The University of Chicago Press, 1987.

Halpert, F. "For Little League's Girls, a Quiet Anniversary." *The New York Times*. May 29, 1989: 9.

Barely There
Female Reporters in Male Locker Rooms

Susan F. Pingel

Ludtke v. *Kuhn*, 461 F. Supp. 86 (S.D.N.Y. 1978)

On September 17, 1990, two separate but related incidents occurred that revived issues related to equal access of female reporters to male locker rooms. In Cincinnati, Sam Wyche, head coach of the Cincinnati Bengals football team, denied *USA Today* reporter Denise Tom access to the locker room for postgame interviews. In Massachusetts, reporter Lisa Olson of the *Boston Herald* enjoyed locker room privileges, but endured lewd actions and obscenities directed at her by several members of the New England Patriots football team.

These incidents came twelve years after then *Sports Illustrated* reporter Melissa Ludtke waged a legal battle to crack the males-only monopoly on the door to the New York Yankees' locker room. Neither Tom's nor Olson's case led to a similar court challenge. Aside from this and other differences, certain issues are similar in all these incidents. Do the players have the right to privacy and, if so, to what extent? Do female reporters enjoy the right to equal treatment similar to their male counterparts, including access to the postgame locker room? Ludtke's action led to the first court decision addressing some of the constitutional issues and ramifications on both sides of the locker room door. Despite the 1978 decision in Ludtke's favor, the two highly publicized 1990 incidents show that personal attitudes and actions are difficult to counter.

For the New York Yankees, historically no strangers to controversy on or off the baseball field, 1977 was a year of particularly poor media relations. Manager Billy Martin arbitrarily banned reporters from the players' lounge, thereby leading majority owner George Steinbrenner to lament the loss of free coverage and advertising generated by the media. Later the media spotlight focused on the successful efforts of the Yankees to defeat the Los Angeles Dodgers in the World Series. During the World Series, however, the Yankees denied reporter Ludtke, then in her mid-twenties and a four-year veteran of the magazine, access to the locker room. That action led Ludtke and her employer, Time, Inc., to file suit in 1978 against the New York Yankees, Major League Baseball, and the City of New York. They claimed Ludtke's civil rights were violated since she was not treated the same as male sports reporters. Specifically, the plaintiffs maintained that Ludtke's due process and equal protection rights as guaranteed by the Fourteenth Amendment to the Constitution were compromised. The Fourteenth Amendment guarantees to all citizens "equal protection" and a right of "due process." The United States Code allows persons to bring a civil action when they claim that their constitutional rights have been violated by a state or "under color of State law." Ludtke's claim of violation of her constitutional rights centered around her claim that she was denied equal protection of the laws of the state of New York and that her First Amendment right to freedom of speech was violated. Separately she contended that New York's equal accommodation statute was violated.

At the time of the suit, Ludtke was one of twenty-two sports reporters at *Sports Illustrated.* Standing at the head of the group on the opposite side of the locker room door was Major League Baseball's commissioner, Bowie Kuhn, who had declared a blanket exclusion of female reporters in clubhouses and locker rooms. Male reporters could be allowed in on a space-available basis. The legal referee appointed (by chance) to determine the outcome was Federal District Court Judge Constance Baker Motley, the only female judge of the United States District Court for the Southern District of New York. Prior to her appointment to the bench, Motley had worked in the South with other lawyers, including Thurgood Marshall, laying some of the legal groundwork for the civil rights movement.

Judge Motley's initial task involved determining if there was sufficient state action necessary to claim a denial of constitutional rights. The state action issue became key to the continuation of the case when the parties did not compromise on access. Although privately owned, the Yankee franchise played in publicly owned Yankee Stadium. To keep the Yankees from moving, the landlord, New York

City, had just gone through considerable expense in modernizing and renovating Yankee Stadium. By special statute the New York State legislature authorized leasing the stadium to the Yankees rather than to the highest bidder. Further, the lease agreement stated that the Yankees were "to comply with all present and future federal, state, and local laws." The court found enough proof that the state action tests applied to the Yankee organization.

With the state action question answered, the court moved to the substantive issue of whether the female reporter had been denied equal protection. Ludtke showed that her treatment differed significantly from her male counterparts. The legal burden then shifted to the defendants to prove excluding female reporters served the interests of the government. Commissioner Kuhn maintained that his exclusionary policy protected the players' personal privacy while changing clothes, promoted the image of baseball as a family sport, and preserved traditional notions of decency and propriety.

The court agreed that the players had a constitutional right to privacy but did not determine that this justified the League's exclusionary policy. Television cameras broadcasted, live and immediately, scenes from the 1977 World Series' locker rooms. Millions of people, male and female, viewed these scenes. Players maintained their privacy through the use of backdrops and towels. These, or similar methods, could be used to safeguard a player's privacy from female reporters. The court found it unnecessary to reach a decision on the plaintiff's other claims. Ludtke won her argument for equal access. This decision, however, only gave female sports writers equal access to the locker rooms in Yankee Stadium.

Female sports writers are a distinct minority in the field of sports reporting. Receiving the assignment, however, is the easy part. Postgame locker room activity provides the "scoops" sports fans crave. All reporters are usually under tight postgame deadlines, but male reporters with easier access to locker rooms have a distinct advantage. The common practice for female reporters seeking interviews, prior to (and for some teams), even after the decision in the Ludtke case, involved waiting for the athletes to emerge from behind locker room doors. Or, female reporters asked male colleagues or the team's public relations staff to request the presence of particular players. Not all the athletes showed up in a timely manner. Generally, these interviews might generate less interest than immediate postgame ones. Some teams tried using a separate interview room. No reporters, male or female, preferred this "programmed" approach to the more informal and spontaneous locker room setting. The Ludtke decision recognized these inequities when female, and not male reporters, were denied locker room access.

There are major differences between the Ludtke, Tom, and Olson situations. Olson and Tom did not seek legal recourse to gain access unlike Ludtke. The National Football League (NFL) handled the investigation in house. In both instances the persons and/or the teams involved were fined by the NFL. Wyche received the largest individual fine, about $30,000. Olson settled out of court, but as of a few years after the incident, some of the Patriots players involved still had not paid their fines. For fear of incurring lawsuits, NFL officials expressed reluctance to collect fines for off-field behavior.

Olson's arguments differed from Ludtke's. Olson based her claim on a violation of her Title VII rights. According to the United States Supreme Court, sexual harassment in the workplace may be pursued as sexual discrimination under Title VII. The Patriots players, however, could not in any way be considered employees of Olson's newspaper. She might have done better to seek a common-law action.

The state action issue is significantly different as well. Only three major league baseball stadiums are privately owned and virtually all of the football stadiums are publicly owned. The Patriots play in a privately owned NFL stadium. Consequently, Olson could not have claimed a violation of her First and Fourteenth Amendment rights in the same manner as Ludtke. The Bengals, however, play in a publicly owned stadium. The exclusion of Tom might have been a violation under similar provisions to Ludtke's case.

In the last decade of the twentieth century, equal access and equal treatment are still issues as the two highly publicized 1990 incidents, and less well known events, reveal. This situation exists despite a 1985 NFL rule allowing equal access for male and female reporters. This rule does not always have the full support of players, coaches, and owners. Obviously it works better when it receives total endorsement. The National Basketball Association and the National Hockey League have allowed equal access without major incidents. In 1991 two states introduced legislation to bar reporters in all locker rooms for thirty minutes after the end of a game; the bills, however, did not become law.

Ludtke commented on the Olson situation, ". . . the battles that I and others waged for equality . . . did not bring an end to discrimination. They only kept the most overt forms from showing. We've learned that changing the rules doesn't necessarily alter attitudes."

Selected Bibliography

Brennan, M. "Civil Rights in the Locker Room: *Ludtke* v. *Kuhn.*" *Comm/Ent* 2 (Summer 1980): 645–669.

Rasnic, C. "Illegal Use of Hands in the Locker Room: Charges of Sexual Harassment and Inequality from Females in the Sports Media." *Entertainment and Sports Lawyer* 8 (Winter 1991): 3–6.

Sobel, L. *Professional Sports and the Law.* New York: Law-Arts Publishers, Inc., 1977 and 1981 Supplement.

Watson, V. "The Men's Room." *The Quill* 75 (January 1987): 20–24.

Major League Baseball Called for Balk!

Marchell M. Austin

Postema v. National League, et al., 91 Civ. 8507, (New York, 1992)

Over the centuries, various institutions, including politics, religion, and professional sports, have helped to mold many American social values. Women and minorities have made huge strides in politics and religion, gaining positions of power in each. The owners and administrators of professional sports, however, have kept that institution largely a white-male sanctuary. Public criticism regarding racial discrimination in hiring practices has recently plagued baseball owners. Through all this criticism there is another discriminatory act by professional baseball that requires attention. This is sexual discrimination in hiring practices charged by former umpire Pam Postema against professional baseball. Postema's allegations stem from many situations that occurred during the years 1977 to 1989, when she was a baseball umpire.

Postema's umpiring career started in 1977 when she applied to Al Somer's Umpiring School in Daytona Beach, Florida. She believed that umpiring would be one way of participating in a game she loved. Her application, of course, was turned down, as there had never been a female at the school before, and "there wasn't even a women's rest room on the premises." After threatening a lawsuit, Postema was finally admitted and completed the course, ranking 17th out of 130 students. Postema's newfound skills turned into a passion for umpiring and into gainful employment when she obtained a position in the Gulf Coast (Rookie) League. She continued working her way up through the A and AA leagues, and also umpired winter baseball in Venezuela. Within six years she advanced to the Triple A Pacific Coast League, the highest level below the majors.

During her tenure as an umpire, Postema had many accomplishments. She was selected to officiate the Venezuelan All-Star game and worked home plate as the umpire for the Hall of Fame exhibition game between the Atlanta Braves and the New York Yankees. In 1988 and 1989 Postema was chief of her umpiring crew and umpired major league spring training games, which were often the precursor to a major league position. Notwithstanding these honors, Postema was subjected to continual offensive acts of sexual harassment, gender discrimination, and abuse by managers, coaches, other umpires, and baseball administrators. She was spat upon, called offensive names, and was a victim of malicious derogatory remarks. Among the vulgar acts included the time that Postema came out to home plate only to find a frying pan resting on top of it, or the time she was kissed on the lips by a manager, in front of 18,000 fans as he turned in his lineup card. Postema, however, refused to be deterred by any of these acts. She constantly took action against derogatory types of conduct through warnings, ejections, and official reports and charged that although these incidents were well known throughout baseball, no one in baseball administrative leadership took any action to correct or stop them.

On several occasions, the press was told that because she was female, she had to do twice as good a job as a male umpire. Dick Butler, then special assistant to the president of the American League and former supervisor of umpires, told *Newsday* and the *Los Angeles Times* that Postema "realizes that she has to be better than the fellow next to her. She's got to be better because of the fact that she's a girl. I'm not saying it's fair, but it exists and she's not going to change it." Also, Bob Knepper, then pitching for the Houston Astros, told reporters in 1988 that women had no place in baseball, a statement which brought national press coverage to Postema and generated widespread public controversy.

During the 1989 season, Postema and her partner were the only two minor league umpires working major league spring training who were not given the opportunity to fill in for vacationing or ill major league umpires, while male umpires with less qualifications and experience were given such chances. At the end of the 1989 season, Postema received a negative written performance evaluation which alleged that she had a "bad attitude," even though she had been rated better than average earlier in the season.

In November of 1989, Postema was unconditionally released when the National and American Leagues were not interested in considering her for employment as a major league umpire. Initially, Postema did not pursue legal action because, as she mentioned in her book, it was a relief to be free from malicious harassment and discrimination. But after being away from the sport she loved for a while, Postema realized she had to take action, not only for herself, but for all women who will ever try to succeed in a male-dominated profession. A formal charge of employment discrimination was filed in April, 1990, with a lawsuit following later that year. Postema's legal action asked for the first umpiring vacancy in the major leagues, damages, and an injunction to prevent further discrimination.

The defendants have made several motions for dismissal of the case, including the claim that there were no vacancies during those times when Postema was in line for a major league position. The National and American Leagues also tried to obtain dismissal on the grounds that Postema waited too long before she filed a discrimination charge. Both motions were denied. The judge also found that the American and National Leagues were not exempt from the suit through baseball's exemption to antitrust laws.

It is unfortunate that discriminatory hiring practices have been allowed to tarnish the image of America's grand old game. If baseball is to remain linked with American values, the judicial system will need to decide if employment discrimination practices are also synonymous with America.

As Postema's suit moved through the legal system, another former female umpire sought legal relief. In 1992, Teresa Cox brought a federal lawsuit against several defendants, including the National and American Leagues, alleging harassment and abuse by male umpires. Late in 1993, Postema and Cox settled their lawsuits out of court. In so doing, they agreed not to reveal terms of the financial settlement but both expressed satisfaction with the outcome. Part of the settlement also stipulated that they would not seek to umpire in the major leagues. Major league umpiring, therefore, continues to remain off-limits to aspiring females.

Selected Bibliography

Garrity, J. "Waiting for the Call." *Sports Illustrated*. March 14, 1988: 26–27.

Keenan, S. "The Umpress Strikes Back." *Sports Illustrated*. July 30, 1984: 44–45.

Postema, P. and G. Wojiechowski. *You've Got to Have Balls to Make It in This League: My Life As an Umpire*. New York: Simon and Schuster, 1992.

Index of Cases

Cases featured in an essay appear in bold type.

Index of Names and Subjects